Praise for *Strategy Strikes Back: How* Star Wars *Explains Modern Military Conflict,* edited by Max Brooks, John Amble, ML Cavanaugh, and Jaym Gates

"Illuminating."—LAWRENCE D. FREEDMAN, *Foreign Affairs*

"Over the course of history, our single greatest vulnerability has been a failure of imagination. *Strategy Strikes Back* confronts that vulnerability. The future may not evolve precisely as these authors suggest, but evolve it will. As it does, we will discover that some of tomorrow's challenges will prove to be timeless, and others, surprisingly new. Learning to imagine now will be time well spent."—GEN. MARTIN DEMPSEY, former chairman of the Joint Chiefs of Staff

"You might be forgiven for thinking the never-ending *Star Wars* franchise was simply a cash cow built of sequels, spin-offs and toys. But the space saga is actually helping further the discussion about military strategy right here on Earth."—CHAD JONES, *San Francisco Chronicle*

"*Star Wars* is just as much a foundational mythology of our time as *The Iliad* was a long time ago. *Strategy Strikes Back* ingeniously uses that world far, far away to help readers take a look at our wars here today." —P. W. SINGER, best-selling author of *Wired for War* and coauthor of *Ghost Fleet: A Novel of the Next World War*

"Anyone with a basic knowledge of the *Star Wars* universe is sure to enjoy the creative parallels used by these esteemed authors to simplify complex topics. Avid fans with deep knowledge of this universe cannot help but embrace these parallels, think through them more deeply, and dig even deeper into them as they try to support or argue against the authors while also showing off their superior knowledge of their favorite series of movies." —STEVE LUCZYNSKI, *Strategy Bridge*

WINNING WESTEROS

WINNING
WESTEROS

How *Game of Thrones* Explains

Modern Military Conflict

EDITED BY MAX BROOKS, JOHN AMBLE,

ML CAVANAUGH, AND JAYM GATES

FOREWORD BY JAMES STAVRIDIS

POTOMAC BOOKS | *An imprint of the University of Nebraska Press*

All rights reserved. Potomac Books is an
imprint of the University of Nebraska Press.
Manufactured in the United States of America.

Library of Congress Cataloging-in-Publication Data
Names: Brooks, Max, editor. | Amble, John,
editor. | Cavanaugh, ML, editor. | Gates, Jaym,
editor. | Stavridis, James, writer of foreword.
Title: Winning Westeros: how Game of thrones
explains modern military conflict / edited by
Max Brooks, John Amble, ML Cavanaugh, and
Jaym Gates; foreword by James Stavridis.
Description: [Lincoln]: Potomac Books, an
imprint of the University of Nebraska Press,
[2019] | Includes bibliographical references.
Identifiers: LCCN 2019001186
ISBN 9781640122215 (cloth: alk. paper)
ISBN 9781640122369 (epub)
ISBN 9781640122376 (mobi)
ISBN 9781640122383 (pdf)
Subjects: LCSH: Game of thrones
(Television program) | Strategy on television.
Classification: LCC PN1992.77.G35
W55 2019 | DDC 791.45/72—dc23
LC record available at
https://lccn.loc.gov/2019001186

Set in Arno Pro by Mikala R. Kolander.
Designed by N. Putens.

CONTENTS

FOREWORD

JAMES STAVRIDIS

During my long career in the U.S. Navy, and especially when I was a young naval officer, my reading habits were defined by two types of books: history and fiction. The first gave me a flavor for the rich tradition of naval service across the centuries, from Themistocles at Salamis to Nelson at Trafalgar to Nimitz in the Pacific. Every sailor knows the stories of these admirals and their battles, and they likewise became for me inspirational characters whose standards I tried to match, as well as strong links in the long chain of naval history and tradition. From them, I learned what it meant to be a fighting sailor.

But it was from novels that I learned how to be a naval officer. Where histories and biographies naturally focus on the great admirals and their fleets, Patrick O'Brian's *Master and Commander* series gave me much more particular insight into the challenges faced by ships and their captains—in our own time just as much as in Nelson's navy. Great novels like O'Brian's—or Michael Shaara's *The Killer Angels* or Nicholas Monsarrat's *The Cruel Sea* or even classic poems like *The Odyssey*—engaged my mind in a different way and trained me to raise my sights from asking, "What happened?" to asking, "What if . . . ?"

What-if questions are the root of strategic thinking. Because the outcomes are not a matter of historical record, I have always found these questions easier to ask when reading works of fiction. Tracing the imaginary career of Captain Jack Aubrey through O'Brian's novels, I constantly asked myself what I would do in the situations he faced. Time and again, I found that this mental exercise paid off when I encountered similar situations in real life. The Aegis destroyers I sailed in might have been much more high-tech than the wooden men-of-war of Captain Aubrey's day, but the challenges of discipline, the tension of preparing for battle, and the pressures of command are enduring elements of naval life.

This idea, of course, applies equally well to film and television. There is much leadership to be gleaned in superb films like *The Caine Mutiny Court Martial* or long-format television such as *The Winds of War*. In today's world of series television, there is no more global strategic plotline than that of *Game of Thrones*. The series follows the exploits of a series of contenders for control of a fictional world. There is significant geopolitical and leadership theory, some magic and witchcraft, angry but tamable dragons, walking dead, much swordplay, brutal intrigue, and family quarrels. If you simply equate the magic and the dragons to emerging technology, the tamable dragons to nuclear weapons, and the swords to guns, it is easy to find yourself in the world of global strategy.

In the following chapters, some of our nation's finest strategic thinkers apply this what-if approach to the fictional world of the *Game of Thrones* series. Their conclusions are incisive, and I applaud them for sharing them publicly. In addition to meaningful contributions to strategic literature, these essays also make for seriously fun reading. Naturally, I am most attracted to Euron Greyjoy, the psychopathic king of the Salt Throne, who truly appreciates sea power. He seems to be channeling Alfred Thayer Mahan and classic sea power theory when he tersely (and correctly) says, "Build me a thousand ships, and I will give you this world."[1]

I encourage all readers to apply the what-if technique to these chapters while reading—and not only to the fictional circumstances they describe but also to the authors' conclusions. After all, one of the greatest benefits of reading fiction is the variety of interpretations it allows. We all know what happened at Trafalgar, but Westeros offers nearly unlimited opportunities to ask ourselves, "What if?" The lessons from the struggles to dominate this fictitious world echo quite clearly into our own.

In 1967 the real-life Rear Admiral J. C. Wylie wrote, "I do not criticize the amateur strategist. On the contrary, I believe deeply that strategy is everyone's business. Too many lives are at stake for us not to recognize strategy as a legitimate and important public concern."[2] More than a half century later, strategy remains as important and lamentably understudied as ever. I salute the authors, editors, and readers of this book for making it their concern.

Today, as ever, the real world is in search of more thoughtful and effective strategies. *Winning Westeros* is a powerful strategic tool, coupled with the enjoyable experience of watching *Game of Thrones*, to think through global strategy. Let's get underway.

NOTES

1. David Benioff and D. B. Weiss, "The Door," season 6, episode 5, dir. Jack Bender, *Game of Thrones*, aired May 22, 2016, on HBO.
2. J. C. Wylie, *Military Strategy: A General Theory of Power Control* (Annapolis MD: Naval Institute Press, 1967), v.

PART 1

People and War

1

Mycah's Parents Didn't Get a Vote

MAX BROOKS

No one likes to imagine they're a nobody. That wouldn't be much of a fantasy. When we watch a show like *Game of Thrones*, we imagine we're Jon Snow or Daenerys Targaryen or that cool guy with the eyepatch and the flaming sword. We don't imagine we're the dude who gets squashed by the falling bell when Cersei blows up the Sept of Baelor. Nobody fantasizes about being Random Shmuck #17 who gets stabbed by the Sons of the Harpy when they run riot through the fighting pit of Meereen. And I'd be hard pressed to find anyone who shows up to Comicon dressed like Mycah the butcher's son.

And why would anyone want to be? Mycah was a powerless peasant murdered for being in the wrong place at the wrong time. But imagine if we were that powerless peasant. Or his parents. Who would speak up for us? A lawyer? A reporter? An elected representative? Westeros doesn't have any of the institutions that protect the weak from the strong, the same institutions that too many of us take for granted.

Out here in the real world, we complain about the compromises, inefficiency, and slow-grinding gears of democracy. Recently, some have gone

3

even further, calling for the "deconstruction of the administrative state." And while democracy's enemies continue to strengthen and multiply, too many of its defenders can't even be bothered to vote. Because that's what voting feels like to many of us—a bother, a hassle, a pointless, boring chore.

And why shouldn't it? How many of us have experienced the horrors of totalitarian regimes? Russian assassinations, Venezuelan starvation, Chinese execution-backed censorship. Those real-life events get less attention from us than a TV show like *Game of Thrones*. And that is exactly why *Game of Thrones* is so important for our time; it is a "stark" reminder of why democracy matters.

If we don't like being governed by a deep state, imagine being ruled by a man who literally *is* the state. "King takes what he wants," Ned Stark laments to his wife in season 1, episode 1. And lamenting is all he can do, because any infantile, psychotic impulse is law. From wars to taxes to murdering babies. Like a "wheel," to quote Daenerys, "crushing those on the ground."

And who's going to save us from that wheel? According to the story, the answer doesn't lie in a better system but a better person. The notion of a good king, someone with the supposed right—and by "right," we mean the freak accident of birth—is the only way that more Mycahs don't end up dead on their parents' doorsteps.

At the point of this writing—on the cusp of season 8, the final season—we're supposed to be rooting for Westeros's benevolent power couple, Jon Snow and Daenerys. Both are good people—honest and kind, with a genuine moral compass that, we hope, will point the way to a future of peace and prosperity for all.

But what if it doesn't? What if, as Missandei warns, "it only takes one arrow" to destroy the hopes and dreams of millions? And what if there's a second archer on a grassy knoll that gets Jon as well as Daenerys? Who takes over? And why? Will it be civil war all over again? Isn't that why Westeros fell into chaos in the first place, because King Robert got himself killed in a hunting accident? That's exactly why our codified, legalized, Oswald-Booth-proof line of succession exists today. To ensure that our lives aren't held hostage to chance, that random tragedy doesn't descend into anarchy.

But let's say Daenerys and Jon live to a ripe old age, which in a world of magic and dragon's blood could be centuries long. Who's to say that they'll always remain the benevolent rulers we're getting to know and love. Not every tyrant starts out tyrannical. A lot of them had nothing but the best intentions. If you don't believe that old-timey saying that "power corrupts, and absolute power corrupts absolutely," just ask the ghosts of Fidel Castro and Muammar Kaddafi.

And if that happens, if those Dear Leaders eventually decline into paranoid, vindictive mass murderers? What checks and balances does Westeros have in place to stop them? The army? That's what stopped Daenerys's father, the "Mad King." The only difference now is that Daenerys still has her two dragons, and that is a very powerful metaphor for our world. Despots throughout time have feared coups as surely as popular uprisings. That's why they've kept their own dragons called the Praetorian Guard, the Savak, and the SS.

But let's say there's no need for a king slayer. Let's say John and Daenerys, "Johnerys," rule with the same fair, wise hand as Caesar Augustus. Then what? Would they have another baby-killing prince like Joffrey? That's the inbred danger of passing down power through blood. But if the storyline about Daenerys's barren womb is true and they have to choose an heir, does that make the people of Westeros any safer?

Maybe Tyrion Lannister would rule for a time, marry a nice prostitute, sire a decent heir and maybe even grand heir, but as long as power remains absolute, it leaves the throne open for a future maniac. Our founding fathers understood this from our own history. They knew that any system that allowed Augustus would eventually spawn Caligula.

This is why George Washington, in the footsteps of Cincinnatus, refused an American throne. In 2018 *Game of Thrones* is a fantasy. In 1776 it was everyday life. The framers of our Constitution saw what happens when a handful of drunken, incestuous, and, in the case of King George III, mentally ill mob dons have direct control over millions of subjects. The whole reason our founders established an administrative state was to protect us from a man like Louis XIV, who declared, "I *am* the state."

That is why we are citizens, not subjects. That is why our Constitution is our king. And unlike Aerys, Balon, Brynden, Robert, Randyll, Ramsay, Rickon, Viserys, Drogo, Hoster, Lysa, Joffrey, Mance, Olenna, Doran, Stannis, Robb, Roose, Tommen, and Walder, our ruler is immortal. Cersei had a point in tearing up the last "piece of paper" from her husband. The words spoke for a person whose power died with him. The words "We the people" speak to the power in all of us.

By choosing to live behind a wall of shared ideals, we ensure that no butcher's son can be butchered. Our administrative state protects every child, and while "constitutional democracy" doesn't exactly roll off the tongue quite like "game of thrones," I like the sound of the former much more than the latter. And so should you.

2

A House to Be Feared

JONATHAN P. KLUG

The vibrant nature of *Game of Thrones* starts with the creative genius of author George R. R. Martin and his ability to blend his vivid imagination with the realism of history. His approach includes grounding characters with actual historical figures and combining history with unique personalities, creating an array of rich characters who seem to be alive with motives and personalities—Martin's is not a story of two-dimensional heroes or villains. Apart from the White Walkers and their undead horde, as well as sadistic Ramsay Bolton, the distinction between heroes and villains is blurred or unclear. *Game of Thrones* characters are complex and unique, and Martin makes their decisions carry a price, often causing life in Martin's world to be Hobbesian—nasty, brutish, and short.[1] Individuals must be painfully careful and lucky to survive, and the heads of the noble houses must think strategically if their families are to survive, let alone thrive. House Lannister and its patriarch Tywin Lannister are the best exemplars of the practice of strategic art in *Game of Thrones*, and this is the focus of this chapter. Just as Tywin and the Lannisters unintentionally taught the Starks, they can

7

teach us much about modern conflict, such as the importance of wealth in the exercise of power and the use of military art.

In an interview, Martin points out that *Game of Thrones* is in part homage to England and its War of the Roses (1455–85), as Martin bases the Starks on the historical Yorks and modeled the Lannisters on the Lancasters.[2] In the same way, the historical basis for Lord Tywin Lannister King is Edward I (1239–1307), rumored to have literally scared servants to death and earned the sobriquet the "Hammer of the Scots." From season 1 until his death in season 4, Tywin Lannister leads House Lannister and hammers his foes. Although he will not win any Father of the Year awards, he focuses on his house, its power, and its future. During his initial on-screen appearance, he sets the tone for all his future actions. As he systematically cleans a deer carcass, he lectures his eldest son Jaime: "It's the family name that lives on. It's all that lives on. Not your personal glory, not your honor—family. Do you understand?"[3] These are the words of a stoic, clinical, and experienced strategist attempting to educate his eldest son and spur Jaime to adopt the same long-term, strategic mindset.

While vital, Tywin's strategic mindset would be of little use without resources. The inhabitants of Westeros seem to know the Lannisters' unofficial motto: "A Lannister always pays his debts"; of all the noble houses, the Lannisters are the richest. At first blush, it may appear that the Lannisters are rich because they are powerful; however, they are powerful because they are rich. The Lannisters' major source of wealth is the many gold and silver mines in their territory, the Westerlands, making it one of the richest regions in Westeros. In fact, one of the most productive gold mines lies beneath Casterly Rock, the Lannisters' ancestral stronghold. This fortification sits above the Sunset Sea and the city of Lannisport, which is one of the great ports of the Seven Kingdoms, a bustling commercial center, and the home of the powerful Lannister fleet. Naval theorist Alfred Thayer Mahan would have agreed that the Lannisters were a maritime power, as they politically support maritime efforts, enjoy a large volume of seaborne trade, possess a large trading fleet, and maintain a large navy, although they lack the colonies that Mahan argued were necessary for sea power.[4] Navies, armies, and allies are expensive, but they are necessary to accumulate wealth from mines and maritime commerce and to secure business investments, which overall makes Tywin Lannister the wealthiest man in Westeros.

Lannister wealth underpins their power, not unlike Great Britain during the era of Pax Britannica, or the United States after World War II. From the eighteenth century to the middle of the twentieth century, Great Britain's "sinews of power" started with wealth.[5] In the twentieth century, the United States' wealth was the foundation of the "arsenal of democracy" and the post–World War II superpower.[6] Like these two powers at their zenith, the Lannisters leverage their wealth to build power and, at the same time, used power to make wealth, creating a virtuous circle of building wealth and power.

The Lannisters also understand finances, as they know how to leverage their wealth by securing loans. The Iron Bank of Braavos is the most important source of loans, continually extending the Lannisters credit based on their mineral wealth and Tywin's track record of sound investments. During his short stint as the master of coin, Tyrion Lannister has concerns that the enormous expense of the War of the Five Kings could force the Lannisters to mortgage their future or not be able to win the war due to insufficient funds. Ominously, the Iron Bank previously funded the enemies of rulers who failed to pay what they owed, of which Tyrion is aware. After winning the War of the Five Kings, Tywin reveals to his daughter, Cersei, that the Lannisters' gold mines had run dry three years previously, driving both Tywin and Cersei to trust no one and increase their willingness to accept risk to maintain their strategic position and secure additional strategic advantage. The alliance with the Tyrells was one of these strategic risks, and it would prove to be a costly decision.

To win the War of the Five Kings, the Lannisters often had to accept risk, and accepting risk is part of using military art to achieve your objectives. For those unfamiliar with the term, military art is broken into the following components: strategic art, operational art, and tactics. Strategic art is "defined as the skillful formulation, coordination, and application of ends, ways, and means to promote and defend the national interests."[7] Successful strategic art achieves the desired set of conditions and thereby secures strategic advantage, which the Lannisters did by winning the War of the Five Kings.[8] Operational art is a series of efforts "successively developing one after another, logically connected to one another, united by the commonality of the ultimate aim, each one achieving limited intermediate aims which in their totality represent an operational pursuit."[9] Robb Stark's efforts against the Lannisters, when viewed together as an overarching campaign, are an example of operational art. Tactics are the pursuit of victory on the battlefield through the application of combat power, and Tyrion's use of wildfire during the crushing defeat of Stannis Baratheon at the Battle of the Blackwater is an example of successful tactics.

Strategic art, operational art, and tactics each require a different perspective and mindset to practice effectively, but they are also interconnected and interdependent. As Russian military theorist Aleksandr Svechin wrote more than a century ago, "all branches of military art are closely associated with one another: tactics takes the steps from which an operational leap is formed; strategy points out the path."[10] Because it points out the path, so to speak, strategic art is the most important component of military art, and operational art and tactics are the materials for strategic art. Tactics are the most dynamic component of military art, as they are subject to the evolution of technology and military techniques, which for *Game of Thrones* includes magic and mythical creatures such as giants, wights, White Walkers, and dragons. The changes in tactics may, in turn, impact operational art, as dragons provide a form of operational maneuver, for example. Operational art provides the context for the tactical level of warfare and tactics, and successful operational art, in turn, facilitates strategic art.

Returning to Tywin Lannister's first scene in *Game of Thrones*, he emphasizes the importance of the near term to his son, although still clearly thinking strategically, when he says, "The future of our family will be determined in these next few months. We could establish a dynasty that will last a thousand years, or we could collapse into nothing, as the Targaryens did." His mention of "these next few months" indicates operational thinking about the forthcoming military campaigns and battles that would be necessary to achieve his strategic goals. Concerning military art, his focus on the future of his family underscores that he is practicing strategic art, his campaign design is a demonstration of operational art, and his battlefield leadership later in the series indicates his tactical abilities.

U.S. Air War College professor Everett Dolman describes strategy as "an idea . . . about the future in anticipation of the probable and preparation for the possible."[11] Strategy deals with the highest levels of statecraft and war and is an unending process. However, who wins at the tactical level is straightforward, as it usually is evident when a battle has a victor. This is also true at the operational level, as it is often clear if a campaign has a victor; however, who "wins" at the strategic level is not always so clear, as it is possible to win a war but lose strategic advantage in the aftermath. In other words, victory is not a strategic concept. At first this notion may seem strange, but because strategy never ends, it is a constant competition without an ultimate victory. Put another way, those who practice tactics and operational art maximize choices within the given rules and constraints provided by strategic art. Those who practice strategic art pursue strategic advantage by manipulating the rules and limitations, thereby changing the context and conditions that circumscribe and shape tactical and operational actions.[12]

Earlier in the *Game of Thrones* series, Robb Stark also demonstrates a growing understanding of Dolman's ideas. After the Starks capture Jaime Lannister, Robb brings him before his mother, Catelyn Stark. During this discussion, Jaime Lannister challenges Robb to fight man-to-man as champions for their houses. Robb wisely responds, "If we do it your way, Kingslayer, you'd win. . . . We're not doing it your way."[13] Robb lives to fight another day and marry a woman he loved, but this breaks the arranged marriage that was the basis for the Stark alliance with the Freys. This sowed the seeds of his undoing. Sadly, Robb did not understand that the Freys would turn on him, nor does he foresee the Lannisters changing the nature of the game with a secret agreement with the Freys and the Boltons, which culminates with the Red Wedding assassination of Robb's pregnant wife, Robb, and his mother.

Naturally, and ironically, the Lannisters' practice of strategy writ large teaches the Starks, making those who survive more capable in the long run. For example, when the honorable Ned Stark confronts Cersei Lannister, he naively assumes that Cersei would follow the same norms of honor that he did. Cersei, however, focuses on power, not honor. She explains the simple nature of *Game of Thrones* to Ned Stark and the audience: "You win, or you die."[14] Sadly for House Stark, Cersei's statement is prescient, as her newly crowned son, King Joffrey, has Ned beheaded, ignoring Cersei's protests. Despite Joffrey's short-term sadistic glee, however, this action sets off cascading effects that still reverberate in the story. The only bit of Cersei's advice that Joffrey seems to heed is, "Anyone who isn't us is an enemy."[15] Although Ned, Robb, and Catelyn die, Sansa and Arya live and learn.

Sansa Stark learns strategy the hard way—from her horrible experiences with the Lannisters, Littlefinger, and the Boltons. Cersei Lannister starts Sansa's strategic education, but Cersei's intention certainly is not to help the teenage Stark girl. Nevertheless, Sansa recalls those hard days and comes to understand their bitter lessons. Sansa's second unintentional master, Littlefinger, uses her as a pawn for his advancement, first in his takeover of the Vale of Arryn and then by wedding Sansa to Ramsay Bolton in an attempt to ultimately become Warden of the North. Just before leaving Sansa with the Boltons, Littlefinger points out that she had "learned to maneuver from the very best."[16] Littlefinger, however, does understand Ramsay Bolton's strategic skills and the depth of his sadistic nature. Again, Sansa learns at great personal and familial expense. All of this adds up to a strategic education par excellence. In Littlefinger's short trial, we see this education come to fruition. It is delightful to watch Sansa turn the accused's "little game" and other smug, but extremely instructive, comments against him. "I'm a slow learner, it's true, but I learn."[17] Sansa's final words to Littlefinger before Arya slits his throat are: "Thank you for all your many lessons, Lord Baelish. I'll never forget them."

Arya, too, learns much from the Lannisters. While he fights Arya's older brother, Robb Stark, Tywin Lannister has Arya Stark serve as his cupbearer, although he does not know her identity. With delightful irony, Tywin provides her with valuable strategic lessons and insight. One of the most important examples is when Tywin discusses the history of Harrenhal with Arya, teaching her about unexamined assumptions and manipulating the nature of the contest. The Lannister patriarch's comments resonate perfectly with Dolman's theories when he explains how the great fortress fell to Aegon Targaryen's dragons, as "Harrenhal was built to withstand an attack from the land. . . . But an attack from the air, with dragonfire? Harren and all his sons roasted alive within these walls. . . . Aegon Targaryen changed the rules."[18]

This chapter's discussion on the strategy of House Lannister in *Game of Thrones* underlines the timeless nature of strategy. This is why Sun Tzu's *Art of War*, Thucydides's *History of the Peloponnesian War*, Kauṭilya's *Arthashastra*, Machiavelli's *The Prince*, Clausewitz's *On War*, Jomini's *The Art of War*, Mahan's *The Influence of Sea Power upon History*, Corbett's *Some Principles of Maritime Strategy*, and other works retain so much value today.[19] In fact, Michael Handel attributes the longevity and preeminence of works such as these to "the underlying logic of human nature, and by extension of political action," which, he argues, "has not changed throughout history."[20] To better understand modern conflict, we can use these theorists and other authors' works in conjunction with *Game of Thrones* to help us appreciate the ageless relationship of money and power as well as the enduring mindset necessary to successfully wield military art to maintain or achieve strategic advantage.

NOTES

1. Thomas Hobbes, *Leviathan* (Harmondsworth, UK: Penguin Books, 1968), chap. 13, para. 9.
2. Mikal Gilmore, "George R. R. Martin: The Rolling Stone Interview," *Rolling Stone*, April 23, 2014, https://www.rollingstone.com/culture/culture-news/george-r-r-martin-the-rolling-stone-interview-242487/. See also "Real History behind Game of Thrones (Explained by Historians and George R.R. Martin)," A, YouTube video, 40:14, July 14, 2016, https://www.youtube.com/watch?v=Odw3Nxdqq4o.
3. David Benioff and D. B. Weiss, "You Win or You Die," season 1, episode 7, dir. Daniel Minahan, *Game of Thrones*, aired May 29, 2011, on HBO.
4. Alfred T. Mahan, *The Influence of Sea Power upon History, 1660–1783* (1890; repr., New York: Dover Publications, 1987), 71.
5. John Brewer, *The Sinews of Power: War, Money and the English State, 1688–1783* (Boston: Unwin Hyman, 1989), 32–39.
6. R. Craig Nation, "National Power," in *U.S. Army War College Guide to National Security Policy and Strategy*, ed. J. Boone Bartholomees Jr., 5th ed. (Carlisle PA: Strategic Studies Institute, U.S. Army War College, 2012), 151.
7. Richard A. Chilcoat, *Strategic Art: The New Discipline for 21st Century Leaders* (Carlisle PA: Strategic Studies Institute, U.S. Army War College, 1995), 3.

8. Strategic advantage is defined as a position of strength of a nation, coalition, or nonstate actor relative to another nation, coalition, or nonstate actor. The position of strength could be one of several factors, such as political, military, economic, social, information, infrastructure, physical environment, or time. Chilcoat, *Strategic Art*, 3.

9. Nikolai Varfolomeyev, "Strategy in an Academic Formulation," in *The Evolution of Soviet Operational Art, 1927–1991: The Documentary Basis*, ed. David Glantz (London: Frank Cass, 1995), 42.

10. Aleksandr Svechin, "Strategy and Operational Art," in *The Evolution of Soviet Operational Art, 1927–1991: The Documentary Basis*, ed. David Glantz (London: Frank Cass, 1995), 22.

11. Everett Carl Dolman, *Pure Strategy: Power and Principle in the Space and Information Age* (New York: Frank Cass, 2005), 1.

12. Dolman, *Pure Strategy*, 1–4.

13. David Benioff and D. B. Weiss, "Baelor," season 1, episode 9, dir. Alan Taylor, *Game of Thrones*, aired June 12, 2011, on HBO.

14. Benioff and Weiss, "You Win or You Die."

15. David Benioff and D. B. Weiss, "Lord Snow," season 1, episode 3, dir. Brian Kirk, *Game of Thrones*, aired May 1, 2011, on HBO.

16. Dave Hill, "Sons of the Harpy," season 5, episode 4, dir. Mark Mylod, *Game of Thrones*, aired May 3, 2015, on HBO.

17. David Benioff and D. B. Weiss, "The Dragon and the Wolf," season 7, episode 7, dir. Jeremy Podeswa, *Game of Thrones*, aired August 27, 2017, on HBO.

18. David Benioff and D. B. Weiss, "A Man without Honor," season 2, episode 7, dir. David Nutter, *Game of Thrones*, aired May 13, 2012, on HBO.

19. Sun Tzu, *The Art of War*, trans. Samuel B. Griffith (New York: Oxford University Press, 1963); Thucydides, *The Landmark Thucydides: A Comprehensive Guide to the Peloponnesian War*, ed. Robert B. Strassler (New York: Simon and Schuster, 1998); Kautilya, *The Arthashastra* (New York: Penguin Books India, 1992); Niccolò Machiavelli, *The Art of War*, trans. Ellis Farnsworth (New York: Da Capo Press, 1965); Niccolò Machiavelli, *The Discourses of Niccolò Machiavelli*, trans. Leslie J. Walker (Boston: Routledge and Paul, 1975); Niccolò Machiavelli, *The Prince*, trans. Luigi Ricci, revised by E. R. P. Vincent (New York: New American Library, 1952); Carl von Clausewitz, *On War*, 1st ed. (Princeton NJ: Princeton University Press, 1989); Antoine-Henri de Jomini, *The Art of War*, trans. U.S. Military Academy (London: Greenhill Books, 1992); Mahan, *Influence of Sea Power upon History*; and Julian S. Corbett, *Some Principles of Maritime Strategy* (1911; repr., Annapolis MD: Naval Institute Press, 1988).

20. Michael I. Handel, *Masters of War: Classical Strategic Thought*, 3rd ed. (New York: Routledge, 2000), 2.

3

Fear or Love

Insights from Machiavelli for Those Who Seek the Iron Throne

LIAM COLLINS

In his seminal work, *The Prince*, Italian political theorist Niccolò Machiavelli famously asked "whether it is better to be loved than to be feared, or the reverse."[1] Machiavelli answered that it is better to be feared than loved but warned against fear spurring hatred. In *The Prince*, he offered a number of other useful insights, and his work has been so influential that *Machiavellian* is now a word defined as "being or acting in accordance with the principles of government analyzed in Machiavelli's *The Prince*, in which political expediency is placed above morality and the use of craft and deceit to maintain the authority and carry out the polices of a ruler" or "characterized by subtle or unscrupulous cunning, deception, expediency, or dishonesty."[2] His treatise, or discourse, aims to advise a prince, the sixteenth-century city-state ruler in Italy, how to remain in power. Ultimately, he argues that the ends justify the means.

Who was Machiavelli? Machiavelli was an Italian philosopher, politician, diplomat, historian, author, and has been called the father of modern political science.[3] He was "born in a tumultuous era in which popes waged acquisitive wars against Italian city-states, and people and cities often fell from power as France, Spain, the Holy Roman Empire, and Switzerland battled for regional influence and control. Political-military alliances continually changed, featuring condottieri (mercenary leaders), who changed sides without warning, and the rise and fall of many short-lived governments."[4] In many ways, it was not unlike the world of Westeros.

When addressing "whether it is better to be loved than feared, or the reverse," in chapter 17 of *The Prince*, Machiavelli starts with an idealistic approach, similar to that of a Greek philosopher, stating, "I say that every prince ought to wish to be considered kind rather than cruel."[5] But he quickly transitions to a more pragmatic, or Machiavellian, approach when he writes, "Nevertheless [the prince] must take care to avoid misusing his kindness. Cesare Borgia was considered cruel; yet his cruelty restored Romagna, unified it in peace and loyalty." He continues, "If this result is considered good, then he must be judged much kinder than the Florentines who, to avoid being called cruel, allowed Pistoia to be destroyed."[6] In other words, the prince and the people are better off when ruled by fear, as opposed to love.

Machiavelli quickly dispenses with the notion that you can be both feared and loved, "since the two rarely come together." He argues that "anyone compelled to choose will find greater security in being feared than in being loved."[7] In making his elegant case that fear always trumps love, Machiavelli writes,

> [Men] are ungrateful, fickle, dissembling, anxious to flee danger, and covetous of gain. So long as you promote their advantage they are all yours, as I said before, and will offer you their blood, their goods, their lives, and their children, when the need for these is remote. When the need arises, however, they will turn against you. The prince who bases his security upon their word, lacking other provision, is doomed; for friendships that are gained by money, not by greatness and nobility of spirit, may well be earned, but cannot be kept; and in time of need, they will have fled your purse. Men are less concerned about offending someone they have cause to love than someone they have cause to

fear. Love endures by a bond which men, being scoundrels, may break whenever it serves their advantage to do so; but fear is supported by the dread of pain, which is ever present.[8]

While many kings and lords of Westeros heeded Machiavelli's words and prized fear over love, they failed to mind the advice from the second half of the chapter, in which Machiavelli states, "Still a prince should make himself feared in such a way that, though he does not gain love, he escapes hatred."[9] King Aerys Targaryen, the Mad King, lost the throne when he was slain by Jaime Lannister, a member of his own Kingsguard. While *Game of Thrones* starts long after Aerys Targaryen was deposed, it is clear that while he inspired fear throughout the kingdom, there was little love for him. Even his own daughter, Daenerys, said of him, "I know what my father was. What he did. I know the Mad King earned his name."[10]

King Joffrey was both feared and hated, and thus, he lasted less than three years on the Iron Throne before being poisoned by Petyr Baelish and Lady Olenna Tyrell at his wedding feast. His own acting Hand called him "a vicious idiot for a king."[11] Tywin Lannister, Lord of Casterly Rock, probably the most feared of all the lords, wasn't even loved by his own family. In fact, he inspired so much hatred that it ultimately resulted in his own son killing him with a crossbow.

King Robert Baratheon didn't appear to be personally loved or feared, as he spent most of his time drinking and whoring, but he wasn't particularly hated either. Given that he deferred the duties of running the kingdom to his Hand and his Small Council, it seems likely that the council was able to administer an appropriate level of fear within the population of Westeros, since he was able to maintain his rule for seventeen years.

Both Ned Stark, as Warden of the North, and his son, Robb Stark, as King in the North, chose to rule by love, as opposed to fear, but this did not bear well for either of them. Ned ultimately found his head on a spike, while Robb's decapitated body was unceremoniously paraded around on a horse with his own dire wolf's head above his body. Robb was betrayed by both Theon Greyjoy, whom he viewed as a brother, and Lord Bolton, one of his bannermen. This would come as no surprise to Machiavelli given his belief that men "are ungrateful, fickle," and "cowardly" and will "turn against you" and that "relying entirely on their promises" brings ruin. Given that so few followed Machiavelli's advice, it should come as no surprise that many leaders of Westeros came to a premature end. The Starks failed to grasp that fear works best because you can't trust people to always be loyal through affection.

Likewise, Orys I attempted to rule by love, having been described as a just leader. He was applauded for his reforms by nobles and commoners alike, but in the words of Tywin Lannister, "he wasn't just for long." Shortly after Joffrey's death, Tywin described Orys's fate to Tommen: "He was murdered in his sleep after less than a year by his own brother. Was that truly just of him, to abandon his subjects to an evil that he was too gullible to recognize?"[12]

So why did the rulers in Westeros fail so miserably? One thought might be that it was a tough environment and leaders simply didn't last long. Sure, it was a Hobbesian world in which "the life of man [was] solitary, poor, nasty, brutish, and short,"[13] but even in that era, Robert Baratheon maintained his reign for seventeen years and the Mad King lasted twenty-four. A more plausible explanation is that many of the rulers failed because they simply lacked an adviser like Machiavelli with "subtle or unscrupulous cunning, deception, expediency, or dishonesty." Simply put, success largely depended on having a Machiavellian Hand, and Tyrion Lannister was the rare Machiavellian in Westeros.

Like Machiavelli, Tyrion was a historian, politician, diplomat, and philosopher. While he was disadvantaged, having been born a dwarf in that era and hated by his father for "killing" his mother, he was still a Lannister, so he never had to want for money or work a steady job, at least until his father appointed him acting Hand of the King. When not whoring or drinking, he was a voracious reader. On the ride north to Castle Black, Tyrion told Jon Snow, "My brother has his sword, and I have my mind, and a mind needs books like a sword needs a whetstone. That's why I read so much."[14] While Tywin was away fighting Robb Stark's Army of the North, Tyrion performed superbly as acting Hand to King Joffrey. He found that his study of history made him well suited for the job and that he had a knack for deceit and deception. His genius ultimately saved King's Landing from nearly certain defeat, and he was able to magnificently manage despite a boy king who lacked the maturity to rule.

By comparison, most other Hands failed miserably. Ned Stark was too idealistic and principled to serve as Hand, lacking "unscrupulous cunning" and "deceit." He may have been a great warrior, battlefield leader, and friend to King Robert, but he was a terrible Hand. He refused to condone the killing of Daenerys on the moral ground of her being a child and, thus, left a threat with a legitimate right to the throne alive. And rather than arresting Cersei upon discovering that the father of her children is not the king but her brother, he did the honorable thing and allowed her twenty-four hours to flee the city. A much more cunning Cersei used this time, instead, to consolidate power and plot against Ned. As Cersei tells him, "When you play the game of thrones, you win or you die. There is no middle ground."[15] Ned simply failed to understand how to play the game, and it led to his demise.

Likewise, the Onion Knight, Davos Seaworth, failed as a Hand. Born in Flea Bottom, the poorest slum in King's Landing, Davos lacked the formal education of Tyrion, and in fact, he couldn't even read until the third season. Too often his advice was clouded by his disdain for the Lord of Light religion. Prior to the attack on King's Landing, he convinces Stannis to leave the red priestess behind. While it can't be certain that the outcome would have been different had she accompanied Davos, it is reasonable to conclude that her sorcery likely would have changed the outcome, given that she was able to defeat Renly's numerically superior army without a single sword being drawn. Like Ned, Davos was too principled for the Machiavellian environment of Westeros, where the ends justify the means, and focusing on principled means can often result in death, as Machiavelli writes, "The way men live is so far removed from the way they ought to live that anyone who abandons what is for what should be pursues his downfall rather than his preservation."[16]

Tywin Lannister's performance, having served stints as Hand of the King to the Mad King, King Robert, and King Joffrey, was somewhat mixed. He was a master at placing "political expediency ... above morality and [using] craft and deceit to maintain the authority and carry out the policies of a ruler." However, the manner in which he executed deceit to accomplish "political expediency" only incited hatred. Tyrion wisely argued that the treacherous feast of the Red Wedding violated acceptable norms of the day. The dialogue between the two shows the nuanced but extremely important difference and why Tyrion is the Machiavelli of Westeros. While discussing the Red Wedding, Tywin asked, "Do you disapprove?" Tyrion responded, "I'm all for cheating; this is war. But to slaughter them at a wedding. . . . The Northerners will never forget." To which Tywin responded, "Good. Let 'em remember what happens when they march on the South."[17] Tyrion understood that even during this anarchic period there are rules as to how the game is played and that you put yourself and your family at great risk with the hatred that is spawned if you violate the rules.

What of the Spider and Littlefinger? While both were on the Small Council and both were exceedingly cunning and operated in a Machiavellian manner, they had different clients from that of Machiavelli's prince. When Varys visited Ned Stark in his cell after being imprisoned, Ned asked, "Who do you truly serve?" Varys's response was clear: "The Realm, my lord. Someone must."[18] While the Spider served the realm, Petyr Baelish, perhaps the most dangerous man in Westeros, served only himself. In the end, both rivaled Tyrion for the ability to operate effectively in the Machiavellian world of Westeros, but only Tyrion's goal was to help "the prince" maintain his rule.

What else can be learned from Machiavelli? Machiavelli is very critical of conscripts, stating, "Mercenaries and auxiliaries are useless and dangerous; and any ruler who keeps his state dependent upon mercenaries will never have real peace or security, for they are disorganized, undisciplined, ambitious, and faithless. Brave before their allies, they are cowards before the enemy."[19] In Westeros there is much debate about the reliability of mercenaries, but their record is fairly strong. When discussing them, Barristan Selmy argues that "men who fight for gold have neither honor nor loyalty; they cannot be trusted." However, Jorah Mormont argues, "They can be trusted to kill . . . if they're well paid."[20]

Yet in *Game of Thrones*, mercenaries and sellswords performed remarkably well and were more reliable than many lords. The Stone Crows, led by Shagga, son of Dolf; the Burned Men, led by Timett, son of Timett; and the Black Ears, led by Chella, son of Cheyk, were reliable and fought valiantly for Tyrion at the Battle of the Green Fork, for the price of a few weapons and a small amount of gold. Likewise, Bronn was extremely loyal to Tyrion, and it was clear that his loyalty was not tied to gold alone. Bronn was anything but "ungrateful, fickle, dissembling, [and] anxious to flee danger."[21] Tyrion put him in constant danger, and never once did Bronn attempt to evade. By contrast, nobles, including Theon Greyjoy, Lord Bolton, and Lord Walder Frey, turned out to be much less reliable.

While the world today is much different from sixteenth-century Italy, or the imaginary world of Westeros, Machiavelli's words still hold true. During the Iraq War, fear held greater persuasive power than love. While al-Qaeda in Iraq subscribed to a twisted version of Sunni Islam, a vast majority of the more moderate Sunni population had no love for al-Qaeda in Iraq, but those same moderates supported the terrorist group out of fear. The brutal tactics carried out by its leader Abu Musab al-Zarqawi held the population in check. But eventually his brutality turned fear into hatred, and the Sunni population turned on him.

There were at least four isolated attempts by Sunni tribes to realign with coalition forces prior to the Sunni Awakening, but each attempt failed, as they were unable to muster the required strength to defeat al-Qaeda. With the coalition unable to provide security, the attempts quickly fell apart, and the Sunni tribes returned to tacit support for al-Qaeda out of fear. The fourth attempt failed when al-Qaeda killed most of the group's leaders. The Sunni Awakening only succeeded because the U.S. surge provided the additional forces necessary to safeguard the Sunni tribes and protect them from al-Qaeda retaliation for supporting the coalition.[22] Had al-Qaeda practiced less brutality, it might have been able to maintain its hold over the Sunni population. Likewise, if the United States understood the power of fear sooner, it might have been quicker to surge troops to support the tribes.

While modern nation-states do not use mercenaries per se, they do use proxies. The United States has used proxy forces in Syria; Iran supported proxies in Iraq; and Russia uses South Ossetian forces to advance its interests in Georgia, as well as street gangs and thugs in the Donbas region of eastern Ukraine and elsewhere. Machiavelli, however, would not be surprised to find that the performance of these modern-day mercenaries can be extremely poor. Criminals often make poor agents, as they are often extremely unreliable and may look for ways to exploit their state sponsor.[23] While the United States might avoid criminal proxies, it is not immune to problems; the United States spent over $500 million to train what ultimately amounted to a mere five fighters in Syria, before shutting down the program in 2015.[24]

In the end, the many kings and lords of Westeros would have fared better if they had had a Machiavelli to advise them. The Stark lords failed because they thought it was better to be loved than feared. Lord Tywin and King Joffrey were right in their belief that it was better to be feared than loved, but they failed because their actions inspired hatred. The most important action that a king or lord of Westeros could have done to ensure regime stability was to select the right Hand and Small Council and heed their advice. As Tywin wisely advised Tommen, "A wise young king listens to his counselors and heeds their advice until he comes of age. And the wisest kings continue to listen to them long afterwards."[25] Unfortunately, few possessed the skills to be a Machiavellian Hand. It required cunning, deception, education, and perhaps most importantly, an understanding that the ends justify the means, and sometimes immoral means must be used to achieve the desired ends. Given that Tyrion was one of the few Machiavellians in Westeros, it should come as no surprise that life in *Game of Thrones* was "solitary, poor, nasty, brutish, and short."

NOTES

1. Niccolò Machiavelli, *The Prince*, trans. Daniel Nonno (1966; repr., New York: Bantam Books, 2003), 65.
2. Dictionary.com, s.v. "Machiavellian," accessed May 22, 2018, https://www.dictionary.com /browse/machiavellian.

3. Mikko Lahtinen, *Politics and Philosophy: Niccolò Machiavelli and Louis Althusser's Aleatory Materialism* (Chicago: Haymarket Books, 2009), 115.

3. Mikko Lahtinen, *Politics and Philosophy: Niccolò Machiavelli and Louis Althusser's Aleatory Materialism* (Chicago: Haymarket Books, 2009), 115.

4. "Niccolò Machiavelli—A Brief Introduction," *Niccolò Machiavelli Blog*, October 13, 2017, https://nicolomachiavelliblog.wordpress.com/2017/10/13/first-blog-post/.

5. Machiavelli, *The Prince*, 65.

6. Machiavelli, *The Prince*, 65.

7. Machiavelli, *The Prince*, 66.

8. Machiavelli, *The Prince*, 66.

9. Machiavelli, *The Prince*, 66.

10. David Benioff and D. B. Weiss, "Hardhome," season 5, episode 8, dir. Miguel Sapochnik, *Game of Thrones*, aired May 31, 2015, on HBO.

11. Tyrion tells Joffrey, "We've had vicious kings, and we've had idiot kings, but I don't know if we've ever been cursed with a vicious idiot for a king!" Vanessa Taylor, "The Old Gods and the New," season 2, episode 6, dir. David Nutter, *Game of Thrones*, aired May 6, 2012, on HBO.

12. David Benioff and D. B. Weiss, "Breaker of Chains," season 4, episode 3, dir. Alex Graves, *Game of Thrones*, aired April 20, 2014, on HBO.

13. Thomas Hobbes, *Leviathan; or, The Matter, Forme, and Power of a Common-Wealth Ecclesiastical and Civill* (1651; Project Gutenberg, 2009), https://www.gutenberg.org/files/3207/3207-h/3207-h.htm.

14. David Benioff and D. B. Weiss, "The Kingsroad," season 1, episode 2, dir. Tim Van Patten, *Game of Thrones*, aired April 24, 2011, on HBO.

15. David Benioff and D. B. Weiss, "You Win or You Die," season 1, episode 7, dir. Daniel Minahan, *Game of Thrones*, aired April 24, 2011, on HBO.

16. Machiavelli, *The Prince*, 61–62.

17. David Benioff and D. B. Weiss, "Mhysa," season 3, episode 10, dir. David Nutter, *Game of Thrones*, aired June 9, 2013, on HBO.

18. George R. R. Martin, "The Pointy End," season 1, episode 8, dir. Daniel Minahan, *Game of Thrones*, aired June 5, 2011, on HBO.

19. Machiavelli, *The Prince*, 52.

20. David Benioff and D. B. Weiss, "Second Sons," season 3, episode 8, dir. Michelle MacLaren, *Game of Thrones*, aired May 19, 2013, on HBO.

21. Machiavelli, *The Prince*, 66.

22. Stephen Biddle, Jeffrey Friedman, and Jacob Shapiro, "Testing the Surge: Why Did Violence Decline in Iraq in 2007?" *International Security* 37, no. 1 (2012): 7–40.

23. Mark Galeotti, "The Kremlin's Newest Hybrid Warfare Asset: Gangsters," *Foreign Policy*, June 12, 2017.

24. Paul McLeary, "The Pentagon Wasted $550 Million Training Syrian Rebels. It's About to Try Again," *Foreign Policy*, March 18, 2106.

25. Benioff and Weiss, "Breaker of Chains."

4

The Source of Tyrion Lannister's Unlikely Survival and Success

JOE BYERLY

Of all the players in *Game of Thrones*, Tyrion Lannister would probably not make anyone's short list of likely survivors of season after season of intrigue and violence. He's small in stature, he has a drinking problem, and his chances of catching venereal disease are extremely high. There are many characters who possessed quality traits that made them better candidates for survival, and yet Tyrion outlasts them all: the noble and strong Ned Stark lost his head in season 1; the Achilles-like Oberyn Martell had his skull crushed in season 4; and the ruthless and Machiavellian Tywin Lannister met his demise in a particularly unfortunate setting, also in season 4. Among the heroes and villains of Westeros, how does a man who stands at only four feet five inches and has a penchant for heavy drinking and enthusiastically patronizing bordellos make it so far in the game of thrones?

Tyrion had two habits that became his competitive advantage and enabled him to overcome his many disadvantages. First, he read *a lot*. Through reading, he gained an understanding of history and internalized years of vicarious experiences. These books gave him the mental models with which to maneuver through multiple complex situations within the

Seven Kingdoms. Second, he built a large and diverse network of people who not only contributed to his development but kept him alive.

Reading

When we are first introduced to Tyrion, we learn that he likes to read. On the way to the Wall, while everyone else prepared to camp for the night, he found a quiet spot and began reading a book that he had borrowed from Winterfell's library. Jon Snow interrupted him and asked why he read so much. Tyrion pointed out that because of his physical attributes, he would never be a swordsman or a great warrior, but he had something that he could continually improve and strengthen. "My brother has his sword, and I have my mind," he tells Jon Snow. "And a mind needs books like a sword needs a whetstone."[1]

As the seasons progress, Tyrion's practice of reading bears fruit in the form of his firm grasp of human nature, history, and war. For instance, he played a pivotal role in the Battle of the Blackwater, when he used deception to destroy Stannis Baratheon's fleet. Tyrion had zero experience with sieges prior to the battle, so he spent time educating himself. He read *An History of the Great Sieges of Westeros*. From his study, he likely saw patterns in the sieges of history and learned from past successes and failures.

The enemy's strategy included a simultaneous attack against King's Landing from land and sea. But during the naval assault, Tyrion had the Iron Fleet leave and Blackwater Bay filled with wildfire, a highly flammable liquid. As the fleet drew close, thinking their victory secured, Tyrion ignited the water, destroying the majority of Stannis's ships. In reading multiple histories of Westeros, he knew how to shape his deception so as to lull the enemy fleet into a false sense of security, thus allowing the wildfire to damage the most ships. Tyrion's mix of reading and experience continued to develop and strengthen his understanding of warfare.

General Dwight D. Eisenhower, another student of war, similarly used deception in 1944 to draw Hitler's forces away from the Normandy landing sites. He created a narrative that played into the Nazis' beliefs regarding Allied capabilities and intentions, causing them to predict that the Allies wouldn't attack until they had good weather and that they would land around the Pas de Calais area, not Normandy.[2]

As Daenerys Targaryen wrestled with using overwhelming force to defeat Cersei Lannister and become the new ruler of Westeros, Tyrion advised her against it. He explained that if she wanted to win, she needed to better understand her adversary first. He told her, "You need to take your enemies' side if you are going to see things the way they do. And you need to see things the way they do if you are going to anticipate their actions, respond effectively, and beat them."[3]

Neither Tyrion's use of deception at the Battle of the Blackwater nor his advice to the Mother of Dragons is likely to have come from his limited experiences. They were the result of the insights he gained from reading. Because of his love of books, Tyrion developed mental models that allowed him to outthink, outsmart, and outmaneuver the various contenders for the Iron Throne in Westeros.

So what are mental models? How did Tyrion develop them from reading? Mental models are lenses through which we view the world, developed through a lifetime of personal experiences and education.[4] Once stored in our brains, they help us quickly understand the world and influence how we take action. Mental models are the reason two individuals—say, for example, a Lannister and a Stark—can look at the same information and draw two very different conclusions. The types and variances of experiences, and how we make sense of them, will determine how our mental models are shaped.

It is important to remember that our models are only as good as the inputs. If we fail to feed our brains with varied experiences or quality literature, then our models will be limited in scope. Since we know that Tyrion did not grow up gaining war experience from campaigning like his brother, Jaime, then he had to develop his mental models through the vicarious experience that comes from reading.

Tyrion's use of reading to build mental models is a practice that has proven its value beyond the shores of Westeros. Throughout history many of our greatest battlefield commanders and strategists also saw the value of reading. For example, in the opening of *The Prince*, Niccolò Machiavelli wrote that he valued "the knowledge of the actions of great men, learned by me from long experience with modern things and a continuous reading of ancient ones."[5] The military strategist Carl von Clausewitz also commented on the power of mental models when he discussed *coup d'oeil*—the ability to quickly appraise a battlefield's terrain—as a prerequisite to military genius in his book *On War*.[6] General George Patton took extensive notes on Frederick the Great, Napoleon Bonaparte, Ardant du Picq, and Helmuth von Moltke, studying not only their successes but also their failures.[7] And more recently Secretary of Defense James Mattis wrote, "Thanks to my reading, I have never been caught flat-footed by any situation, never at a loss for how any problem has been addressed before. It doesn't give me all the answers, but it lights what is often a dark path ahead."[8]

Like Mattis, Tyrion's practice of reading helped him quickly comprehend situations and develop a way forward that proved successful. He survived not because he was a Lannister but because he relied on the vicarious experiences gained through reading history and absorbing the past.

While reading filled in a lot of the gaps in Tyrion's knowledge, however, there were still gaps. To fill them, he relied on the second aspect of his competitive advantage: his networks.

Networks

Throughout the series, Tyrion comes into contact with a cast of people who fell well outside the elite social circles of King's Landing or Casterly Rock. In doing so, he built a diverse network of people who contributed to his development and, on several occasions, saved his life.

A review some of the key relationships Tyrion developed over the course of seven seasons makes clear the remarkable utility of his networks. He befriended Jon Snow early in season 1. He also traveled to the Wall and spent time in the Night's Watch with Maester Aemon and Jeor Mormont. He teamed up with the sellsword Bronn, from whom he learned about many of the harsh realities of combat. He formed an alliance with the hill tribes in the North (and led them into battle). As the Hand of the King, he interacted with members of the Small Council, including the conniving

Varys. And finally, he found himself in the camp of Daenerys Targaryen, planning an invasion of Westeros among a motley crew of former slaves and seasoned warriors. Tyrion is so connected that a network study published in an academic journal concluded that he is one of three main characters in *Game of Thrones*.[9]

These connections are significant because a body of research shows how our networks are critical to professional success. In his book *Friend of a Friend: Understanding the Hidden Networks That Can Transform Your Life and Your Career*, David Burkus argues, "Being connected to a strong network provides major advantages—access to diverse skills and perspectives, the ability to learn private information, and the type of expertise and influence that makes it easier to attain power."[10]

Time and time again, Tyrion's network helped shape his outlook by exposing him to diverse skills and perspectives. We know that Tyrion read several books in preparation for the Battle of the Blackwater. However, there were gaps between the harsh realities of siege warfare and what was written in books. Bronn filled those gaps by explaining how the breakdown of society starts during the siege. Bronn's insight gave Tyrion the impetus to develop a plan that quickly defeated Stannis Baratheon's forces rather than delaying for a future breakout.

Tyrion's connections also provided him with "private information" and "the type of expertise and influence" that Burkus describes, which "make it easier to attain power." After Tyrion killed his father, Tywin, he met Varys once again during his escape from Westeros. Varys invited him to help bring Daenerys into power and finally bring peace to Westeros. When one door shut on Tyrion, his network opened another. When he finally met Daenerys and became part of her inner circle, Varys again provided him with assistance. Varys's own personal network became an extension of Tyrion's, helping him to govern Meereen in Daenerys's absence.

Throughout history, successful leaders have surrounded themselves in times of conflict with people who provided them with diverse viewpoints and opposing thought. Abraham Lincoln placed three former opponents who ran against him in the election of 1860 in his cabinet during the Civil War.

This helped him better understand the challenges he would face in uniting the Union, let alone seeking to reunite the entire country. During Operation Iraqi Freedom, General Stanley McChrystal surrounded himself with members of the State Department, the Central Intelligence Agency, and other key agencies (all with different and sometimes opposing cultures) so that he could approach complex problems through a whole-of-government lens.[11]

What Does Tyrion's Experience Teach Us about Being a Player in Today's Game of Thrones?

Tyrion Lannister was not born with the physical attributes of someone most likely to succeed in the highly contentious environment of Westeros. However, he did understand that he possessed opportunities to improve his chances. And so do we.

Tyrion invested in his personal development through a lifelong habit of reading. He studied the past to understand the present. He understood war and human nature and used this to his advantage throughout the series. We can make the same investment as Tyrion and prepare ourselves for the conflicts that lie ahead. Statesmen and military leaders throughout history faced many of the same problems we see in today's geopolitical environment. As retired lieutenant general H. R. McMaster once wrote, "People fight today for the same reasons Thucydides identified 2,500 years ago: fear, honor and interest."[12] In the end, the richness of our mental models will determine through what lens we see the world and the actions we take. There is no easier way to do that than through reading.

Tyrion also supplemented his reading with the knowledge gained from large, diverse networks. He learned from sellswords, bastards, queens, and schemers. We may not come into contact with characters as outlandish as those Tyrion meets in the Seven Kingdoms, but we can build a network of diverse personalities and social circles who can help fill our gaps. Authors Will Richardson and Rob Mancabelli call this a "personal learning network," which they define as "a set of connections to people and resources both offline and online who enrich our learning."[13] Problems like state competition, the rise of violent extremist organizations, and failing governance are not going to be well managed by leaders with narrow sets of skills. Wicked problems require leaders who are well rounded and who see those problems from multiple angles. We can only gain that through surrounding ourselves with people who help expand our own thinking.

Tyrion Lannister could never have competed with the likes of his brother, Jaime; the Stark men; or the Martells in direct combat. That would have played to his weaknesses. So he took another route—and that is one of the greatest lessons he offers us. He played to his strengths. He fed his curiosity through self-study and cultivated his network through constant personal contact. He succeeded in war, not by the sword, but by a more subtle approach. At first glance, much like our evaluation of Tyrion, the only way to win wars is by the sword. Tyrion teaches us that there's more to it than that. We only need to find our competitive advantage and bring that with us to our own game of thrones.

NOTES

1. David Benioff and D. B. Weiss, "The Kingsroad," season 1, episode 2, dir. Tim Van Patten, *Game of Thrones*, aired April 24, 2011, on HBO.

2. Milan N. Vego, *Joint Operational Warfare: Theory and Practice* (Newport RI: U.S. Naval War College Press, 2009).

3. David Benioff and D. B. Weiss, "Beyond the Wall," season 7, episode 6, dir. Alan Taylor, *Game of Thrones*, aired August 20, 2017, on HBO.

4. Gary Klein, *Streetlights and Shadows: Searching for the Keys to Adaptive Decision Making* (Cambridge MA: MIT Press, 2009), 41.

5. Niccolò Machiavelli, *The Prince*, trans. Harvey C. Mansfield, 2nd ed. (Chicago: University of Chicago Press, 1998), 3–4.

6. Carl von Clausewitz, *On War*, trans. Michael Howard and Peter Paret (Princeton NJ: Princeton University Press, 1976), 102.

7. Roger H. Nye, "Whence Patton's Military Genius," *Parameters* 21, no. 4 (Winter 1991–92): 60–73.

8. Jill R. Russell, "With Rifle and Bibliography: General Mattis on Professional Reading," *Strife*, May 7, 2013, http://www.strifeblog.org/2013/05/07/with-rifle-and-bibliography-general-mattis-on-professional-reading/.

9. Andrew Beveridge and Jia Shan, "Network of Thrones," *Math Horizons*, April 2016, https://www.maa.org/sites/default/files/pdf/Mathhorizons/NetworkofThrones%20%281%29.pdf.

10. David Burkus, *Friend of a Friend: Understanding the Hidden Networks That Can Transform Your Life and Your Career* (New York: Houghton Mifflin Harcourt, 2018), 8.

11. Stanley A. McChrystal, Tantum Collins, David Silverman, and Chris Fussell, *Team of Teams: New Rules of Engagement for a Complex World* (New York: Portfolio, 2015).

12. H. R. McMaster, "The Pipe Dream of Easy War," *New York Times*, July 21, 2013, https://www.nytimes.com/2013/07/21/opinion/sunday/the-pipe-dream-of-easy-war.html.

13. Will Richardson and Rob Mancabelli, *Personal Learning Networks: Using the Power of Connections to Transform Education* (Bloomington IN: Solution Tree Press, 2011), 2.

5

The Mother of Dragons

Defiant Leadership for Uncertain Times

RICK MONTCALM

Uncertainty is a hallmark of conflict. What Carl von Clausewitz called the fog and friction of war, uncertainty is the combined result of unpredictable circumstances that arise during war, the imperfect knowledge on which commanders must make decisions, and the impossibility of guaranteeing success, even under the best conditions. No amount of information and preparation can remove it entirely, but overcoming it is paramount. Uncertainty is persistent and omnipresent, and it is the fiery kiln in which men and women are transformed into leaders.

Early in *Game of Thrones* we are introduced to Daenerys Targaryen, daughter of a fallen king and pawn in her brother's selfishly ambitious pursuit of his family's lost throne. By the end of season 2, we find Daenerys a widowed khaleesi, born again as the Mother of Dragons and leader of a diminished Dothraki khalasar. With the passing of her husband, Khal Drogo, Daenerys's power, position, and identity are in question. Through sheer will, an unwillingness to accept her present condition, and a spirit of defiance when dealing with those who look down on her and the ragged Dothraki, Daenerys showcases the effect a leader can have in uncertain times. In so doing, she offers an archetype of the masterful leaders who have affected the course of history on real-world battlefields.

The lore of the defiant leader is not limited to fiction. The U.S. Army's own doctrine on leadership recognizes the role that uncertainty plays in command. Its leadership manual on what the U.S. Army calls "mission command" states that leaders "understand and use human relationships to overcome uncertainty and chaos and maintain the focus of their forces."[1] Leadership is a human endeavor, one based on principles of trust, understanding, cohesion, and accepting risk. This is true from the tactical through the strategic levels, in conflicts past and present, in the real world and in Westeros.

After a long journey through the Red Waste in season 2, Daenerys and her khalasar arrive at the gates of Qarth, a great and prosperous city run by a council of wealthy merchants and nobles known as the Thirteen. She and her people are initially denied entry into the city when Daenerys refuses to display her beloved dragons, apparently destined to perish in the Garden of Bones outside the city gates. When she and her small group of followers— diminished from the arduous journey to the city—eventually gain entry, they are immediately immersed into a world of treachery hiding beneath a veil of false wealth and affluence. This is not unlike young military leaders and commanders in far flung combat zones like Iraq and Afghanistan, wading through unclear circumstances to best understand their environment.

In short order, Daenerys's dragons are kidnapped by a mystical group called the Warlocks, and several of the Dothraki are murdered. Daenerys is forced to find the dragons through a series of challenges in the House of the Undying, overcoming illusions of personal desire intended to lure her away from reality. She perseveres and destroys her captors, and her treasured dragons are restored to her. Daenerys leaves Qarth on a ship, newly enriched with the gold loot from her erstwhile captors' homes. Qarth presented primarily a personal challenge for Daenerys but is important because it is the first instance in which she prevailed on her merits and gained the personal confidence paramount for any leader. She demonstrated the golden rule for any good military leader, whether King Leonidas at Thermopylae or Dick Winters in *Band of Brothers*: the mission and soldiers always come before care for self.

Next, the khaleesi and her Dothraki followers sail for Astapor in Slaver's Bay to purchase an army, eight thousand enslaved men of the Unsullied. Throughout her first encounters with the masters in Astapor, she is clearly not taken seriously. It takes a remarkably audacious gambit before the masters recognize what a formidable opponent Daenerys represents—too late to save their own lives. Under the guise of trading one of her beloved dragons for the army, Daenerys liberates the slaves of Astapor, frees the Unsullied, and defeats the masters of the city.

Uninterested in being a slave master, Daenerys gives the Unsullied the choice to leave as free men or continue to serve voluntarily as soldiers. Inspired by this new approach, the Unsullied all remain, and Daenerys adds "Breaker of Chains" to the growing list of honorifics that speak to the regard in which her leadership is held. Her nation of followers grows, not because of subjugation, but because of genuine leadership in uncertain circumstances. Daenerys's defiance was an incredible gamble but was based firmly on an understanding of how to exploit the masters' perception of her weakness and naivete and how to leverage the tools at her disposal, her dragons, as well as on an understanding that having a willing army would surely prove more powerful than brokering in slaves. She arrived in Slaver's Bay as an honorable leader but emerged as a trusted commander.

A later scene in Yunkai is very similar. Facing the three leaders of the Second Sons, the sellsword army paid to secure the city, Daenerys is once again insulted by men who underestimate her. She offers them terms, which are quickly scorned by two of the three. One of the leaders, Daario Naharis, sees gravity in her presence and words, beheads the other two, and pledges the loyalty and service of the Second Sons to her cause. Daario leads an infiltration of Yunkai, helping in the slave liberation and overthrow of the city's masters. The khaleesi, the Mother of Dragons and Breaker of Chains, finds her band of followers again swelling by freed slaves singing *mhysa* (mother) at her in gratitude, inspired not by fear but by her willingness to rebuff uncertainty, challenge tradition, and lead followers rather than lord over subjects.

After liberating the enslaved populations in Astapor and Yunkai, Daenerys Targaryen and her army continue their conquest into the city of Meereen.

After Daario quickly defeats the city's champion in a duel, Daenerys launches barrels of broken slave chains over the walls. Here, the slaves are more reluctant to revolt, until the Unsullied inspire them to action. But with the success of her conquests, Daenerys also sees her population of enemies growing larger and bolder. Because of uprisings in Astapor and Yunkai as new self-proclaimed rulers and leaders vie for control, Daenerys remains in Meereen as queen to solidify her rule. She recognizes that the grasp of her control is fleeting and that the future of her queenship is uncertain. She decides to lead rather than continue her conquest, accepting that she is unlikely to be able to rule over seven kingdoms if she is unable to control three cities.

The situation in Meereen is perilous. In short order, Daenerys is forced to expel Jorah the Andal, a once-trusted friend and adviser whose past as a spy against Daenerys is exposed, and soon after, the infamous Sons of the Harpy begin a campaign of terror, killing Unsullied soldiers and civilians in an effort to reinstate slavery. Since the death of her beloved Khal Drogo and unborn son, Daenerys has never found herself more alone and isolated from the things she trusts and loves than in Meereen. Following an assassination attempt in the fighting pits by the Sons of the Harpy, Daenerys flees on Drogon's back. After a failed peace negotiation, Daenerys's small kingdom appears to be in peril, with recently displaced masters encircling her on all sides.

As enemy ships lay siege to Meereen, Daenerys reappears and destroys her adversaries. The Mother of Dragons has repeatedly used a combination of force and promise of freedom to grow her kingdom. In the case of Meereen, she displays the full might of her force, securing her position as commander, leader, and queen. Where influence fails, Daenerys compels her detractors with force. Even on the precipice of disaster, she remains defiant and sure of her place. Her most faithful followers never waver. They trust her promise of freedom and protection, as she repeatedly emerges at exactly the right moment, and makes the right decisions, to secure victory. This is precisely what the modern U.S. Army asks of its leaders—to place themselves at an operation's decisive point to best influence a battle. Daenerys continuously does this, placing herself where she can best shape events.

Daenerys's defiance and focus serve her well as her army and dragons mature, and her sights are once again set on her birthright and ultimate prize—the Iron Throne and rule over the Seven Kingdoms of Westeros. Through the fifth, sixth, and seventh seasons of *Game of Thrones*, her full evolution from pawn to young leader to destined ruler becomes apparent. She has overcome doubt and poor advice to become surrounded by a fiercely loyal and capable inner council, and she finds herself risen from the bonds of slavery to command a massive alliance of ground and naval forces. Her journey remains littered with misfortune and setbacks—she loses both her navy and one of her dragons in the process. But her tenacity endures, and her ability to command matures. The Mother of Dragons and Breaker of Chains continues to lead confidently through uncertainty at every turn, and her destiny seems more certain every time she defies doubt and emerges victorious.

Consider the parallels to the siege of Bastogne, the fierce battle between German forces and the tremendously outnumbered, surrounded, and underestimated American forces at the eponymous Belgian town in December 1944. Part of the larger Battle of the Bulge, Bastogne sat at the intersection of seven roads, a critical juncture for German forces aiming to control and bring reinforcements into the port of Antwerp. The Germans considered their success a guarantee, and the Americans found themselves on the precipice of peril.

On the eve of battle, on December 22, the German commander sent a note to Brigadier General Anthony McAuliffe, the American deputy commander of the 101st Airborne Division, calling for a peaceful surrender. The Americans had fewer men and fewer weapons and were poorly supplied. McAuliffe's notorious response was one word—"NUTS!" That single word signaled the division's refusal to give ground and galvanized American resolve in that harsh winter. In the days leading up to Christmas, American victory was uncertain. By the end of January 1945, the surrounding German forces were defeated. To this day, the First Brigade, 101st Airborne Division, is known as the Bastogne Brigade.

Rewinding a bit further to World War I, the U.S. Marines fighting in France's Belleau Wood in the summer of 1918 provide another example of leadership amid war's uncertainty. Like their counterparts a quarter century later at Bastogne, the marines faced far superior and recently reinforced German forces. With Russia's withdrawl from fighting on the eastern front, German strength in France was steadily increasing. American, French, and British forces were fighting to halt the westward momentum of more than five German divisions east of Paris. In early June, German forces penetrated French defensive lines, prompting the Americans to call up their reserves, which included elements of the Fourth Marine Brigade under the command of Brigadier General James Harbord.[2]

The retreating French forces implored the U.S. Marines to withdraw to trenches farther from the front lines. Instead, Harbord ordered his marines to fix bayonets and dig in to hastily prepared defensive positions. Over the next several days, the marines would repeatedly beat back advancing German forces, holding the line against attack after attack. When called to retreat by the French, an American officer named Captain Lloyd Williams replied, "Retreat—Hell, we just got here!"[3] This defiance is emblematic of the U.S. Marine leaders during this battle and would ultimately allow American forces to take Belleau Wood and halt German advances.

In the cases of both Bastogne and Belleau Wood, the tactical victories were immeasurably important, and the tenacity of the soldiers and marines has led to mythic remembrance of these battles. Though the triumphs cannot be entirely attributed to the commanders, the role of the leaders in those battles is difficult to overstate. There are certainly similarities between Daenerys, McAuliffe, and Harbord during their tactical engagements, but the greater lesson is seen in the strategic outcomes their leadership had during times of uncertainty and potential peril. All three are pillars of creativity, audacity, and defiance—their willingness to stand firm when victory was uncertain, inspiring those who might otherwise doubt their prospects of success, is an essential component of their tactical and strategic victories.

Daenerys Targaryen is no soldier or marine. Though her story is one of nearly continuous conflict, she never occupied trenches like those of Belleau Wood or suffered a brutal winter like Bastogne's in 1944. Nevertheless, she repeatedly found herself in positions of tactical and strategic disadvantage, and she suffered advisers who often doubted her abilities and her vision. In spite of all of this, the Mother of Dragons indignantly stared down overwhelming odds and bested daunting adversaries with a sense of purpose and self-assured vision of victory. She understood the value of earned loyalty over coerced obeisance, and when her people suffered, she shared in that suffering. Her inexperience was overcome by defiance and purpose, and her victories were secured by her daring when dealing with those who underestimated her as a warrior and leader.

NOTES

1. Headquarters, *Mission Command*, Army Doctrine Reference Publication 6-0 (Arlington VA: Department of the Army, May 2012), 2–17.
2. Allan Millett, "Death and Life at the Three Pagoda Pass," MHQ—*The Quarterly Journal of Military History* 6, no. 1 (Autumn 1993): 68–79.
3. Alexander Merrow, Gregory Starace, and Agostino von Hassell, "Belleau Wood," *Marine Corps Gazette* 92, no. 11 (November 2008): 43–47.

6

Lessons for Command from Khaleesi's Rise

ERICA IVERSON

Over a century later, the lessons of the Great War (World War I) continue to be salient and relevant, not only to our own world but to *Game of Thrones* as well. One main challenge facing the Allied Forces in defeating the Central Powers of Austria-Hungary, Germany, Bulgaria, and the Ottoman Empire was their lack of a unity of purpose. One Allied Force with disparate missions representing the "discredited, disjointed political strategy of governments not working in harmony" required a unified mission to bring the countries together for more effective command and control.[1]

Similarly, the hybrid factions of the Seven Kingdoms—divergent (and often conflicting) thrones, banners, militaries, religions, and cultures—unite under the command of Queen Daenerys Targaryen in the Great War, as winter has arrived at last to Westeros.[2] Her rise to power, given tumultuous obstacles and sacrifices, has real-world implications for leaders and commanders alike. As queen commander of a massive joint military force with land, air, and naval assets, Daenerys Targaryen commands a successful campaign through the development of four key components: (1) a core team of advisors, (2) strategic alliances, (3) trained forces, and (4) a unified strategy. These military campaign objectives shape the trajectory for Queen Daenerys's role as commander in the war against the existential threat facing the Seven Kingdoms.

With Targaryen blood running through her veins, Daenerys knows that she is destined to rule and that little can interfere with her ambitions; however, the road to greatness is hard to go alone. Embracing this tradition, Daenerys Targaryen's rise began with one political advisor, Jorah Mormont, who is well versed in the political landscapes in both Westeros and Essos. Throughout the HBO series and books, she selects and develops her cabinet much as Queen Elizabeth I of England did when she took the throne in 1558.[3] Both were very young rulers, both were the last-surviving children, and both were heavily influenced by an intimate circle of male advisors, including courtiers and bureaucrats who know the intricacies of politics, diplomacy, and leadership. The forty-five-year reign of Queen Elizabeth I during England's Golden Age was marked by her reliance on an elite council of advisors, namely Lord Burleigh (William Cecil) and Francis Walsingham.

Similarly, Queen Targaryen's circle includes Aegon Targaryen (aka Jon Snow) as her deputy in command; Tyrion Lannister, Hand of the Queen, as the chief of staff; historian Sam Tarly; cultural advisor Missendei; and intelligence advisor Lord Varys. To supplement her tactical military maneuvering are military advisors Grey Worm, commander of the Unsullied, and Daario Naharis, commander of the Second Sons, who serve in a reserve capacity in Meereen. Collectively, Daenerys's cabinet offset her inexperienced military training and political savviness of Westeros and offer loyalty, specialized expertise, and jurisprudence.

Likewise, each advisor has a different relationship with Queen Daenerys: Tyrion cautions, Varys coddles, Jorah obsesses, Grey Worm protects, and Jon Snow obliges. Military commanders, especially at war, rely on their staff to provide them the most germane, timely information to help them make the most informed decisions. Lives depend on it, so selecting the right advisors is imperative.

Equipped with this varied staff of advisors, Daenerys utilizes them to expand her influence by focusing on key houses that could serve as strategic allies. While vengeance is a strong motivator for Houses Tyrell and Martell, whose fate is all but confirmed, it is House Greyjoy's breakaway naval fleet and, more importantly, the King in the North with all the banners in support of him that bolster Daenerys's command. Convinced by seeing the very real, existential threat of the Army of the Dead, Queen Targaryen's objective shifts from King's Landing and taking the Iron Throne to focusing all forces, allies, and assets to fight the White Walkers, thus adding the Army of the North to her expanding coalition. Victors in military conflict often succeed because they have more and better of something, hence military supremacy—whether that is capacity, capability, or competence, often achieved through the diversification of assets through building coalitions and alliances.

Winston Churchill once famously said that "there is only one thing worse than fighting with allies, and that is fighting without them."[4] An alliance requires sharing goals while maintaining national interests. This often requires compromise from coalition partners, but having a shared objective provides unity of purpose and unity of effort, as seen with the seventy-nine partners that make up the Global Coalition against Daesh.[5] Alliances are crucial to succeed in any form of military conflict, and both allies and partners are an integral part of national security. As such, the unclassified summary of the 2018 National Defense Strategy—which provides guidance and direction for the U.S. Armed Forces—emphasizes that for the United States, our "allies and partners provide complementary capabilities and forces along with unique perspectives, regional relationships, and information that improve our understanding of the environment and expand our options."[6]

Queen Targaryen requires a vast force to fight the Army of the Dead . . . and win. With only two sides in the Great War, the living and the dead, the choice appears fairly easy; however, not all are yet convinced of the impending threat coming from the North. With newly forged alliances comes a substantial increase of assets and capabilities. The fighting forces under the command of Daenerys Targaryen accumulate mass power projection—land power; sea power; and in the case of dragons, air power. The military force she builds to fight the White Walkers was strengthened over a succession of victories, battles, and negotiations. The mélange of warriors follow Queen

Daenerys for different reasons: the Dothraki horse warlords follow power, the formerly enslaved Unsullied follow her strength, the Second Sons mercenaries follow money, and the Army of the North follows Jon Snow, who follows his queen.[7]

Prussian general Helmuth von Moltke the Elder wrote in 1871 that "no plan survives contact with the enemy,"[8] and the Targaryen theater campaign plan of Essos and Westeros epitomizes this. While her first husband Khal Drogo helped give Daenerys confidence and status as the khaleesi, it was from his death, and from her new status as the Mother of Dragons, that Daenerys gained notoriety and power as queen. The port cities in Essos (Qarth, Astapor, Yunkai, and Meereen) as well as Vaes Dothrak became strategic conquests on the drive toward Westeros. For Queen Targaryen, it was made crystal clear not that winter was just coming but that winter had arrived, as the Great War began with the killing and turning of one of her three beloved dragons. While her Machiavellian endgame is to rule over the Seven Kingdoms, Daenerys's end state is survival for humanity so that she has a kingdom left to rule.

The Targaryen campaign required several branches of the strategic plan, deviations including a delayed stay in Meereen for regional stability, being captured by the Dothraki khals but gaining a khalasar of fighting horse warriors, and surviving two marriages and three assassination attempts; yet Queen Targaryen is stronger after all of it. The best leaders are able to devise strategies that are well thought out yet flexible, as Napoleon Bonaparte posited that "plans of campaign may be infinitely modified according to the circumstances."[9]

In the evolution of the khaleesi's command, as both a political and military leader, a few notable lessons emerge.

Lesson 1: Know when to use diplomacy or military measures as a means to an end. Machiavelli wrote in *The Prince* that it is important for a leader, both military and political, to understand warcraft, which encompasses myriad areas that include military strategy and tactics, political dynamics and foreign policy, geography, and diplomacy.[10] Knowledge and proficiency in these areas will help differentiate when to use military force and when to use diplomatic means to achieve ends. For Daenerys, the political threat standing in her way to the throne is Queen Cersei Lannister; however, Daenerys chooses diplomacy by parlaying with House Lannister, rather than using military means to forcibly take King's Landing. Kinetic action, or military measures, often comes at the cost of blood and treasure for both sides, so it is often used as a last resort when diplomatic means fail. Luckily, Daenerys's Hand of the Queen, Tyrion Lannister, knows both queens better than anyone and serves in a critical role advising Daenerys and Cersei to unite rather than fight, as they both share a common enemy.

Lesson 2: Earn respect without compromising your values. While eating a raw stallion heart may not be an acceptable norm, doing so earned the khaleesi instant respect from the Dothraki. Respect is a double-edged sword; it must be both given and earned. Speaking to the Dothraki, she reminds them, "I'm not any khal—I will ask more of you than any khal has ever asked of his khalasar," and the warriors rally behind her.[11] With regard to politics, societal culture, and social change, respect goes a long way by remaining loyal to oneself and subordinates. Quite simply, Queen Targaryen earns respect because she gives it, much as Boudicca, queen of the Iceni tribe in Britannia, whose story became legendary during the reign of Queen Elizabeth I and who also shares many historical similarities with Daenerys, led a rebellion of one hundred thousand tribespeople against armored, trained Roman legions in AD 60. Both women fought for their people and their freedom, ready at any cost. Boudicca told her warriors, "If you weigh well the strengths of our armies you will see that in this battle we must conquer or die."[12]

Lesson 3: Put people first, and show compassion always. By definition, command means taking responsibility for something,[13] which means tending to the general welfare of your subjects. One of Queen Targaryen's many strengths is the compassion she has for people, nurturing to the extent that the Yunkish freed slaves refer to her as *mhysa* or "mother." Balancing justice and mercy, Queen Targaryen offers a choice of bending the knee or death to the captured Lannister and Tarly army and helps the Dothraki conquer their biggest fear, crossing the Narrow Sea.

The success of a leader can be marked in victories—in battle, in deals, in treaties. However, even military commanders who can successfully lead an army can see downfall if they fail to care for their soldiers. Testament to the leadership of Jon Snow, the King in the North, is the pledging of loyalty to him by many houses in the North, including Houses Manderley, Glover, and Cerwyn, after they previously refused to fight alongside and for him. Knowing how and when to balance compassion, justice, and mercy is a true test of leadership.

Lesson 4: Leadership knows no gender. Westeros has no shortage of queens and ladies in charge. Queen Yara Greyjoy and Queen Daenerys Targaryen share a moment when they vow to be better rulers than their fathers.[14] Queen Targaryen's character could be inspired from a number of warrior queens in history, including Artemisia I of Caria—named after Artemis, Greek goddess of the hunt—who served as the naval commander for King Xerxes of Persia; Queen Zenobia of the Palmyrene Empire (now Syria), known as a freedom fighter who led her empire to conquer Egypt, Anatolia, and Syria; and Boudicca, who is still celebrated as a national heroine in the United Kingdom and universally as a fighter of freedom and justice.

Daenerys is no stranger to insults, often by men disregarding her intelligence, and becomes more emboldened in each season to rise against adversity. She gives as she gets—like in the book *A Storm of Swords*, when she retorts back to Prendahl na Ghezn while in Yunkai: "Woman? Is that meant to insult me?"[15] As a warrior queen, she uses her dragons as a negotiation tool to threaten annihilation, while using them as a power projection to demonstrate the capabilities of her firepower. Saying "dracarys" is the equivalent of giving the green light to launch missiles with the intent to annihilate, and she does not hesitate to say it. There is little that Daenerys's character cannot do.

Queen Daenerys Stormborn's assembled forces, leaders, and allies are in for the fight of their lives. While the Great War promises magnitudes of casualties comparative to the two world wars our world has faced, this war between the living and the one-hundred-thousand-strong Army of the Dead is a matter of survival for humanity—not money, not power or the throne, not honor, not greed. The khaleesi's rise to power begins when she arises from the smoldering ashes of her khal, and it evolves to riding her dragon above her united force to save the living.

Daenerys Targaryen's ascent is an upward rise from losing everything she ever loved to becoming a wife; a mother; a khaleesi; a politician; a warrior; a leader; and above all, a queen. Leaders today need to be equipped with a command toolkit of diplomacy, respect, compassion, and leadership skills both in peace and wartime. Dragons are merely a perk. Whatever the fates have in store for the Targaryen bloodline in the game of thrones, with fire and with ice, Queen Targaryen will go to her grave fighting for her people, as did Queen Boudicca. Tacitus quotes Boudicca as she was riding with her daughters in a chariot, rallying thousands to their deaths under her lead: "We British are used to women commanders in war; I am descended from mighty men. . . . I am fighting as an ordinary person for my lost freedom, my bruised body, and my outraged daughters. . . . Consider how many of you are fighting and why! Then you will win this battle or perish. That is what I, a woman, plan to do—let the men live in slavery if they will."[16] In war, everything is put on the line. To win or to perish is better than the alternative of being enslaved; that is what Daenerys and Boudicca will be remembered for, in life and in death.

NOTES

1. Tasker H. Bliss, "The Evolution of Unified Command," *Foreign Affairs* 1, no. 2 (1922): 2.
2. The queen's full title is Daenerys of the House Targaryen, the First of Her Name, the Unburnt, Queen of the Andals, the Rhoynar, and the First Men, Queen of Meereen, Khaleesi of the Great Grass Sea, Protector of the Realm, Lady Regnant of the Seven Kingdoms, Breaker of Chains, and Mother of Dragons.
3. Meghan Single Hurst, "No Ordinary Woman: Historical Inspirations behind the Mother of Dragons," *Tower of the Hawk*, June 16, 2015, https://hawkstower.wordpress.com/2015/06/16/no-ordinary-woman-historical-inspirations-behind-the-mother-of-dragons/.
4. "Chequers, 1 April 1945," International Churchill Society, accessed November 13, 2018, https://winstonchurchill.org/uncategorised/quotes-slider/2014-11-3-16-25-06/.
5. For a complete list of the Global Coalition against Daesh, see their "Partners" web page at http://theglobalcoalition.org/en/partners/.
6. Jim Mattis, *Summary of the 2018 National Defense Strategy* (Washington DC: U.S. Department of Defense, 2018), https://www.defense.gov/Portals/1/Documents/pubs/2018-National-Defense-Strategy-Summary.pdf.

7. The Army of the North includes all those banners of the North, the Brotherhood without Banners, the Free Folk, the Night's Watch, and the Vale—all under the leadership of Jon Snow, the King in the North.

8. Helmuth von Moltke, "Über Strategie" [On strategy] (1871), in *Moltkes Militärische Werke*, ed. Großer Generalstab, 14 vols. (Berlin: E. S. Mittler, 1892–1912), 2, part 2:291–92.

9. General Burnod, ed., *Napoleon's Maxims of War*, trans. George C. D'Auilgar (Philadelphia PA: David McKay, 1902), maxim 2. See also Mads Brevik, etext, "The Military Maxims of Napoleon," Digital Attic, 2001, http://www.digitalattic.org/home/war/napoleon/.

10. Niccolò Machiavelli, *The Prince*, trans. W. K. Marriott (1532; Project Gutenberg, 2006), chap. 14, https://www.gutenberg.org/files/1232/1232-h/1232-h.htm.

11. Bryan Cogman, "Blood of My Blood," season 6, episode 6, dir. Jack Bender, *Game of Thrones*, aired May 29, 2016, on HBO.

12. Jone Johnson Lewis, "Boudicca (Boadicea): How Boudicca led a Celtic Revolt against Roman Occupation," ThoughtCo., last updated September 19, 2018, https://www.thoughtco.com/boudicca-boadicea-biography-3528571.

13. *Cambridge Dictionary*, s.v. "Command," Cambridge University Press, accessed November 13, 2018, https://dictionary.cambridge.org/dictionary/english/command.

14. David Benioff and D. B. Weiss, "Battle of the Bastards," season 6, episode 9, dir. Miguel Sapochnik, *Game of Thrones*, aired June 19, 2016, on HBO.

15. George R. R. Martin, *A Storm of Swords* (New York: Bantam, 2003), chap. 42, loc. 46710, Kindle.

16. Cornelius Tacitus, *The Annals*, in *Complete Works of Tacitus*, trans. Alfred John Church and William Jackson Brodribb (New York: Random House, 1942; edited for Perseus by Sara Bryant, 2011), bk. 14, chap. 35, http://www.perseus.tufts.edu/hopper/text?doc=Perseus%3Atext%3A1999.02.0078%3Abook%3D14%3Achapter%3D35.

7

From Brienne of Tarth to Lyanna Mormont

Shifting Attitudes about Women in Combat

KELSEY CIPOLLA

Towering over her opponent, clad in armor and a helmet and artfully wielding a sword, Brienne of Tarth fought her way onto screens at a time when *Game of Thrones* was more known for showing women in brothels than on battlefields.

It quickly became evident that as a woman warrior, she was as much of an outlier in Westeros as a blonde Baratheon. After Brienne bested Ser Loras Tyrell in combat at a tournament celebrating King Renly Baratheon, the crowd of onlookers was shocked when she revealed herself to be a woman and even more surprised when she asked to be named to Renly's Kingsguard, the elite force dedicated to protecting its ruler.

Although Renly cheerfully granted her request, deeming her "a very capable warrior,"[1] it was clear that to the vast majority of his forces, the idea of a woman fighting was not just unexpected but undesirable. A woman of noble birth who has eschewed the title of "lady" in favor of pursuing a life of honor and service through her skills in battle, Brienne is mocked, threatened, and abused for attempting to occupy a traditionally male role as well as for her appearance—solidly built, she has a shock of short, blonde hair; stands taller than many men; and dresses in armor or simple, more gender-neutral garb as opposed to traditional gowns.

In Westeros, martial endeavors are almost entirely left to men, although there are some notable exceptions: Visenya Targaryen was a fierce warrior and dragon rider along with her brother, Aegon, and her sister, Rhaenys. The women of Bear Island are skilled with weapons because the men of the island are often out at sea fishing, leaving them vulnerable to attacks, and Lady Maege Mormont served as a soldier and commander in Robb Stark's army in the War of the Five Kings, which claimed her life.

On the Iron Islands, Yara Greyjoy becomes the commander of a fleet despite the deeply rooted misogyny in her culture. Oberyn Martell's three eldest daughters are extensively trained in combat, and over the course of the series, we see Arya Stark transform from a young girl interested in weapons to a lethal assassin.

But for the most part, it's easy to imagine Brienne's experience as the most typical for women who see themselves as warriors. While other characters put their skills to use carrying out their own agendas, win acceptance by conforming to misogynist culture, or come from backgrounds where their pursuits are relatively accepted, Brienne wants to be a soldier and serve with honor but finds herself limited and, at times, endangered by those around her.

Unfortunately, like Brienne, women in the United States who pursue careers in the military, especially those who hope to obtain combat roles, have historically faced a steep uphill climb, both in society and within the military—but that may be changing.

Overcoming Obstacles

Opponents of women in combat often point to gender differences, questioning whether women have the physical strength to match their male peers and how that might threaten military readiness. More insidious (and less often stated outright) are enduring sexist beliefs about women's roles and abilities, which can translate into negative views on women serving in the military generally but especially in combat positions. One study found that military-affiliated students hold significantly more negative attitudes about women in combat compared to civilian students, although they had similar views on women serving in the military in general: "The military's historic exclusion of women in official combat roles may inadvertently have served to reinforce sexist beliefs (e.g., that women are weak) that lead to negative attitudes toward women in combat."[2]

Changing engrained beliefs is a tall order, but Brienne proves herself more than physically capable time and time again. When she's tasked with delivering legendary warrior-turned-prisoner Jaime Lannister back to his father in King's Landing in exchange for the safe return of Sansa and Arya Stark to their family, Jaime wastes no time setting on her, questioning whether she is in fact a woman and referring to her as a beast. As the two travel, he continues to take aim at her appearance, sexuality, and fighting prowess.

"All my life, men like you have sneered at me, and all my life, I've been knocking men like you into the dust," she replies.[3]

When several soldiers confront the pair, laughing in Brienne's face before recognizing Jaime and moving to attack, Brienne makes quick work of them. Later, Jaime attempts to escape and steals a sword, dueling Brienne while shackled. Despite his reputation as the best swordsman in Westeros, she is about to beat him when they are taken captive. Later in the series, we see her defeat the Hound, another warrior known for his skill and brutality.

Women in our own military have proven their skill and valor on a grand scale. More than 9,000 women have been awarded Army Combat Action Badges and 1,000 U.S. Army women medics have received the combat medical badge. More than 150 women have received Army Commendation Medals and Bronze Star medals with a valor distinction, which denotes "acts of heroism involving conflict with an armed enemy." Two U.S. Army women have received Silver Stars since World War II, presented for "gallantry in action against an enemy of the United States."[4]

While those figures are small compared to the total number of awards and decorations given—for example, more than 120,000 Combat Action Badges and 17,000 Combat Medical Badges were presented during the same period—these women earned recognition despite being officially restricted from combat at the time they were honored.[5] And it's worth noting that unlike in Westeros, where opposing forces engage in crushing head-to-head battles, many U.S. service members do not engage in close combat. Since World War II, almost 90 percent of combat deaths occur among a group—primarily infantry units—comprised of less than 4 percent of the Department of Defense's uniformed strength.[6]

The harassment Brienne endures is also likely all too familiar to women in the service. Despite efforts to integrate women into the military over the last few decades, service women identify gender bias as one of the biggest challenges they face personally and as a community.[7] And sexual harassment and assault in the military continue to be disturbingly common—more than 20 percent of active duty women surveyed indicated they experienced sexual harassment and 4.3 percent indicated experiencing sexual assault in the previous year.[8] Many choose not to report it, fearing retaliation.

Fighting for a Place

Throughout her journey, Brienne continues to endure mistreatment, but she also finds those willing to learn from her expertise and recognize her value as a warrior and protector. Brienne ultimately rescues Sansa from her sadistic, abusive husband, Ramsay Bolton, and reunites her with her brother, Jon Snow.

Together, Jon and Sansa work to rally allies to overthrow Ramsay and take back their ancestral home, Winterfell. In the process, they meet a very different kind of warrior woman, ten-year-old Lady Lyanna Mormont, the daughter of Maege Mormont, who is now the head of House Mormont, as well as Bear Island. She is convinced to join their cause and pledges her small force to them, even riding with them into the Battle of the Bastards, although she does not participate.

In Lyanna, we get a glimpse at a new future for women in Westeros, women who lead confidently and fight ferociously without being subjected to the mistreatment Brienne experiences so frequently. After Jon, Sansa, and their allies win back Winterfell, Lyanna is the lone female voice in a crowd of northern nobles, yet she's also the one who first proclaims Jon Snow the

King in the North. When Jon orders all children—boys and girls—over the age of ten to be trained for combat and is met with resistance from the nobles, particularly Lord Glover, Lyanna defends the idea passionately, while Brienne looks on in surprise.

"I don't plan on knitting by the fire while men fight for me. I might be small, Lord Glover, and I might be a girl, but I am every bit as much a northerner as you," Lyanna says. "And I don't need your permission to defend the North. We'll begin training every man, woman, boy, and girl on Bear Island."[9]

Although there are extenuating circumstances—like an impending army of White Walkers that needs fighting—the idea of training girls for combat is revolutionary by Westeros's standards.

Our military has undergone its own considerable shift. Although women have been recognized for their service in combat roles since the American Revolution, for most of U.S. military history, women's positions were primarily clerical or in support of military medical services. More service roles opened during World War II, and the move to an all-volunteer force, paired with a new focus on equal opportunities for men and women, led to a continued increase in the number of women in the military as well as fewer barriers to their entry and more prospects, though there were restrictions placed on combat roles.[10] The most recent version, in 1994, the Direct Combat Exclusion Rule, excluded women from assignment to units below the brigade level whose primary mission is to engage in direct combat on the ground, meaning they could not serve in artillery, armor, infantry, and other such combat roles that engaged with an enemy on the ground with weapons while being exposed to hostile fire and a high probability of direct physical contact.[11]

Even in the face of these barriers, women continued to seek out opportunities to serve. As warfare evolved to be less linear, many found themselves serving in roles that were not intended to engage in direct combat but were still in combat zones and under fire. Although women weren't allowed to serve in combat positions, they were nonetheless often subjected to the same risks.

A New Era

In January 2013, then secretary of defense Leon Panetta rescinded the Direct Combat Exclusion Rule on women serving in previously restricted occupations, opening closed combat-arms occupational specialties and noncombat specialties assigned to combat units.

Between 2013 and December 2015, 111,000 positions were opened to women, and on December 3, 2015, then defense secretary Ash Carter announced that all combat roles would be open to women who were able to meet the required standards across all branches of the military. The change opened nearly 220,000 additional jobs, giving women the opportunity to drive tanks, fire mortars, lead infantry soldiers into combat, and serve as Army Rangers and Green Berets, U.S. Navy SEALs, U.S. Marine Corps infantry, U.S. Air Force parajumpers, and more.[12]

Since the announcement, women have entered jobs previously closed to them, operating in a multitude of combat billets across the Marine Corps, and graduated from the U.S. Army's Infantry or Armor Basic Officer Leader's Course.[13] Six hundred female army soldiers are in infantry, armor, and artillery positions that were only recently opened to women, and twelve women have now graduated from Ranger School.[14] (Only about 3 percent of U.S. Army men are Ranger qualified.)[15]

"I was thinking of future generations of women," now captain Kristen Griest, one of the first two women to graduate as a Ranger, said about the experience. "I would like them to have that opportunity, so I had that pressure on myself."[16] The pressure that comes with having to prove not only your personal abilities but the abilities of your gender will hopefully dissipate as more women see themselves represented in combat roles and attitudes shift within the military, as well as the general public.

Further growth is likely on the horizon. As of March 2018, women make up 16.4 percent of all active duty military, but they account for 25 percent of the students enrolled at the U.S. Air Force Academy, 20 percent of West Point's student body, and 26 percent of the U.S. Naval Academy.[17] And the House Armed Services Military Personnel Subcommittee recently urged military branches to recruit more women, as fewer young people meet the qualifications to serve.[18]

Although the U.S. military still has room for improvement when it comes to providing a safe and supportive environment for women in the service, the opening of all roles sends a clear message about the value of women and their contributions.

"When I became secretary of defense, I made a commitment to building America's force of the future," Carter told reporters while announcing the change. "In the 21st century, that requires drawing strength from the broadest possible pool of talent. This includes women."[19] Like Jon Snow, he recognized the value in bringing women into the fold, not just as a step toward inclusivity but as a practical way of strengthening a fighting force and protecting people.

In the few years since the combat ban was lifted, women have already shown that they don't need the bar to be lowered for them. Instead, they are rising to the standards that many felt would be too challenging. In December 2016 a female officer completed the U.S. Army's rigorous selection process for the Seventy-Fifth Ranger Regiment, making her the first woman to join a special operations unit.[20] Ten months later, a lieutenant became the first woman to graduate from the U.S. Marines Corps' demanding Infantry Officer Course, becoming the first female U.S. infantry officer.[21] And Captain Griest and fellow Ranger School graduate Captain Shaye Haver both transferred out of their previous positions to become infantry officers, paving the way for mentorship and female role models within units.[22]

Lyanna Mormont would be proud.

NOTES

1. Bryan Cogman, "What Is Dead May Never Die," season 2, episode 3, dir. Alik Sakharov, *Game of Thrones*, aired April 15, 2012, on HBO.

2. Lauren Cunningham and Margaret M. Nauta, "Sexism as a Predictor of Attitudes Toward Women in the Military and in Combat," *Military Psychology* 25, no. 2 (March 2013): 166–71.

3. David Benioff and D. B. Weiss, "The Prince of Winterfell," season 2, episode 8, dir. Alan Taylor, *Game of Thrones*, aired May 20, 2012, on HBO.

4. Ellen Haring, "Do Military Women Want Combat Jobs? The Survey Numbers Say Yes—And So Do More Than 9,000 Combat Action Badges," *Foreign Policy*, April 24, 2014, http://

foreignpolicy.com/2014/04/24/do-military-women-want-combat-jobs-the-survey-numbers
-say-yes-and-so-do-more-than-9000-combat-action-badges/.

5. United States Army Human Resources Command, "Awards and Decorations Statistics by Conflict," accessed July 4, 2018, https://www.hrc.army.mil/content/Awards%20and%20decorations%20statistics%20by%20Conflict.

6. Robert H. Scales, *Scales on War: The Future of America's Military at Risk* (Annapolis MD: Naval Institute Press, 2016), 5.

7. Service Women's Action Network, "SWAN Releases 1st Annual Survey of Service Women and Women Veterans," press release, November 14, 2016, https://www.servicewomen.org/press-releases/swan-releases-1st-annual-survey-of-service-women-women-veterans/.

8. Lisa Davis, Amanda Grifka, Kristin Williams, and Margaret Coffey, eds., *2016 Workplace and Gender Relations Survey of Active Duty Members* (Alexandria VA: Office of People Analytics, May 2017), http://www.sapr.mil/public/docs/reports/FY16_Annual/Annex_1_2016_WGRA_Report.pdf.

9. David Benioff and D. B. Weiss, "Dragonstone," season 7, episode 1, dir. Jeremy Podeswa, *Game of Thrones*, aired July 16, 2017, on HBO.

10. Kristy N. Kamarck, *Women in Combat: Issues for Congress* (Washington DC: Congressional Research Service, December 13, 2016), https://fas.org/sgp/crs/natsec/R42075.pdf.

11. Les Aspin, "Direct Ground Combat Definition and Assignment Rule," Department of Defense memorandum, January 13, 1994, https://www.govexec.com/pdfs/031910d1.pdf.

12. Cheryl Pellerin, "Carter Opens All Military Occupations, Positions to Women," U.S. Department of Defense, December 3, 2015, https://www.defense.gov/News/Article/Article/632536/carter-opens-all-military-occupations-positions-to-women/.

13. Shawn Snow, "Where Are the Female Marines?" *Marine Corps Times*, March, 5, 2018, https://www.marinecorpstimes.com/news/2018/03/05/where-are-the-female-marines/.

14. David Vergun, "Army Vice Chief of Staff: Women Vital to 'Strength of Our Army,'" Army News Service, March 13, 2018, https://www.army.mil/article/202035/army_vice_chief_of_staff_women_vital_to_strength_of_our_army; Matthew Cox, "12 Female Soldiers Have Now Graduated Army Ranger School," Military.com, April 9, 2018, https://www.military.com/daily-news/2018/04/09/10-female-soldiers-have-now-graduated-army-ranger-school.html.

15. Mark Thompson, "America: Meet Your First Female Rangers," *Time*, August 20, 2015, http://time.com/4005578/female-army-rangers/.

16. Thompson, "America."

17. Defense Manpower Data Center, "DoD Personnel, Workforce Reports & Publications," s.vv. "Active Duty Military Personnel by Service by Rank/Grade (Updated Monthly)," "March 2018 (Women Only)," available at https://www.dmdc.osd.mil/appj/dwp/dwp_reports.jsp; U.S. military academy percentages were taken from the institutions' respective 2016 web pages in the *U.S. News and World Report* college rankings.

18. Ben Werner, "Military Branches Are Doing More to Recruit Women into Active Duty," U.S. Naval Institute News, April 13, 2018, https://news.usni.org/2018/04/13/service-branches-want-more-women.

19. Dave Philipps and Matthew Rosenberg, "All Combat Roles Now Open to Women, Defense Secretary Says," *New York Times*, December 3, 2015, https://www.nytimes.com/2015/12/04/us/politics/combat-military-women-ash-carter.html.

20. Meghann Myers, "This Woman Will Be the First to Join the Army's Elite 75th Ranger Regiment," *Army Times*, January 18, 2017, https://www.armytimes.com/news/your-army/2017/01/18/this-woman-will-be-the-first-to-join-the-army-s-elite-75th-ranger-regiment/.

21. Kevin Lui, "In a Landmark First, the U.S. Marines Now Has a Female Infantry Officer," *Time*, September 26, 2017, http://time.com/4956767/us-marines-first-female-infantry-officer/.

22. Emma Moore and Andrew Swick, "The (Mostly) Good News on Women in Combat," Center for a New American Security, April 19, 2018, https://www.cnas.org/publications/reports/an-update-on-the-status-of-women-in-combat.

8

You Know Something, Jon Snow, about the Qualities of a Strategic Leader

P. W. SINGER AND ML CAVANAUGH

"Jon Snow" and "strategic genius" are certainly terms that don't seem to go together.

While Jon is one of the most beloved of characters in *Game of Thrones*, Ned Stark's bastard son is often viewed like his "father"—a hero, but not a very smart or strategic one.[1] Viewers see this in everything from Littlefinger's sneering appraisal of him to Jon's performance in the Battle of the Bastards, where he easily fell into Ramsay Bolton's trap. Indeed, even the first love of his life, Ygritte, a fiery Free Folk, perhaps best sums up how Jon has generally been perceived: "You're brave. Stupid, but brave."[2]

But just as the Bastard of Winterfell's actual birth history turns out to be more than once presumed, it's time to reevaluate how Jon Snow is viewed as a strategic leader. Far from just having great hair and sword skills, Jon Snow shares many of the attributes that have made the real world's great supreme military commanders so successful, particularly one of the most revered in U.S. history, George Washington. Jon Snow serves as a reminder that the qualities of just one man can shape the course of an entire war.[3] As the sellsword-turned-knight Bronn once put it, "Men win wars. Not magic tricks."[4] Ultimately, leaders make decisions, and decisions make history. And Jon Snow's personal characteristics suggest that he just might be bound for greatness as a strategic leader.

The Education of Jon Snow

It may be a cliché, but it is also an entirely valid lesson in both *Game of Thrones* and the real world: leaders are both made and born. The dynamic relationship between inherent qualities and learned attributes is often what determines a leader's trajectory in life and conflict.

Jon Snow possesses the personal magnetism with which so many high-performing leaders are born. The often indescribable, but very real, *power of persuasion and attraction* that gets others to follow has repeatedly shaped history. In the American Revolution, one of the most crucial moments happened not in battle but when the tall, attractive George Washington strode into the Second Continental Congress on May 9, 1775, wearing a tailored military uniform of his own design. The often-disagreeable leaders there unanimously voted in Washington, who looked the part, as the commander of the new American army.[5] Throughout the war, Washington would carry himself in a similar way that captured the imagination of his contemporaries. Historians have also noted the way he used his noble aloofness to strategic advantage in keeping himself above the age's often-petty personal politics.[6]

We see the same qualities in Jon Snow, as others are naturally drawn toward him and defer to him. Both the newest recruits to the Night's Watch and its senior commander, Jeor Mormont, quickly recognize that Jon is special, a friend to be made and a future leader to be molded. Indeed, when the Wall is attacked by hordes of Free Folk led by former Night's Watch brother Mance Rayder, who similarly has been impressed by Jon, the young man takes command of the Wall's defense, an act that no one questions despite his clearly lesser rank.[7] When Jon then orders his friend Grenn and five others to go down to protect the inner gate because giants are poised to breach the Wall, Grenn's group knows precisely what this means—their own likely deaths. But they still fight on, for a very simple reason, as Grenn tells the unit, "You heard Jon." Jon knew what to do, and the brothers of the Night's Watch trusted him, even when he was not formally in charge of them.

That Jon Snow, like Washington, was born with a quality of personal magnetism doesn't mean that he was destined for leadership. Joffrey also looked the part, and he was anything but a great leader. Indeed, with the circumstances of his birth clouded in mystery, Jon's early days were instead defined by hardship that would prove crucial to his development and later leadership success. Jon gained *personal resilience* through an early life as the outsider Bastard of Winterfell and then suffered his father's beheading, as well as the loss of his brothers Robb and Rickon. Similarly, George Washington lost his father at age eleven and then his brother Laurence (who had become his "surrogate father") at twenty.[8] Both were forced to take on early responsibilities and develop the *mental and emotional toughness* that often defines the best leaders. Such difficulties in childhood track with the unfortunate experiences of many other successful American leaders, including Alexander Hamilton, Abraham Lincoln, Ulysses S. Grant, Dwight D. Eisenhower, Bill Clinton, and Barack Obama, among others.[9] But a broader study of over four hundred high-performing individuals also found that more than 75 percent had difficult childhoods.[10] As spymaster Lord Varys says, "Any fool with a bit of luck can find himself born into power. But earning it for yourself? That takes work."[11]

It is this intersection of natural talent and early difficulty that leads Jon to build another important attribute, *the ability to move across diverse settings.* Early in the series, he laments to Tyrion the twin life of a bastard, knowing the lord's family but having to eat among the lower born. Yet this dual experience provides Jon the knowledge and skills of a noble as well as an awareness and authenticity that endeared him to his troops and common folk. He understood situations from multiple perspectives, bringing to the game of thrones both the bottom-up and the top-down view that arguably no one else in Westeros could. Being able to move easily among the high and the low born has characterized many real-world leaders as well. Washington both was the equivalent of Virginia nobility and also spent his early years working as a professional surveyor, which he started at age sixteen on a farm and revisited later while enduring difficult frontier expeditions (the equivalent of being beyond the Wall).[12]

In constructing these capabilities, Snow and Washington were formed and fashioned by exceptional mentors. Ned Stark raised Jon Snow and taught him not just how to wield a sword but everything from the *communication skills* a good general would need in battle to the *strong moral code* a respected leader brings to critical relationships. Despite what Jon's nemesis Ser Alliser Thorne might say ("You have a good heart Jon Snow. It'll get us all killed"), the reality is that these codes are often the pathway to victory.[13] Leaders who are known to be guided by a code are considered more trustworthy by others and are thus able to build and maintain coalitions and alliances.[14] Amoral or immoral actors don't work well with others, and when they do, it is at best transactional and short-term.

An apt illustration is provided by Littlefinger, who's trusted by nobody. As a result, his power is brittle and unreliable. In contrast, Jon continually builds a loyal network of followers, partners, and allies that is both sustainable and ever growing. It is not coincidental that Jon is the series's only leader to be elected to leadership, twice, of radically different organizations, in much the same way that Washington was voted as both commander of the new American army and then president of the new United States.

It isn't that Jon Snow or George Washington were men of moral perfection or even always lived up to their codes. We often see Jon fall short. He violated his Night's Watch oath with Ygritte, and then he lies to Tormund that there were one thousand men at Castle Black, an act of military deception.[15] So too, Washington was a flawed man who accepted slavery around him and who was also devious enough to run a series of spy rings. In a sense, this duality of *a moral code, but peppered with pragmatism,* is what allows Jon to succeed in a world where an inflexible Ned Stark was unable to survive, just as it allowed Washington to win a war that melded high moralities and low realities.

Jon's practical education continued after he parted from Ned, when Jon "took the black" and was selected to serve as personal steward to Lord Commander Jeor Mormont. In Mormont's fate, there is a striking echo to

George Washington's own pre–Revolutionary War mentor. In 1755 Washington served as British general Edward Braddock's senior American aide and learned how large armies were organized, but he also witnessed the consequences of military operations that fail to understand their foes or operating environment. Like Mormont's expedition past the Wall, Braddock's campaign to retake Fort Duquesne from the French would end in disaster and Braddock's own death.[16]

Jon Snow at War

These internal qualities and early years of experience and mentorship prepared Jon well for the Great War, which many sensed was coming.[17]

Jon showed himself to be *personally courageous*, which would seem to be unstrategic.[18] But influenced by his mentors, Jon knew that such displays had real battlefield benefits. Much is made of Jon's one-man charge during the Battle of the Bastards, but what is often forgotten is the psychological tactic he employed when he called out Ramsay Bolton before the fight: "Will your men want to fight for you when they hear you wouldn't fight for them?"[19]

In a similar manner, Washington understood that, at some point, the strategic crosses with the personal in wars that hinge on the human element. He led from the fore at key moments—from the famous crossing of the Delaware River to the Battle of Monmouth, where he singlehandedly rallied the troops, with a display of personal courage that turned the battle. Both men's bravery, though, is not limited to the physical but is also on display in the mental realm through their difficult decisions and hard calls. Jon knew that it would divide the Night's Watch to bring the Free Folk into an alliance, but he did it anyway.[20] Washington knew that it would be unpopular to evacuate cities like New York and then Philadelphia, but he still made that choice, because it had to be done.

Jon's bravery is balanced by his grasp of the war's two crucial strategic insights. The first is a recognition of the most essential elements of the war, the key goals and actions upon which the entire conflict will turn. Prussian general and war theorist Carl von Clausewitz would undoubtedly approve.[21]

In the American Revolution, it was Washington's realization that to continue fighting and sustain his army was of the utmost importance. The enemy could capture the young nation's largest cities, but these were empty losses, as long as the Continental Army remained in the fight. Washington's key objective was to keep the war going. Similarly, Jon recognizes that survival is the essence of victory in his war.[22] In a war for humanity, to outlast is to win.

Jon's second realization is the crucial importance of alliances. When Jon becomes the lord commander of the Night's Watch, he recognizes that the White Walker threat is more important than anything else. His core insight is simple and powerful—"Winter is coming. We know what's coming with it. We can't face it alone."[23]

In ruling the North, Jon leaned into alliances. In contrast to Stannis Baratheon and then Ramsay Bolton, Jon understood that even in the most hierarchical system, to follow is still a choice, so he makes a point to draw in and unite instead of command and compel. Even when he has good reason to punish the families that pulled their support from House Stark, Jon chose leniency over punishment, in part due to his moral code but also in the name of building a bigger coalition.

Jon Snow unites disparate groups, families, and banners in a way that mirrors how George Washington realized that his role was about much more than winning battles—his larger responsibility as commander was to bring together those whom he once described as "a mixed multitude of people under very little discipline, order or government."[24] Washington ultimately turned this mixture into a professional and then victorious army and then into a nation. In this cause, much like Jon, Washington was willing to look past the petty jealousies from other commanders, like Continental Army generals Henry Lee and Horatio Gates, who thought he shouldn't lead, as well as the constant swirl of unnecessary infighting and conspiracy.

The payoff for both commanders' focus on alliance building was the ability to attract and leverage the aid of ever more varied forces from afar, which would prove crucial to victory. The Free Folk and the Knights of the Vale are akin to the disparate coalition of allies like the French, Dutch, and

Spanish, who joined the fight against Great Britain. In proving their ability to build and maintain wide-ranging alliances, Washington and Snow benefitted from foreign forces in a way that their foes, who repeatedly alienated allies, could not.

In the pursuit of these twin goals, neither Jon Snow nor George Washington showed perfect judgment. Each made mistakes along the way, from Washington's early attempt to defend New York City to Jon's hard-charging, headlong rush into battle with Ramsay Bolton. But what they did show is the key attribute of flexibility and an ability to continually learn while still in command. As Washington himself once advised, we should "derive useful lessons from past errors . . . for the purpose of profiting by dear bought experience."[25] When Washington realized that his soldiers could not hold key cities, he shifted to a Fabian war of delay, maneuver, and opportunistic counterattack.[26] Then after Valley Forge and the training revolution it provided, followed by the French arrival into the war, he shifted back toward seeking major battle.

Jon Snow's original instinct is to fight with what he has and to hold the Wall with available resources.[27] When he sees how powerful the White Walkers are, he realizes that this approach will not work against a foe with seemingly infinite resources of (dead) manpower. He then seeks to shift the balance through new alliances (with the Free Folk and Queen Daenerys) and new weapons (dragonglass and dragons).

Compare this with how Stannis Baratheon handled his battles. Despite being, as Ser Davos Seaworth puts it, the "most experienced commander in Westeros,"[28] Stannis was too proud and inflexible to admit that he made a major strategic miscalculation in driving his army to a snowy destruction, in much the same way the once genius but then rigid Napoleon did in Russia.

Losing Fights and Battles, Winning Wars (and Thrones?)

History's great strategic leaders often look better in hindsight. George Washington was continually attacked by contemporary critics for being a "weak general," a critique with some merit as at the time he was losing battle after battle.[29] Indeed, Washington arguably lost more battles than any other general in American history.[30] Jon Snow similarly seems to pale in strategic genius compared to his contemporaries and has no great victory of his own to claim.

And yet each leader brought to their roles a series of personal qualities and experiences that allowed them to succeed at what matters most, to recognize the key nature of the wars they were in, and to build the necessary alliances to achieve final strategic victory. Just as George Washington is now remembered fondly for the supreme leadership qualities he needed to win the Revolutionary War and to become the father of his country, the once discounted Bastard of Winterfell may well end up being remembered as "first in war" and "first in peace" in all the Seven Kingdoms.

NOTES

1. While Ned Stark is not Jon Snow's biological father, Ned did raise Jon Snow, and Jon considered Ned his father throughout the series. As such, this essay will refer to Ned Stark as Jon Snow's father.

2. Vanessa Taylor, "The Old Gods and the New," season 2, episode 6, dir. David Nutter, *Game of Thrones*, aired May 6, 2012, on HBO.

3. See Daniel L. Byman and Kenneth M. Pollack, "Let Us Now Praise Great Men: Bringing the Statesmen Back In," *International Security* 25, no. 4 (Spring 2001): 107–46.

4. David Benioff and D. B. Weiss, "The Ghost of Harrenhal," season 2, episode 5, dir. David Petrarca, *Game of Thrones*, aired April 29, 2012, on HBO.

5. David Hackett Fischer, *Washington's Crossing* (Oxford: Oxford University Press, 2004), 17.

6. See Joseph J. Ellis, *His Excellency: George Washington* (New York: Alfred A. Knopf, 2004), 273; Edmund S. Morgan, *The Genius of George Washington* (New York: W. W. Norton and Co., 1980), 7; Ron Chernow, *Washington: A Life* (New York: Penguin Press, 2010), xx.

7. David Benioff and D. B. Weiss, "The Watchers on the Wall," season 4, episode 9, dir. Neil Marshall, *Game of Thrones*, aired June 8, 2014, on HBO.

8. Ellis, *His Excellency*, 8–10.

9. Ron Chernow, *Grant* (New York: Penguin Press, 2017), 18, 12, 17; Victor Geortzel and Mildred George Geortzel, *Cradles of Eminence, Second Edition: Childhoods of More Than 700 Famous Men and Women*, updated by Ted George Geortzel and Ariel M. W. Hansen (1962; repr. Scottsdale AZ: Great Potential Press, 2004), 64–65.

10. Geortzel and George Geortzel, *Cradles of Eminence*, 282–83.

11. David Benioff and D. B. Weiss, "The Wars to Come," season 5, episode 1, dir. Michael Slovis, *Game of Thrones*, aired April 12, 2015, on HBO.

12. "Surveying," in *George Washington Digital Encyclopedia*, ed. Joseph F. Stoltz III (Fairfax County VA: Mount Vernon Estate, 2012), http://www.mountvernon.org/library/digitalhistory/digital-encyclopedia/article/surveying/.

13. David Benioff and D. B. Weiss, "The Dance of Dragons," season 5, episode 9, dir. David Nutter, *Game of Thrones*, aired June 7, 2015, on HBO.

14. For example, Queen Cersei unhesitatingly accepts Jon Snow's word, because she knows "Ned Stark's son will be true to his word." David Benioff and D. B. Weiss, "The Dragon and the Wolf," season 7, episode 7, dir. Jeremy Podeswa, *Game of Thrones*, aired August 27, 2017, on HBO.

15. Bryan Cogman, "Kissed by Fire," season 3, episode 5, dir. Alex Graves, *Game of Thrones*, aired April 28, 2013, on HBO.

16. Peter Cozzens, "Rivals and Partners in a New World," *Wall Street Journal*, May 19–20, 2018.

17. Benioff and Weiss, "Dragon and the Wolf."

18. Tywin Lannister, considered among the most strategic players in the game, preferred to command well behind the lines, far from any personal risk.

19. David Benioff and D. B. Weiss, "Battle of the Bastards," season 6, episode 9, dir. Miguel Sapochnik, *Game of Thrones*, aired June 19, 2016, on HBO.

20. Jon does so with the support of Maester Aemon's advice to "kill the boy, and let the man be born"; Bryan Cogman, "Kill the Boy," season 5, episode 5, dir. Jeremy Podeswa, *Game of Thrones*, aired May 10, 2015, on HBO

21. Carl von Clausewitz would have described such a strategic leader as possessing an "intellect that, even in the darkest hour, retains some glimmerings of the inner light which leads to truth; and second, the courage to follow this faint light wherever it may lead." Carl von Clausewitz, *On War*, ed. and trans. Michael Howard and Peter Paret (Princeton NJ: Princeton University Press, 1976), 102. For more on this subject, see the rest of Clausewitz, *On War*, bk. 1, chap. 3.

22. All the more so when you consider that he even survived death.

23. Cogman, "Kill the Boy."

24. U.S. Army Center of Military History, "Washington Takes Command of Continental Army in 1775," U.S. Army, June 5, 2014, https://www.army.mil/article/40819/washington_takes _command_of_continental_army_in_1775.

25. George Washington quoted in Cozzens, "Rivals and Partners in a New World."

26. See Dave R. Palmer, *George Washington's Military Genius* (Washington DC: Regnery History, 2012), originally published as *The Way of the Fox* (Westport CT: Greenwood Press, 1975). For more on Fabian strategies, see James Holmes, "Fabian Strategies, Then and Now," *War on the Rocks*, September 17, 2015, https://warontherocks.com/2015/09/fabian-strategies -then-and-now/.

27. Before the Battle of the Bastards, Sansa told Jon, "We need more men." Jon responded, "We fight with the army we have." David Benioff and D. B. Weiss, "No One," season 6, episode 8, dir. Mark Mylod, *Game of Thrones*, aired June 12, 2016, on HBO.

28. Benioff and Weiss, "Dance of Dragons."

29. "The Conway Cabal," in *Virtual Marching Tour of the American Revolutionary War*, UShistory .org, accessed June 1, 2018, http://www.ushistory.org/march/other/cabal.htm.

30. David Hackett Fischer, "Washington's Crossing" (public lecture, Pritzker Military Museum and Library, Chicago IL, January 5, 2018).

PART 2

Technology and War

9

The Lessons of Viserion and Technological Advantage

JONATHAN E. CZARNECKI

Truth in advertising: I will come clean from the first. I want Daenerys Targaryen to gain the Iron Throne. She's the one who's made the heroine's epic journey. She's quite literally walked through fire. Dany expresses intelligence, cunning, ruthlessness, compassion, and utter determination. And she's raised dragons.

Throughout the *Game of Thrones* televised series, the side of Daenerys Targaryen held an asymmetric (biological) technology edge that no other side can match—she had three dragons (Drogon, Rhaegal, and Viserion), and everyone else had none. This advantage lasted until the final episode of season 7. In that storyline, the White Walker king killed Viserion and resurrected the dragon as a wight (effectively a zombie). At the conclusion of the episode, the king used Viserion to destroy the Wall, which had protected Westeros from the White Walkers for thousands of years. Winter has come to the homeland kingdoms of Westeros.

The dissolution of Dany's advantage is a fable from which we in the U.S. national security community can learn, or more accurately relearn, four important lessons that accompany any technological advantage: (1)

technological advantage is fleeting; (2) all technological advantages leak to the enemy; (3) technological advantages work both ways—for us and against us; and (4) technological advantage disables as well as enables us.

Technology is one important, even vital, context within which conflicts are confronted and fought; and as Colin Gray so wisely reminds us, contexts are everything in war.[1] These lessons are especially relevant at a time when the U.S. military is witnessing an apparent dissolution of its formidable technological advantages, especially in comparison with the military of the Peoples' Republic of China (PRC), and when the United States is attempting to reassert that advantage through a national defense strategy that would focus on implementing and expanding an idea called the "third offset."[2]

The third offset can be thought of as a successor to the 1990s-era revolution in military affairs. It is a strategic effort to provide the United States with a lasting technological advantage in much the same manner that the previous two offset strategies did. The first, in the 1950s, emphasized nuclear technologies; the second, in the late 1970s and early 1980s, emphasized precision, intelligence, stealth, and space technologies. The third offset strategy focuses mostly on cyber and artificial intelligence technologies.[3]

Four Lessons on the Dissolution of Technology Advantage

If Daenerys Targayen or her key advisors, Tyrion Lannister and Missandei, had access to the archives that included our own historical Earth, they would have found many cases of the ephemeral nature of technological asymmetry in war, impressive dragons notwithstanding. Horses, chariots, armor, iron blades, wind power, muskets, cannons, steam power, telegraphy, radar and sonar, aircraft, tanks, machine guns, missiles, nuclear weapons, and cyber-domain technologies are just some of the imaginative, clever ways that humans have figured out how to kill their own kind, only to witness their enemies very quickly learning how to develop and use a similar technology, and usually improve it in some way to keep the competitive cycle moving ever onward.

The first lesson is that all technological advantages are fleeting at best.[4] Even dragons. Enemies adapt—sometimes they steal your technology (or resurrect it, in the case of Viserion), sometimes they develop a counter, sometimes they change their actions so as to make your advantage irrelevant. The time between introduction of a new technology and a counter generally has been declining over history.

For example, during the early stages of World War II, the British and Germans engaged in the Battle of the Beams, in this instance radio beams that would guide German bombers during night attacks to their targets. The Germans began their effort in September 1939; by May 1941 they had shifted their attention east toward the Soviet Union. During that brief period, the Germans introduced no less than three major radio-beam-producing systems, and the British responded to each in turn. Six iterations of navigation technology representing three generations of improvements occurred within twenty months.[5] Comparatively, this pattern of technology introduction and countertechnology adaptation has continued apace in the latest major wars the United States has fought, in Afghanistan and Iraq from 2001 onward. A 2012 Government Accountability Office report on countering improvised explosive devices (IEDs) found that the United States had spent more than $18 billion between 2006 and 2011 on counter-IED efforts, involving 1,340 initiatives, all developed in response to enemy adaptation to U.S. actions.[6]

The second lesson, related to the first, is that all technological advantages eventually leak into other hands. The way the British obtained the counter to the last German technological improvement in radio navigation would have given Daenerys pause. The British found the latest German radio navigation device in a German bomber that was shot down during a night raid; they then reverse engineered the device to produce false signals that misled other German bombers using the device. In similar fashion, the White Walker king reverse engineered (resurrected and turned) a deceased and recovered Viserion to be used for his nefarious purposes.

We can say that the first two lessons lead to the third: that technological advantage works both ways—for our side and also for our enemy. A successful introduction of a technology forces determined enemies to think critically and creatively about the conundrum into which we have forced them. If our foes have any modicum of intelligence (and virtually all do), they will attempt to adapt to and overcome the advantage and its accompanying strategic, operational, or tactical asymmetries. Call it the technology-advantage version of strategy as described by Sean Connery's policeman character in *The Untouchables*: "You want to get [Al] Capone? Here's how you get him. He pulls a knife; you pull a gun. He sends one of yours to the hospital; you send one of his to the morgue. That's the Chicago way!"

The fleeting advantage and the leakage of technology both promote the inadvertent exchange of technologies. When accomplished on a large, national scale, this can lead to extraordinarily violent contests. The British-German naval race preceding World War I led to the Battle of Jutland.[7] The Allied arms race in general during the same period led to a terrific symmetry of forces and doctrine, resulting in complete negation of advantages to either side for almost four years along the western front. All that the respective forces could do was to hunker down, fight, and die. A short-lived, nontechnological advantage of the Germans in 1918 (storm trooper tactics associated with precision artillery barrages) almost broke the stalemate; however, the Allies learned the German tactics; used them with another technology advantage of their own, the tank; coupled them with a new massive influx of raw manpower, the Americans; and crushed the German lines less than five months after the Germans applied their advantage.

Now that Daenerys and her allies have a technological symmetry with their foes, they need to be very careful not to be lured into a strategic stalemate, especially since the enemy literally regenerates itself and additionally can resurrect and turn friendly soldiers who were killed in action.

The fourth lesson, leading from the third, should be clear to readers by now. Technology often disables as much as it enables. This is most unfortunately true when one becomes dependent on that technology for battlefield success. The dependence becomes a form of blindness that makes one vulnerable to exploitation by an enemy. In such circumstances, only bad things can happen.

For a historical reference, Dany and her advisors should pay heed to the American experience at the first naval battle in the Guadalcanal campaign in August 1942, that of Savo Island. The Allies, primarily American with some Royal Australian Navy support, had just wrested Henderson Field on Guadalcanal from the Japanese. They had repelled intense air attacks and, in the tropical heat, had become exhausted. In those days, naval ships were not air conditioned, so the heat was overpowering. Though intelligence had provided repeated findings that a Japanese surface task force was moving south from Rabaul, Allied leadership misread intentions and chose to take defensive naval positions in Savo Sound (soon to be called Iron Bottom Sound for obvious reasons). They wanted their crews to recover from their exertions in battle over the previous two days. The Allied command relied on a technology advantage called radar; this electromagnetic detection and ranging system could, in theory, identify approaching enemy vessels from twenty miles away, even at night.

What the Allied leaders apparently did not know was that detection distance was under ideal conditions and with a more advanced model than their ships had mounted. The real detection distance, under ideal circumstances, was closer to seven miles and then only if the target was within the search cone of the transmitting antenna (which had to be manually turned). When the Japanese approached the Allied formations late in the evening of August 8, 1942, they were outside the cone, and Japanese lookouts using superior night optical technology detected the Americans first. The result was the worst naval defeat at sea (Pearl Harbor being at peace and at anchor) for the U.S. Navy. The Allies relied on radar to provide the warning time to get ready to repel an attack; their situational awareness was disabled by this reliance. It was only because the Japanese ran out of time (they had to be out of Allied air attack range by dawn) that the Allied amphibious fleet avoided the destruction of its protective force.[8]

All in all, having a technology advantage in war is a mixed blessing. One has to be constantly aware of both the opportunities and the limitations afforded by the advantage and must always be prepared for the inevitable enemy counterpunch and adaptation to the advantage. Dany and her dragons, with her numerous allies, must take the Viserion factor into account in order to have a chance to take the Iron Throne from Cersei Lannister. Daenerys must win with something other than the biological technology advantage that is dragon power.

For those of us who must make our way in our real world, these lessons and their implications signal that we must be prepared to adapt in ways that are unaccounted for in the third offset and its successor conceptions. It is worth our time and attention to reflect on what these alternative adaptations could be.

Restoring Asymmetric Advantages

Let us consider three general approaches to rebalancing the military power wheel to our advantage. First, and most obviously, we can envision obtaining some other technological advantage. After all, Jon Snow and Samwell Tarly are now busy in Westeros mining and refining dragonglass into weapons that are lethal to White Walkers. Of course, as noted in the lessons above, that likely will result in a reciprocal adaptation by the White Walkers.

There's also the issue of cost, which does not seem to be such a big issue in *Game of Thrones* but always plays a critical and often deciding role in our world. Pursuit of third offset technologies will be costly; that should be abundantly clear to those with just the most basic understanding of defense research and development and defense acquisition. For example, the F-35 program now is the most expensive weapons system program in history, and the aircraft isn't even fully operational.[9] Similarly, the DDG-1000 destroyer program in the U.S. Navy is so prohibitively expensive that the acquisition program is limited to three platforms; a naval associate of mine calls these ships "works of art" because they're too expensive to truly be tools of the trade. These two current programs illustrate the cost pressures technology advantages place on defense budgets. Coming at a time in which our nation is incurring record deficits and demanding governmental programs to assist everything from health care to infrastructure, such an expensive alternative to rebalancing military power should be assessed as questionable at the very least.

A second alternative approach to the problem of restoring asymmetric advantage might be to explore revitalizing other instruments of national power (diplomatic, informational, military, and economic).

Daenerys might consider applying diplomacy to reengage Cersei Lannister or to make inroads with Cersei's alliance with Euron Greyjoy, the leader of the Iron Islands and head of a formidable fleet. Alternatively, she might be able to negotiate with the White Walker king, who in the past has engaged in a form of diplomacy with the wildings north of the Wall; admittedly, this seems a most unlikely task, though it might buy time for her to marshal her forces.

In our world, Ambassador Robert Oakley, former ambassador to Somalia, has said, "If they're talking, they're not shooting." Generally, that is a good thing in a world of proliferating nuclear weapons. We see the potential in the Korean talks about peaceful settlement of the Korean War; we should see the potential that President Emmanuel Macron of France made reference to concerning the Iranian nuclear treaty, the Joint Comprehensive Plan of Action (JCPOA), in his speech to the U.S. Congress. Even if imperfect, Macron said, "there is a framework" that can be improved on.[10]

Information is a second instrument of national power that can be applied as a substitute or complement to technological advantage. This instrument can be expressed through strategic communications or messaging, through disinformation, through network disruption, and through deception and manipulation with the aim of getting inside the minds of relevant parties of interest.[11] Dany could engage Bran Stark, the new Three-Eyed Raven, to use his growing power to see into the past and the future and to manipulate both. Bran has a mental connection with the White Walker king, one that could be exploited . . . but for good or evil?

In our realm, we have seen and continue to experience the results of messaging, of manipulation and deceptive information in our current politics. We know that social media is a decisive tool that can polarize or integrate societies. The power and speed with which information operations can affect massive changes in a polity are frighteningly fast, overwhelming governments' abilities to cope with or respond to information.[12] To date, the advantage of information operations has resided with the offense, the disruptors, whether they be private agents or agents of Russia or the PRC. The challenge for the United States is to be able to reintegrate the social and political messages that enable us to perceive ourselves as a united people working to improve our lot in the world.

Applying the military instrument of power is more than just applying technology, although that surely is and will be a component of future operations. Here, Daenerys and her allies would be well advised to turn to the likes of J. F. C. Fuller and B. H. Liddell Hart of the British or John Boyd of the Americans, for recommendations on how more effectively to apply the substantial military forces she has to overcome the White Walker army now flooding into Westeros. All three would emphasize maneuvers or indirect approaches to attacking the enemy. They would also remind our heroine that war is conducted *simultaneously* at the physical, cognitive, and moral levels. Even if wights are difficult to physically kill, they can be outthought and outfought, and friendly forces can be constantly reminded of the moral imperatives of the human side. Dany, even while leading a coalition, must find a way to quicken her decision cycle so as to effectively paralyze the White Walkers, allowing the humans to strike when and where they can be most effective.

We may believe that our armed forces, those of the United States and its allies, already practice Fuller, Hart, and Boyd very well. Perhaps that can be argued to be the case at the tactical level, but operationally and strategically, that hardly appears to be the situation. Our opponents in the prolonged War on Terror remain potent, if severely damaged. They have an incredible resilience that is derived from the intensity of their *ideas* and *faith* that transcends the blood they have shed on the battlefield. Tactically, we surpass our foes wherever we have met them, but to what end?

In many ways, we seem to be reliving the experience of Colonel Harry Summers's conversation with Colonel Tu of the North Vietnamese Army, allegedly occurring in 1975, in which Summers remarked, "You know, you never defeated us on the battlefield" (n.b., this was an overstatement); Tu responded, "That may be so. But it is also irrelevant."[13] We have fought this war well on the physical level but not so well on the cognitive and moral levels. Our military may argue that the problem is out of their hands because civilian political leaders provide the strategic direction that leads clearly to operations and campaigns, and civilian leadership has been anything but consistent or constant over the course of the war. As Colonel Tu might say, that may indeed be so. But it is also an admission of defeat of a kind—that is, we cannot defeat an idea or a faith, no matter how onerous it seems to us. We should ponder that point the next time we as a nation get the urge to launch a flight of missiles or an armed drone somewhere, for some reason.

Finally, there is the economic instrument of national power that can be applied to the Great War in Westeros. It seems clear that there are manpower limitations in Westeros, especially among the fractured kingdoms. One can suppose that Dany could send emissaries, as indeed Cersei has, to Essos and beyond to obtain additional mercenary armies and navies, as well as for resources to support the same. She certainly has the talent for these types of negotiations in the persons of Tyrion Lannister and Daario Naharis. Both are proven arbitrators and promoters of her cause who increase the probabilities of their success in the Iron Bank of Braavos; and if negotiations fail, Daario's fighting qualities likely would quell any significant disagreements.

Our own application of the economic instrument of national power has been extensive and generally successful. Recently, Korean president Moon Jae-in has credited President Trump's threatened sanctions with renewed North Korean interest in negotiations. The threatened use of sanctions and their removal have also proven a useful tool in the Iranian JCPOA treaty. Finally, targeted sanctions against key wealthy Russian billionaires over the Russian information campaign against the United States have certainly gotten Russian attention to the problem. We should realize that the longer economic sanctions are in place, the more difficult it is to maintain unity of effort among those applying them. That difficulty was one significant problem in the post–Desert Storm Iraqi sanctions regime; they also led to unintended consequences, such as increased suffering among Iraqi people due to lack of access to certain health and agricultural goods.

There is a third way to go about restoring an asymmetric advantage in the war for Westeros now being waged. That way is one of unlimited or, in Clausewitzian terms, absolute war. Truly, the war that is upon Westeros is an existential one: between the humans and nonhumans (White Walkers). The intention of the White Walker invasion of the south—that is, the kingdoms of Westeros—seems clear: to kill and turn all humans into wights. This being the situation and the desired end state of the White Walker king, then Daenerys should consider one of the last ruminations of her father, the Mad King, Aerys Targaryen, who fixated on immolating the entire population of King's Landing with his proclamation: "The traitors want my city . . . but I'll give them naught but ashes. . . . Burn them all."

A scorched-earth strategy that uses wildfire and dragon fire certainly would kill the White Walker army; it would also devastate Westeros for an indeterminate time to come. Akin to the Soviet strategy at the beginning of World War II, this means sacrificing much of Westeros's territory and people. In this case, millions of human inhabitants likely would die, mostly through starvation and sickness. This strategy buys time to build or rebuild armies, as well as acting as a killing mechanism against the northern threat. However, given the extremity of the consequences, Dany likely would perceive this as a last resort.

Here, our comparison between the fictional world of Westeros and our real world comes to an end. The strategic threats that we face, while significant and costly, are hardly existential. The Taliban and the Islamic State are regional entities with occasional global reach. The PRC is mostly a competitor for global economic hegemony, not political dominance. The Russians, however devious and devoted with their information operations, are trying to fight demographic realities—they are losing population, and in the end, population is the essential ingredient for political and economic power. Eventually, the Russians must learn to manage their decline until a semblance of population stability can be restored.

In no instance of the above threats and competition is a scorched-earth option realistic, desirable, or acceptable for the United States. By scorched earth, here I mean the use of nuclear weapons, a far more dangerous and powerful technology than wildfire or dragons. And yet as part of the implementation of the third offset, the United States plans to upgrade and expand its nuclear arsenal over a ten-year period. There are compelling technological reasons for doing so: the existing systems are based on 1960s technologies; our competitors (think Russia) are upgrading theirs; and our existing systems can be changed from area to precision weapons, thus enabling their utility. All well and good.

But do we really want such an asymmetric advantage?

A Wall of sorts that would prevent some as-yet-unknown White Walker threat from our homeland?

And a homeland that looks like Westeros?

Do we really want to play the game of thrones?

NOTES

1. Indeed, Gray has made it his first maxim. See Colin S. Gray, *Fighting Talk: Forty Maxims on WAR, PEACE, and STRATEGY* (Lincoln: University of Nebraska Press, 2009).

2. The phrase "third offset" originated in the Obama administration, where the strategy focused on technological advances. The translation of this strategy into national defense strategy can clearly be read in the Trump administration's *2018 National Defense Strategy* (or at least its unclassified summary). In fact, the strategy was expanded to include adaptation of the department's culture and organizations to these technological ideas. For an example of the initial strategy, see Mackenzie Eaglen, "What Is the Third Offset Strategy," *Real Clear Defense*, February 15, 2016, https://www.realcleardefense.com/articles/2016/02/16/what_is_the _third_offset_strategy_109034.html. For the expansion and implementation of the idea, see Steve Blank, "National Defense Strategy: A Compelling Call for Defense Innovation," *Real Clear Defense*, February 13, 2018, https://www.realcleardefense.com/2018/02/13/national _defense_strategy_a_compelling_call_for_defense_innovation_300284.html.

3. A good summary of the third offset and its predecessors can be found in Robert Martinage, *Toward a New Offset Strategy: Exploiting U.S. Long-Term Advantages to Restore U.S. Global Power Projection Capability* (Washington DC: Center for Strategic and Budgetary Assessment, 2014).

4. My colleague Jan S. Breemer reminds me that the lesson does not always hold. He mentions the case of Greek fire, which remained an advantage to the Byzantines for almost six hundred years. In fact, the actual ingredients of the weapon remain in dispute to this very day.

5. Brian Johnson, *The Secret War* (Barnsley, UK: Pen and Sword Military Classics, 2004).

6. Government Accountability Office, *Counter Improvised Explosive Devices*, GAO-12-861R (Washington DC: Government Accountability Office, August 1, 2012).

7. Earlier, a nineteenth-century naval arms race occurred between Great Britain and France. See Jan S. Breemer, "The Great Race: Innovation and Counter-Innovation at Sea, 1840–1890"

(Corbett paper no. 2, Corbett Centre for Maritime Policy Studies, King's College, London, January 2011).

8. James D. Hornfischer, *Neptune's Inferno: The U.S. Navy at Guadalcanal* (New York: Bantam Books, 2012). Hornfischer provides the most up-to-date history of the Battle of Savo Island; see especially pt. 1.

9. Adam Ciralsky, "Will It Fly?" *Vanity Fair*, September 16, 2013, https://www.vanityfair.com /news/2013/09/joint-strike-fighter-lockheed-martin.

10. Fred Kapan, "L'Etat of the Union," *Slate*, April 25, 2018, https://slate.com/news-and -politics/2018/04/macrons-speech-to-congress-was-a-rousing-rebuke-of-trumps-foreign -policy.html.

11. Timothy L. Thomas still has the best summary of this way of conducting information operations, in his "The Mind Has No Firewall," *Parameters* 28, no. 1 (Spring 1998): 84–92.

12. There is a large and growing body of literature on the political and social effects of information applied by social media. One excellent reference is Cass R. Sunstein, *#Republic: Divided Democracy in the Age of Social Media* (Princeton NJ: Princeton University Press, 2017).

13. Richard Halloran, "Strategic Communication," *Parameters* 37, no. 3 (Autumn 2007): 4.

10

Game of Pwns

Baelish and Varys as Drivers of Modern Conflict

NINA A. KOLLARS

It is tempting to characterize conflict in *Game of Thrones* as one of great power competition, viewing the competition through the lens of realism. It is easy to view the struggle as an anarchic one between similar family structures acting in their own self-interest and building their power to promote familial self-preservation. In short, it is all too tempting to view Westeros as the ultimate Hobbesian playground. As viewers of the popular series will attest, life in Westeros is nasty, brutish, and short. However similar to real-world international relations, a pure-realism viewpoint falls short in understanding the conflict, due to the exclusion of actors who are not part of the major families.

To be clear, the primary factor that initiates conflict in Westeros is not power disparities between families or a product of an anarchic system (as realism would predict) but malicious data manipulation by a nonstate actor. The threat is not dragons or White Walkers but a single hacker, Petyr Baelish—the money lender and brothel owner who attempts to pwn both the Starks and the Lannisters for personal glory and gain and maybe a little bit of schadenfreude.[1]

Certainly, politics and tension exist in Westeros, but conflict between the head families began with manipulated data. The bloodshed begins early in season 1, when Baelish convinces Catelyn Stark that the dagger intended to kill her son belongs to the rival Lannister family's own Tyrion. The events that follow spark a brutal, bloody war between the two families, and as chaos ensues, Baelish manipulates data to sow further political instability, adroitly maneuvering to maximize his own profit and stature. To use Baelish's own words, "Chaos isn't a pit. Chaos is a ladder."[2]

Baelish is neither king nor ruler nor powerful leader in any meaningful sense. Instead, he is a man who deals in information. He excels as an information broker with a network of informants and secrets that he leverages for his own gain—no matter the disruption it causes. In contemporary parlance, Baelish is a black hat hacker. Like the black hats in our reality, Baelish has expert skills in social engineering and is situated within a networked information system. Baelish proves himself to be a most formidable hacker, because he understands how to manipulate data, data systems, and humans. He is the ultimate black hat, because he uses the system entirely for his own gain. He doesn't care about the health of the kingdom, the security of the leadership, or the strength of its military. Baelish wants money, power, and glory, and he uses hacker-like skills to get it. And like any good hacker, he occasionally disrupts the system for the lulz.

Thankfully, another sort of hacker emerges in Westeros to balance the chaos Baelish unleashes. This is Varys, alternately known as the Spider or as the Master of Whispers. As Baelish's archnemesis, Varys is equally as masterful at manipulating information networks. Another hacker of social systems, Varys differs from Baelish in that Varys sees himself as protector and maintainer of the health and well-being of all the citizens of Westeros. No fan of purposeless chaos, Varys sees himself as a stabilizing figure. In contrast to Baelish's black hat role, Varys functions as a white hat hacker, a preserver and protector of system stability.

Still, one should hesitate in just how much comfort to take in Varys's work. In his own words, "I did what I did for the good of the realm."[3] Varys judges for himself, takes action on his own, and helps who he—individually—judges should be aided. In this sense, any temptation to see Varys as an agent subsumed under the state is false. Varys is undoubtedly *also* a nonstate actor. The difference is that he seeks to ensure the well-being of a system he prefers. While he works to pwn Baelish, he isn't always working in favor of the ruling regime. Westeros's cyberraven comms and little bird-mice networks can be just as easily utilized for personal gain as they can for the public good. And while we are tempted to say that Varys is a force for the kingdom's good, his actions aren't always specifically regime preserving. While we can resolutely abhor Baelish for his selfishness, Varys's form of justice could easily run afoul of a regime worth supporting.

This brings us to the driving question of this writing. How might Baelish's and Varys's behavior inform the way we think about modern military conflict? Most broadly, the answer is that the role of nonstate actors capable of manipulating information systems should be among our foremost concerns, both during times of geopolitical competition and during times of open warfare.

Given the increased interconnectedness of modern information systems (spawning more points of potential network vulnerability), the Baelish-Varys pwnage behavior proves increasingly important to understanding contemporary geopolitics.

This writing posits that modern conflict is less a playground for decoration-laden master strategists with their complex militaries and more a utopia for shrewd (often less heroic) hackers with their relatively simple methods of system hacking. More succinctly, the outcome of future conflict will rely more than at any point in the history of warfare on the struggles between white and black hat hackers. It is worth our time to understand what drives these two types of actors and what we can be doing now to prepare for this type of competition.

Black hat hackers operate as self-interested manipulators of information and information systems. Black hats are information brokers, and they do so to benefit themselves—whether it be for glory, riches, or power. Black hats care little about the discord they might sow, so long as it furthers their own private goals. Be it raven scrolls or bots on the internet, we would do well to heed this lesson in the modern era. Beware the disruptive danger of nonstate actors capable of information system manipulation! At best, they make our militaries, governments, and communities less efficient. At worst, they make the systems untrustworthy, and when trust breaks down, clear lines of decision-making go awry. Distrust of information systems is problematic, and black hats only exacerbate that problem. They not only increase criminality and chaos in a system, but they make it easier to blur lines. They literally make it difficult to trust the information systems we rely on to function. One needn't look any further than the current debacle of Russian meddling in our own election systems, feeding polarized media cycles and undermining the public's trust in voting. It is one thing to hack Sony to demonstrate dissatisfaction with a depiction of a North Korean leader—it's another thing when meddling in data causes a nation to doubt its own democratic political processes. And yet here we are.

In terms of military and elite-government decision-making, could this erosion be the cause of a world war? This author finds it unlikely as a first-order cause but worries deeply that it will undermine national reliance on information systems both public and private. Insofar as military decision-making in wartime seeks to enable global joint operations, continues to be pushed downward onto the battlefield, and aims to engage in cross-service and cross-domain operations, the reliability of information within those networks as they cross service, country, or system borders is susceptible to manipulation. Military cooperation, at every level, gets harder.

On the peacetime governance side, it is trustworthy information systems that make it possible to sort democratic states from those merely claiming to be democratic—literally. Transparent processes that communicate the will of the people to government systems and the mutually transparent systems that demonstrate the actions of militaries and government leaders to the public—these are the core mechanisms that separate democracy from other regimes. Information, trustworthy information, connects the heart of a republic to its mind. Undermining trust in that flow undermines democratic regimes, their global cooperation schemes, the international laws they seek to uphold, and ultimately systemic stability.

As such, the Baelish problem is deeper than simple criminal disruption. Baelish is more than a casual black hat hacker making his money on the dark side of the system. He's worse. He not only blurs the distinctions between criminal activities and those that fundamentally alter political power structures, but he also blurs the distinction we draw between wartime activities and peacetime politics. Is Baelish waging war? Is he manipulating? Or is he trying to topple a regime, using methods just shy of overt violence? When something goes wrong, do we blame the Lannisters for the attack using bad data? Or just Baelish's treachery? As it is in Westeros, the same is increasingly true for black hats manipulating the modern system. Increasingly, we are finding that nonstate cyberthreat actors are slippery when it comes to intent, often blurring the lines between criminal economic behavior and state-sponsored political agendas. This is the current and (my guess is) the future reality of the cyberthreat space—it will be harder and harder to discern the difference between criminal and political actors. We may even reach a time when the distinction just isn't useful at all. Advanced persistent-threat actors like North Korea's Lazarus Group are unabashedly both. They make their money hijacking cryptocurrency wallets, and they hack patriotically for the regime.[4]

Consider OceanLotus, a group reportedly working out of Vietnam, whose bailiwick since 2014 appears to be spearfishing (targeted email campaigns intended to make recipients download malware) of manufacturing and hospitality companies operating in Vietnam (both domestic and foreign).[5] Prior to this, however, the Electronic Frontier Foundation indicated that OceanLotus had been found to attack dissidents and journalists in Vietnam since 2013.[6] While it is possible that OceanLotus's political activities were the result of its own preferences, it is equally likely that they were simply paid to do so.

Consider also the case of a group called Codoso based out of China. Codoso is generally described as a freelance Chinese hacking group rather than a state-operated organization. Nevertheless, in 2014 Codoso breached Forbes.com. The attack initially appeared to be a broadly targeted attempt to steal credentials from a highly visited site, but later forensics indicated that the group's interest was in only a select few visitors to the site—specifically defense sector firms.[7]

Black hat freelancing is a rising, vibrant global service industry, made possible through deep-web spaces that enable private communication, dark-web markets, and cryptocurrencies that obscure the transfer of funds. The markets differ between Russian, Chinese, and U.S. sites, but no country is immune to the effects or the birth of these markets. The cost for stolen data services ranges from low-end credit card data sales at approximately one dollar per card to targeted hacking of email accounts at about one hundred dollars each.[8] As new technologies are pushed onto the marketplace, malware can be adapted to attack it. Among the hottest trends in the Chinese service market is the tailoring of malware to mobile technologies that enables mass spamming and phishing attacks.[9] Efforts to stem these services have resulted in a globally uncoordinated and vastly ineffective game of internet whack-a-mole. It will be some time, if ever, before states learn how to manage the rise of the black hat service market—when, that is, states aren't buying into it themselves.

Although it's a tempting response to the threat posed by black hats, the answer is not simply to fight fire with fire and hire white hat hackers. The motivation of the white hat can also be fraught with contradiction for any ruling regime. Working toward the stability of a system isn't the same thing as loyalty to a particular regime. As season after season of *Game of Thrones* demonstrates, Varys changes loyalties as he judges who might preserve the kingdom best. This, in practice, is likely part (though obviously not sufficiently all) of why the U.S. military and intelligence agencies attempt to "grow their own" hack talent, rather than rely on the public pool. Recall that Edward Snowden considers himself a white hat, and frankly, many in the white hat hacking community concur with Snowden's self-labeling. It should function as a sober reminder that just because the United States is a country of free citizens with a democratic process does not mean that white hat preferences for preservation of stability naturally align. And when they do not, data gets stolen and often publicly distributed.

Our intelligence and military communities are well aware of these risks and are still attempting to find a balance between hiring the best talent and protecting against insider threats. This explains why DoD efforts to "Hack the Pentagon," "Hack the Air Force," and similarly (poorly) titled events aren't so much white hat hacking events as they are vulnerability research intended to find security loopholes in publicly facing websites. The DoD wants the capabilities and talent but recognizes that white hats do not necessarily signify love for U.S. national security agencies (not that they necessarily should either—there's a real argument for leaving white hats to do their work as part of a healthy information ecosystem rather than trying to capture them as federal cyberwarriors).

Ideally, the real-world problem of information systems' reliability and modern conflict would be as narrow as that of one or two Baelishes or even just a matter of telling the Baelishes and Varyses apart (something not always possible). Westeros is truly a fantasy world that presents us with two agents who operate at the apex of an information system. In an era of networked connectivity and instantaneous communication, the potential for self-interested information brokers—whether white hat or black—to affect systems is broad and staggering. In this sense, the problem of Westeros's systems pales in comparison to the modern cyberthreat conflict space. The series features two actors who can pwn the system. The truth is that there are tens of thousands of Baelishes and Varyses engaged in a global push and pull for the preservation or corruption of data. Even more confoundingly, being either self-interested or community-preserving is not a consistent state for the hack community—hackers can and do change hats. Meanwhile, states, marketplaces, and communities are caught in the crossfire.

It is often the case that young black hats just learning their trade eventually come to see the error of their ways and turn white hat "before they've been sentenced for their first felonies."[10] For this very reason, Null Space Labs was created by hacker (and penetration-testing consultant) Datagram and his colleagues in Los Angeles to direct the energies of young hackers before they venture down the wrong path.[11] Similarly, crowd-sourced programs on vulnerability research—like those at BugCrowd, where they are known as bug bounties—also provide an outlet for young hack types to make money and develop their skills while operating within the law.[12] But it is equally possible that what began as benign tinkering in cyberspace can turn malicious, particularly for skilled populations in parts of the world where opportunities are few or in places where politics have resulted in disaffected citizens. For talented hackers trying to make money to support their families, there are choices that must be made, and the dark side is sometimes the only option to get paid.

Finally (if the hacking metaphor hasn't already jumped the shark), I offer the following thought on future hacking efforts. As in Westeros, the modern real-world information system is neutral, and those with the capacity to manipulate it can do so either disruptively or as an act of preservation. If the reader will forgive this stretch to the potential artificially intelligent information future, there remains Brandon Stark, who by the end of season 7 has become data omnipotent—he can seek out the data to any question he is asked both backward and forward in time. In doing so, Bran is the one who ends up pwning the pwner Baelish, by revealing Baelish's deception with the dagger. This technological temptation too, however, has its limitations. Bran can only see what he seeks to observe, and as such, his capacity to check against data manipulation is limited by the scope of his question. In this way, similar concerns should be on the forefront of the national conversation about the use of artificial intelligence for national security and military purposes. In May 2018 many extremely talented Google employees tendered their resignations in response to learning that their AI research would be applied to military purposes. We would be wise to step carefully into this space. Information, its manipulation, and the systems that provide it are the deep variables at play in the potential for and exercise of conflict between countries—and they will only be more at play in the conflicts of tomorrow.

NOTES

1. *Pwn* (pronounced "pōn") is a slang term used by hackers to refer to the compromise of someone else's computer or network. Used more broadly, it refers to the domination of one over another. You can pwn or be pwned. The term, according to hack folklore, comes from a typo when the writer was attempting to type the word *own* (as in "you have been owned").

2. In addition, this line from Baelish is obviously crafted for the eponymously titled overall episode, "The Climb." David Benioff and D. B. Weiss, "The Climb," season 3, episode 6, dir. Alik Sakharov, *Game of Thrones*, aired May 5, 2013, on HBO.

3. Benioff and Weiss, "The Climb." The scene between Baelish and Varys is markedly tongue-in-cheek as the two information brokers come together to spar verbally. No small nod to the difference in motivations between the agents.

4. Rosie Perper, "New Evidence Reportedly Puts North Korean Hackers behind a List of High-Stakes Bitcoin Heists," *Business Insider*, January 19, 2018, https://www.businessinsider.com/north-korea-lazarus-group-behind-cryptocurrency-cyber-attack-wannacry-sony-2018-1.

5. Nick Carr, "Cyber Espionage Is Alive and Well: APT32 and the Threat to Global Corporations," *Threat Research*, May 14, 2017, https://www.fireeye.com/blog/threat-research/2017/05/cyber-espionage-apt32.html.

6. Eva Galperin and Morgan Marquis-Boire, "Vietnamese Malware Gets Very Personal," Electronic Frontier Foundation, January 19, 2014, https://www.eff.org/deeplinks/2014/01/vietnamese-malware-gets-personal.

7. Josh Grunzweig and Bryan Lee, "New Attacks Linked to C0d0so0 Group," *Palo Alto Networks*, January 22, 2016, https://researchcenter.paloaltonetworks.com/2016/01/new-attacks-linked-to-c0d0s0-group/; Ericka Chickowski, "Chinese Hacking Group Codoso Team Uses Forbes.com as Watering Hole," Dark Reading, February 10, 2015, https://www.darkreading.com/attacks-breaches/chinese-hacking-group-codoso-team-uses-forbescom-as-watering-hole-/d/d-id/1319059.

8. Pierluigi Paganini, "Pricing Policies in the Cyber Criminal Underground," InfoSec Institute, October 7, 2014, http://resources.infosecinstitute.com/pricing-policies-cyber-criminal-underground/.

9. Pierluigi Paganini, "Chinese Criminal Underground Is Doubled between 2012 and 2013," *Security Affairs*, September 6, 2014, http://securityaffairs.co/wordpress/28074/cyber-crime/chinese-underground.html.

10. Thank you to Casey Ellis at BugCrowd for this line; I'm cribbing directly from a telephone conversation I had with him.

11. For more about Null Space Labs, see their website at https://032.la/, last accessed March 5, 2019.

12. For more on BugCrowd, see the *BugCrowd* blog "About" page, at https://www.bugcrowd.com/about/blog/.

11

WMD in Westeros and Beyond

MAGNUS F. NORDENMAN

Nuclear weapons. Biological weapons. Chemical weapons. Radiological weapons. Tools of violence so uniquely destructive they've earned their own classification: weapons of mass destruction (WMD). And they present some of the most vexing problems for national security policy makers and military leaders today. Their use is considered taboo among most nations, and real-world use of them has been relatively rare since the United States dropped two nuclear bombs on Hiroshima and Nagasaki in Japan in 1945. However, acquiring them remains a priority for various regimes around the world—regimes like those of Syria, Iran, and North Korea. Meanwhile, for decades, nations such as the United States and its allies have been working hard to stop the further spread of WMD and to deter nations that already have them from using them—in turn, cajoling, sanctioning, rewarding, and even invading countries that were perceived as posing a WMD threat to world peace. And for decades, these efforts have been met with decidedly mixed results.

But why do WMD remain an attractive option to some nations if their use is a taboo and even keeping them around will potentially land a government in hot water with the international community? *Game of Thrones* has something to teach us about the power, uses, and risks associated with WMD, on and off the battlefield.

The U.S. military defines WMD as "chemical, biological, radiological, or nuclear weapons capable of a high order of destruction or causing mass casualties."[1] The combatants in Westeros, of course, do not have these particular weapons, but some of the warring houses do, at various times, have access to weapons capable of a high order of destruction and causing mass casualties. Wildfire, created by the Alchemists' Guild in King's Landing, and the dragons that Daenerys Targaryen nurtures from three petrified eggs given to her as a wedding gift both fit the U.S. military's description of WMD.

Unlike our world, there seems to be little that deters the active use of WMD in the war for the Seven Kingdoms. This may be due to fact that very few of the combatants have WMD capabilities, so there is consequently little concern that another party may reciprocate in kind. In effect, there is no deterrence to the use of WMD in Westeros. This state of affairs is not unlike the early period of nuclear weapons, when the United States was the only nation that held them. The two atomic bombs dropped over Japan during World War II carried no risk of retaliation with similarly destructive weapons against targets in the United States, and the early Cold War saw serious discussions about the regular battlefield use of nuclear weapons. This tune changed as nations such as the Soviet Union and China began to acquire their own nuclear arsenals. Alas, the situation in Westeros is quite different.

Let's take a look at the use of WMD during the war for the Iron Throne. It turns out that the contenders in Westeros think about the use of WMD in much the same way as the war-waging states of World War I did, as well as the way in which current dictators, fearful of losing power to either popular uprising or by intervention from the outside, do.

WMD on the Battlefield

In our world, WMD have been used—and in many other cases, their use has been considered—on the battlefield. During World War I, Germany, France, and the United Kingdom used chemical weapons, such as mustard gas, to weaken the defenses of the adversary before launching an attack. Chemical weapons also generated a psychological effect of fear on the adversary, alongside the painful suffering and often death that afflicted those without protection. These weapons were, however, not without drawbacks. The gas would sometimes waft back over friendly lines as the wind changed direction. Later, tactical nuclear weapons were also considered for battlefield use, although such considerations never became reality. The idea was to drop a small nuclear bomb on the enemy's defenses and then assault with tanks and infantry through the hole in the defensive line created by the tactical nuclear bomb.

Military planners also recognize a unique defensive role for WMD. States such as North Korea, Iraq, Libya, and Iran could hardly stand up against conventional assaults by, for example, the United States and its allies. In these cases, regimes turn to the threat of WMD as a guarantee that they will not, someday, be subject to violent regime change by foreign intervention. This, in essence, explains the reluctance of countries like North Korea to give up their nuclear weapons; doing so would leave the country open to a conventional attack that it has no way to withstand.

In *Game of Thrones*, we see wildfire and dragons used both defensively and offensively. During the Battle of the Blackwater, Stannis Baratheon seeks to seize King's Landing and capture the Iron Throne from its occupant (and his nephew), Joffrey Baratheon, by assaulting the city from both land and sea. The city's defenses, led by Tyrion Lannister, are nearly overwhelmed by the multidirectional assault, but Tyrion manages to break Stannis's offensive by using wildfire to destroy much of the attacking naval flotilla. Wildfire turns the tide of the battle in the defenders' favor, enabling them to successfully defend King's Landing.

Later, during Daenerys Targaryen's invasion of Westeros, she uses dragons to great effect against the Lannister army at the Battle of the Goldroad. It is indeed a classic case of using WMD to breach the enemy's line in order to give other ground units the opportunity to exploit the breach. During the battle, the Lannister forces form up to meet the Dothraki cavalry charge, but their formations are overcome by Daenerys's dragons, which burn huge holes in their lines. The mobile Dothraki cavalry charge through these gaps, operating not unlike modern tank forces, to finish the fight against the Lannisters.

We see another case of WMD breaching defenses when the White Walkers use dragon fire to collapse a part of the Wall, along the northern border of the Seven Kingdoms. This example also points toward one of the risks inherent to WMD—the chance, however small, that another actor may seize them and use them for nefarious purposes. In the world of *Game of Thrones*, the White Walkers get their hands on one of Daenerys's dragons; in the real world, counterproliferation activities are driven in part by the fear that a terrorist group might steal a nuclear weapon from an unstable state. As season 7 closes, WMD have enabled the White Walkers to overcome the Wall's defenses, something that they had been unable to accomplish with the weapons they previously had at their disposal.

WMD and Regime Survival

But WMD are not only of interest to states for their value on the battlefield or for their ability to deter a conventional attack by a far stronger adversary. They are also attractive because holding them, and occasionally using them, can keep a regime in power for decades longer than they would otherwise survive. Indeed, most instances of WMD being used since the Second World War have been related to regime survival, rather than combat operations. Former Iraqi dictator Saddam Hussein used chemical weapons against the restive Kurds in northern Iraq in the 1980s. He also used them against Shia Muslims who rose up against him, with the encouragement of the United States, in southern Iraq after Saddam's forces were ousted from Kuwait in 1991.[2] Bashar al-Assad's regime in Syria has also used chemical weapons on several occasions, against rebels and civilians alike, as part of his effort to remain in power during that country's civil war.[3] In this context, the psychological effects of WMD are especially important to a regime, in order to keep the population cowed. Indeed, this is a likely explanation for why Saddam Hussein refused to fully account for his lack of WMD, even when risking an all-out invasion by the United States and its allies in 2003. Publicly admitting he had no WMD could very well have led to uprisings, perhaps supported by Iran, against the regime in Baghdad.[4]

Similarly, in Westeros, rulers use wildfire and dragons to maintain their rule. Cersei Lannister, for example, uses wildfire to kill the High Sparrow and his followers at the Great Sept of Baelor in King's Landing, thereby ending that particular challenge to the House Lannister and its control over the capital. Daenerys Targaryen is also no stranger to using her dragons to strike fear in those who may challenge her. After the Battle of the Goldroad she persuades surviving enemy troops to fall in line by publicly executing Randyll and Dickon Tarly with the help of her dragons.

WMD in the Wrong Hands

A recurring theme within debates about WMD in national security circles is that some regimes cannot be trusted with such weapons due to the regimes' instability, the risk that they might not act entirely rationally, or the fear that they will hand over their WMD to nonstate actors such as terrorist groups that cannot be deterred. This formed part of the rationale for the U.S. invasion of Iraq in 2003 and has consistently been a large part of the debate around North Korea's nuclear weapons capability. Also, after the end of the Cold War, the United States and the West spent considerable sums of money to secure the nuclear weapons of the crumbling Soviet empire, in order to ensure that they, or their components, did not end up on the international black market. In the world of *Game of Thrones*, this is also a very real problem.

Aerys Targaryen—the Mad King—began as a kind ruler of Westeros but was later overtaken by hallucinations and intense paranoia. He executed and tortured many who he thought plotted against his rule. As his actual enemies closed on King's Landing, the Mad King ordered King's Landing and its population to be destroyed with wildfire, all the while believing that he could not be killed by it, thinking himself a dragon in human form. Before he could go through with the plan, Jaime Lannister killed him in the keep, thereby ending not only the Mad King's rule but also that of the House Targaryen.

What *Game of Thrones* Teaches Us about WMD

Game of Thrones points to the inherent attractiveness of WMD to some states and terrorist groups, even as the international community works hard to contain, control, and eliminate these weapons. The use of WMD in the real world is also sure to turn a regime into an international pariah. Witness the Saddam regime in Iraq or the Assad-run state in Syria. But WMD can, if properly applied, turn a military's fortunes on the battlefield, overcome strong defenses, and deter an attack from a superior enemy. In addition, WMD can keep a population in line, wipe out domestic opposition, and keep a ruler in power for a long time. That is why, in spite of ambitious efforts over decades to end their production and use, an array of states and nonstate groups seek to acquire them. And they remain attractive even though seeking and keeping them can mean decades of crippling sanctions, international isolation, and even military strikes. But *Game of Thrones* also points to the inherent risks of developing and maintaining a WMD arsenal and what can happen when a state loses control over its stock or when the ruler is not entirely rational.

The *Game of Thrones* world is one where might makes right, and this is certainly true when it comes to the use of wildfire and dragons in the War for the Iron Throne. Little suggests that our own world will do much better when it comes to WMD.

NOTES

1. *Department of Defense Strategy for Counter Weapons of Mass Destruction* (Washington DC: U.S. Department of Defense, June 2014), 17, https://archive.defense.gov/pubs/DoD_Strategy _for_Countering_Weapons_of_Mass_Destruction_dated_June_2014.pdf.
2. See, for example, Michael Nguyen, "Report Confirms Iraq Used Sarin in 1991," *Arms Control Today,* January 1, 2006.
3. Krishnadev Calamur, "Assad Is Still Using Chemical Weapons in Syria," *Atlantic,* February 6, 2018.
4. Glenn Kessler, "Saddam Hussein Said WMD Talk Helped Him Look Strong to Iran," *Washington Post,* July 2, 2009.

12

The Influence of Sea Power on Westeros

MICHAEL JUNGE

Across the major Westerosi wars, fleets play small but incomparably pivotal roles. Wars are fought and won ashore. Those small roles are so central that even small fleets remain important, to the point that marriages, plots, and promises revolve around fleets more than armies.

The history of Westerosi naval power is largely a narrative of contests between kingdoms, rivals, and violence at sea. The wealth and strength of kingdoms rises and falls with sea commerce and control and has done so since the First Men. The greatest tactic to increase wealth in Westeros is to exclude others, or remove them, from the sea. Whether it be the Dornish trade or blockade as siege, wealth moves or stops moving via the sea. Commerce by sea, while important and often violent, rarely leads to war on land. Even the loss of fleets is seldom seen as a threat to the houses ashore. However, fleets are inseparable from war on land.

While seaborne commerce was not the sole cause of war, wars between kingdoms routinely relied on fleets of ships to bring goods, material, horses, or men to the field of battle. Ships laid and relieved sieges. Control of the seas tipped the balance or modified conduct ashore. Sea power and maritime history are inextricably military history. One does not exist without the other.

Armies are, in relation to fleets, easy to raise. Every holding, every barony, and every kingdom has soldiers organized into some level of army. Skills gained in hunting animals translate easily to armed conflict on land. Not so at sea.

Most kingdoms have, at best, a small fishing fleet. And even then, only those who have sufficient coast and harbors need to be at sea. Fishing boats make poor ships of the line. Fishing boats have one purpose—catching and transporting fish. They are not intended for carrying men or horses, and when fishing boats carry men, armored men, the totals number only in the dozens. If horses are desired, then no men are carried in the same boat. Fishing boats are not armored or armed. They are not solid enough to carry cannon of consequence, and any arms fired from them must contend with the moving sea. It's very different from firing a bow and arrow or a cannon from solid and unmoving land. House Tully thrives on the fact that water of any sort, even an unbridged river, can so retard an army's progress as to give victory to the opponent. And bridges do not yet cross the sea.

What makes a sea power? Alfred Thayer Mahan tells us there are six features: geographic position; physical geography including climate, natural resources, and topography; territorial expanse; population size; population character; and government character.[1] In all of Westeros there are only three fleets: the Royal Fleet, in King's Landing; the Iron Fleet, of the Iron Islands; and the Redwyne Fleet, pledged to House Tyrell and, through them, to the king. The Royal Fleet numbers around two hundred ships; the Iron Fleet, around a hundred. Of these three fleets, only the Iron Fleet has the physical location and individual character to seek sea power. Other houses lack either the geographic location, the topography, the expanse, the population, or the government interest to field a fleet that could become central to its culture and identity.

The North is the largest of the Seven Kingdoms but has been without any sort of real sea power since Brandon the Shipwright sailed south and disappeared; in his grief, Brandon's son, Brandon the Burner, destroyed the remnants of the fleet and any shipbuilding industry. For centuries, no real threat came by way of the sea—only Ironborn raiders, coming and going like the Free Folk, attacked from beyond the Wall, taking and leaving but never seeking to conquer. The White Walkers and Night King, however far off in history, always sought to conquer, destroy, and remain. The history of the North is focused on a single threat, a single great (or greater) power. Winterfell is central to the holding, without interest in the sea. Likewise, the remaining kingdoms are largely ruled from central locations. The government of the North—and with it, its people and character—is not interested in the sea. While extensively bordered by water—the Sunset Sea to the west and the Narrow Sea to the east—the North is far more focused on the Wall and winter.

Even with the largely insignificant emphasis on sea power, the quest for ships and fleets takes up much time, intrigue, and gold. Jorah Mormont knows that gold can buy ships and intercedes, ineffectually at first but with great impact later, against Daenerys's benevolence during a Dothraki sack. Ser Davos Seaworth, the Onion Knight, knows that Stannis can only take King's Landing—and with it, seize the Iron Throne—with ships. In order to acquire ships, Robb Stark goes against his mother's advice by seeking an alliance with Balon Greyjoy. And Daenerys needs ships to cross the Narrow Sea. Even when Daenerys is installed in Dragonstone and begins her conquest of Westeros, her need for and reliance on ships is not finished. To avoid being perceived as a foreign invader, Daenerys sends the Iron Fleet, or the portion controlled by Theon and Asha, south to ferry the Dornish army to lay siege on King's Landing, while the Unsullied sail for Casterly Rock.

Not every hunter is a soldier, and not every guard detachment an army. Some cultures are better suited to war than others. The famed Unsullied and other sellswords provide one direction for war; the standing armies in Westeros, another. Finally, the warlike Dothraki nomads provide a third. Each of these three are isolated in their own place, their own lands. Eddard Stark knew this, telling King Robert, "Even a million Dothraki are no threat to the realm, as long as they remain on the other side of the Narrow Sea."[2]

For the Unsullied, Dothraki, or Seven Kingdoms to ever come into conflict would require more than just desire—it would require a fleet.

As Daenerys begins her conquest, Cersei also seeks allies, choosing an untrustworthy one in Euron Greyjoy, recognizing that the Ironborn "have ships, and they're good at killing."[3] Euron has the remainder of the Iron Fleet and is also good at killing, having led a revolt against King Robert, which included burning the Lannister fleet. Like Daenerys in Meereen, Cersei is willing to offer marriage in return for a fleet. And Cersei's arrangement proves disastrous for Daenerys.

What lessons can the non-Westerosi learn from this? Look back again at the criteria, the needs and foundations, for sea power: geographic position; physical geography including climate, natural resources, and topography; territorial expanse; population size; population character; and government character. In the United States of America a maritime heritage is so enshrined in our culture that we take all six of the criteria for granted. We romanticize the industrial might that brought victory in the Second World War. We are so resource rich that even as our industrial base shrinks, many believe that it can be rapidly reconstituted. With feature films like *The Perfect Storm* and television shows like *Deadliest Catch*, the public sees a fishing industry that is now a fraction of what it once was. Even with more aircraft carriers than the rest of the world combined, we tend to sit comfortably on our laurels; should we?

The American central position—between two benevolent or indifferent neighbors to the north and south and separated from Europe and Asia by oceans to the east and west—will remain. Geography is one of those things that changes little within the life span of countries or even empires. To what extent will climate change, resource depletion, and urban sprawl alter the culture and population of this maritime nation? Much of the physical geography will remain—deepwater ports for instance—but other things are in question.

In 1776 every state (née colony) had coastline to the east. By 1812 three of the eighteen states were landlocked—no matter how grand the Mississippi

River is or how great the Great Lakes are, they are not the sea. By 1860 half the states were landlocked—a ratio that remains today.

Balancing this is that much of the population lives near the coast. In fact, this is true around the globe; 80 percent of the world's population lives within two hundred miles of the sea. The National Oceanic and Atmospheric Administration's *National Coastal Population Report* tells us that 52 percent of Americans live in counties that border the oceans.[4] Of the country's twenty-five largest cities, twelve are on the coasts, and another seven are in coastal states.

Ninety percent of global trade travels by sea, and the United States is by far the biggest consumer of commercial goods and global natural resources. Maintaining global access to the maritime commons is, has been, and will be in the United States' interests. Meanwhile, our merchant fleet ranks twenty-second in the world by tonnage—behind Antigua and Barbuda, Bermuda, Japan, Norway, and even Malta.[5] The United States claims two hundred container ships. By comparison, China has over two thousand.[6]

Among fishing fleets, the story is similar, with the United States ranking roughly sixth behind Indonesia, Japan, Mexico, and Korea and capturing a quarter as much as China and half as much as Peru—both of whom have smaller fleets.

Among navies, however, the United States ranks first. The United States has the most ships, the greatest reach, and the greatest overall firepower. U.S. aircraft carriers total more than the rest of the world combined. Not only are there more of them, but each carrier can carry twice as many aircraft as the next-largest foreign carrier. Like the merchant and fishing fleets, however, the U.S. Navy is in both overall and relative decline.

Like Brandon the Shipwright's travels, China once sailed far across the Indo-Pacific region. During the Ming dynasty (1368–1644), Chinese fleets sailed as far south as Java, as far west as the Persian Gulf and Africa, and possibly as far east as North America. And like Brandon the Burner, in 1433 China burned its fleets and retreated from the sea to remain shore bound for centuries. Now, in the last two decades, the Chinese People's Liberation Army Navy has seen a tenfold increase in defense spending and boasts two aircraft carriers and over a hundred blue water combatant ships.[7] China has increased its reach, routinely operates off the coast of Africa, and is building a naval base in the Horn of Africa. Russia remains a capable naval power with Cold War–era ships and a modernization plan.

George R. R. Martin has admitted that his *Game of Thrones* is Mediterranean centric, Eurocentric, and even Anglocentric.[8] His historical analogies only go so far. Despite the great naval battles and rivalries of the past two thousand years, no country was able to take a position like the United States until the last century. No other country in the world has had the position, geography, topography, climate, population, and government to field both a large army and large navy. But this capability may be short-lived. Aegon Targaryen captured and united Westeros with an army, small fleet, and three dragons. His descendants ruled for three hundred years. For the time, dragons were the ultimate in asymmetric warfare, as they struck fear into the hearts of all men and laid waste to wood, stone, and steel. In time those dragons shrank in stature, until they finally withered away to become shadows of their former selves and their masters went from cruel conquerors to cruel and crazed. A united Seven Kingdoms could not be conquered with an army, small fleet, and three dragons—Daenerys needs a large army, a fleet of warships and transports, and three dragons.

Pax Americana is only in its first century—will it make two more?

NOTES

1. A. T. Mahan, *The Influence of Sea Power upon History, 1660–1783* (Boston: Little, Brown and Company, 1890; Project Gutenberg, 2007), http://www.gutenberg.org/files/13529/13529-h/13529-h.htm.

2. David Benioff and D. B. Weiss, "The Kingsroad," season 1, episode 2, dir. Tim Van Patten, *Game of Thrones*, aired April 24, 2011, on HBO.

3. David Benioff and D. B. Weiss, "Dragonstone," season 7, episode 1, dir. Jeremy Podeswa, *Game of Thrones*, aired July 16, 2017, on HBO.

4. National Oceanic and Atmospheric Administration, *National Coastal Population Report: Population Trends from 1970–2020* (Washington DC: U.S. Department of Commerce; U.S. Census Bureau, March 2013), https://aamboceanservice.blob.core.windows.net/oceanservice-prod/facts/coastal-population-report.pdf.

5. See "Shipping Fleet Statistics: Data Tables (FLE)," Department of Transport, March 28, 2018, https://www.gov.uk/government/statistical-data-sets/shipping-fleet-statistics.

6. United Nations Conference on Trade and Development, *Review of Maritime Transport 2017* (Geneva, Switzerland: United Nations, 2017), 30, https://unctad.org/en/publicationslibrary /rmt2017_en.pdf.

7. Kyle Mizokami, "The Chinese Military Is a Paper Dragon," *Real Clear Defense*, September 5, 2014, https://www.realcleardefense.com/articles/2014/09/05/the_chinese_military_is _a_paper_dragon_107416.html.

8. grrm [George R. R. Martin], July 4, 2013, comment on grrm [George R. R. Martin], "We're Number One . . . ," *Not a Blog*, June 29, 2013, grrm.livejournal.com/326474.html?thread= 17863242#t17863242.

13

Winning the Waves

Sea Power and the Seven Kingdoms

BRYAN MCGRATH

Everyone knows that the *Game of Thrones* world is make-believe. There are no dragons. There are no White Walkers. There is no Night King. What there is, though, is a somewhat accurate representation of the Middle Ages and the power politics that attended them. Central to the *Game of Thrones* world is the importance of sea power, and there are lessons learned in the Seven Kingdoms that apply equally in our modern (real) world.

The world of *Game of Thrones*, like any world, begins with geography. Before the First Men, the Age of Heroes, the Andal Invasion, the Age of Valyria, the Seven Kingdoms, and the Age of the Targaryens, there was the island continent of Westeros, and across the Narrow Sea was the continent of Essos. For a contemporary sense of scale, think of a gigantic Great Britain (Westeros) separated from a Europe-like continent (Essos), with the Narrow Sea providing a considerably larger buffer to Westeros than the English Channel. In other words, the sea is a primary feature of the geography of our story.

And since there is no air travel (save for Daenerys Targaryen) and no steam or combustion engines available for transportation, armies move at the speed (and endurance) of the horse or at the whim of the wind. This essay concerns itself with the latter—specifically, the roles that sea power plays in the Seven Kingdoms.

The Pursuit of Sea Power

Possessing a fleet is a definitional requirement for great power status and influence in the Seven Kingdoms—and a persistent theme throughout the show's seven seasons—as it is in the real world. The United States' founding fathers enumerated "providing and maintaining a Navy" as a power specifically given to Congress. Having a fleet—and the challenge of building and sustaining it—is a constant issue for nations seeking to extend their dominion or to sustain their influence. One of the contestants for the Iron Throne—Daenerys Targaryen—spends six seasons seeking a fleet to transport her army of Unsullied and Second Sons from Essos to Westeros across the Narrow Sea, and it is not until Yara Greyjoy strikes a deal with Daenerys in episode 9 of season 6 that she finally gets one. That Yara's fleet represents a mere fraction of her native Iron Islands' maritime power is the result of her (and her brother Theon's) hasty escape upon Uncle Euron's election as king a few episodes earlier.

Euron also figures prominently in the Lannister family's incessant quest for sea power, first by destroying the Lannister fleet during the Greyjoy Rebellion (during the reign of King Robert Baratheon nine years before the show begins), only to later be defeated in battle off Fair Isle by Robert's brother and Master of Ships, Stannis Baratheon. Stannis's victory at sea over the Greyjoys paved the way for Robert's army to invade the Iron Islands and quash the rebellion, an important result of which was the requirement for Balon Greyjoy to "bend the knee" to Robert and surrender his only surviving son, Theon, to the custody of Lord Eddard (Ned) Stark, Warden of the North. Theon's later perfidy during the War of the Five Kings would bring great anguish to the Starks. King Euron Greyjoy's later alliance with Cersei Lannister (in the opening episode of season 7) provided her with a massive fleet to enable future operations, to include the transport of the ten-thousand-strong mercenary army, the Golden Company, (and war elephants) from Essos to Westeros after Cersei's late season 7 deception of Daenerys and Jon Snow.

Another would-be king of Westeros employing sea power is Stannis Baratheon. As earlier described, Stannis was King Robert's Master of Ships, and upon Robert's death and the succession crisis that ensues, Stannis mounts his claim to the throne from his holdfast at Dragonstone, employing the majority of the Royal Fleet already under his command. The destruction of most of this fleet at the Battle of the Blackwater causes Stannis to seek the support of the Iron Bank of Braavos, where he eventually gains limited financing to rehire the fleet of sellsail pirate Salladhor Saan, who seems to have somehow survived Blackwater with much of his pirate fleet intact. Saan's ships ferry Stannis's depleted army north, where he gains a significant victory over the Free Folk beyond the Wall, although his success proves short-lived.

Cersei Lannister gained access to significant maritime power when Euron Greyjoy presented her with his fleet late in season 7. To that point, the Iron Throne of the Seven Kingdoms had been hobbled by a lack of sea power. When Tyrion Lannister destroyed Stannis's ships employing the Westerosi version of weapons of mass destruction (wildfire), he destroyed ships that had previously belonged to the crown. The Iron Throne's sea power problem was further exacerbated in season 5 when the Iron Bank requested that a portion of the crown's debt be repaid and the Master of Coin Mace Tyrell reported to Cersei that only half of what was requested was available. Recognizing the criticality of recapitalizing the Royal Fleet, Cersei ordered it rebuilt at any cost, including alienating the Iron Bank.

Of the great houses involved in the War of the Five Kings and its aftermath, it appears that only the Starks were without immediate concerns for a fleet. Had Robb Stark survived long enough to march on King's Landing, however, an alliance with a seafaring power would have been critical, as the city would likely have been able to withstand a landward attack and could resupply itself if not cut off from the sea.

The Uses of Sea Power

The Seven Kingdoms employed sea power for many of the same ends for which it is used in the world today, five of which bear closer examination.

Noncombatant evacuation operations (NEO). Jon Snow borrows Stannis Baratheon's fleet—hired from pirate Salladhor Saan—to sail around the east coast of Westeros, past the easternmost Night's Watch post on the Wall at Eastwatch-by-the-Sea, and north to Hardhome. There he was able to save five thousand Free Folk from the Army of the Dead and transport them south to Castle Black and surrounding lands.

War at sea. Although fleets are incredibly important to the political objectives of the contestants in *Game of Thrones,* in seven seasons we are treated to only one blue-water fleet engagement, season 7's third episode. Interestingly, the forces engaged were entirely from the Iron Islands: Euron Greyjoy's larger, more powerful fleet pounced on a portion of Yara Greyjoy's fleet as it was headed to Dorne to ferry Dornish troops north to invest King's Landing under Daenerys Targaryen.

Raids and special operations support. Yara Greyjoy's daring raid on the seat of House Bolton at the Dreadfort in season 4, episode 6, to rescue her brother Theon from the sadistic clutches of Ramsay Snow (bastard son of Lord Roose Bolton) was a classic special operation. Had Theon not been thoroughly broken by Ramsay's torture, the raid would likely have succeeded. Larger-scale raids were successful in destroying the Lannister fleet at Lannisport during the Greyjoy Rebellion (as Jaime Lannister reminds us in season 7 upon meeting Euron at King's Landing) and the portion of Yara Greyjoy's fleet supporting the Unsullied in their attack on Casterly Rock (again, by ships under Euron Greyjoy's command, although, at the time, he was personally busy destroying the other half of Yara's fleet). Additionally, coastal raiding seemed to be the entirety of Balon Greyjoy's plan to create mayhem in the North while Robb Stark's armies marched south in season 2.

Amphibious assault. Two major amphibious landings are attempted in the first seven seasons of *Game of Thrones,* although neither of the attacking forces gained the victories they sought. At the Battle of the Blackwater, Stannis Baratheon's mighty fleet was reduced by Tyrion Lannister's wildfire stratagem, leaving an insufficient landing force to invest the Red Keep in the face of determined resistance and the arrival of Tywin Lannister at the head of his army. Later, in season 7, the Army of the Unsullied attacked Casterly Rock (seat of House Lannister) and encountered little resistance in the approach, landing, or storming of the castle. All of this was, however, part of Jaime Lannister's cunning plan, for as the Unsullied ventured ashore, the ships from which they launched were pounced on by a portion of Euron Greyjoy's fleet.

Transport of armies. Fleets provide armies with essential mobility. Daenerys Targaryen spends much of the first six seasons of *Game of Thrones* trying to obtain a fleet to move her army across the Narrow Sea. The criticality of this mission was reinforced early in the show, in just the second episode, when Ned Stark reassures Robert Baratheon—who was worrying over the possibility of Viserys Targaryen (and his sister, Daenerys) invading Westeros at the head of a Dothraki army—that the Dothraki have no ships. Six seasons later, Daenerys dispatches a portion of Yara Greyjoy's fleet south to Dorne solely to transport its army north to participate in a siege of King's Landing. And in the season 7 finale, Euron Greyjoy feigns terror at the thought of the threat from the Army of the Dead and claims to be withdrawing his fleet to the Iron Islands, when he is sailing across the Narrow Sea to Essos to embark the ten thousand sellswords of the Golden Company to enable Cersei's double cross of Daenerys and Jon Snow.

Lessons We Can (Re-)Learn from Sea Power in the Seven Kingdoms

Fleets are expensive but worth it if you wish to be a great power. Both Daenerys Targaryen and Cersei Lannister must buy, build, and maintain fleets to enable their political and military objectives. Stannis Baratheon's seizure of the Royal Fleet at the beginning of the War of the Five Kings divested the Iron Throne of a powerful tool for military and diplomatic operations, and Cersei hazards the finances of the Seven Kingdoms to recapitalize it. Euron Greyjoy's offer of an alliance (and marriage) appear to have solved her sea power problem for the moment, just as his niece Yara's alliance with Daenerys solved hers. As stated earlier, House Stark entered the War of the Five Kings with somewhat limited political and military objectives, including the rescue of Sansa and Arya Stark from King's Landing and the destruction of House Lannister. Although limited, these objectives were unlikely to be gained without alliance with a maritime power. Fleets take a long time to build and are expensive to maintain. This argues for either ironclad alliances with maritime powers, peacetime investment in naval power, or both.

Sea power alone is not enough. House Greyjoy was, without question, a tremendous sea power. The Greyjoy fleet raided up and down the west coast of Westeros while Robb Stark moved south, and Euron Greyjoy had for years been sailing the fourteen seas, raiding and pillaging before he returned to the Iron Islands to kill his brother Balon and engineer election to his throne. Additionally, Euron's fame had already been won nine years before the *Game of Thrones* events began, from his daring raid at Lannisport, where the Lannister fleet was burned at the waterline. But the Iron Islands had little or no economic diversity, and they were unable to field armies or enter alliances with land powers that gave them the ability to project power, let alone defend their own islands. To be blunt, Euron Greyjoy's cry of "Build me a thousand ships, and I will give you this world" simply does not hold up.[1] The two main powers left standing at the end of season 7 (not counting the Army of the Dead, whose naval power is unknown)—Cersei Lannister and her allies, on one side, and Daenerys Targaryen and her allies, on the other—relied on both powerful sea *and* land forces (with Daenerys also possessing air power). There is wisdom in maintaining a strong, joint force.

Air power changes everything. When the combined slaver fleet attacks the city of Meereen and appears to have Daenerys Targaryen's reign on the ropes, it is ultimately *unchallenged* air dominance—in the guise of three large dragons—that wins the day. The destruction of the slaver fleet provides evidence that it is risky for ships to operate within range of land-based air power without area or self-defense antiair weapons. But air power, too, has its limits, as when Yara Greyjoy's fleet is destroyed by her uncle Euron, causing Daenerys Targaryen to contemplate mounting her dragons in search of Euron. She is ultimately dissuaded by her war council, as they were not in possession of sufficient intelligence necessary to target his fleet.[2]

Defense against weapons of mass destruction is required. Tyrion Lannister's employment of wildfire at the Battle of the Blackwater is a clear use of weapons of mass destruction against a fleet unprepared to combat it. Stannis Baratheon should have invested in better prelanding information about King's Landing—through what we today call intelligence, surveillance, and reconnaissance. Perhaps then he would have learned of the Lannister plan to reactivate the Iron Throne's weapons of mass destruction program, originally begun under the Mad King, Aerys II. Lacking sufficient protection against wildfire, Baratheon would have been advised to land his force elsewhere and then march on King's Landing.

Sea Power and the Final Battle

There is little in the *Game of Thrones* series to minimize the impact of sea power and much that reinforces it. No power without a fleet is of consequence, and the most powerful forces are buttressed by significant fleets. Great armies are made mobile, daring raids are attempted, fleet engagements are undertaken, and crafty deceptions are accomplished—all with sea power. No element of military power is as important to the objectives of the major combatants as is sea power, for as awe-inspiring as Daenerys Targaryen's dragons are, her army was useless while it was in Essos. Cersei Lannister's victories are also underwritten by sea power—the sea power of Euron Greyjoy.

It remains to be seen what role sea power will play in the eighth and final season. The Golden Company ferried by Euron Greyjoy will arrive to supplement Cersei Lannister's forces. But at that point, the three major armies (the dead, Daenerys's, and Cersei's) will all occupy the same land mass (Westeros), and we will likely see grinding land warfare, supplemented by considerable air power from both the dead and Daenerys's forces. But Daenerys—whose rise from bargaining chip in her brother's pursuit of the Iron Throne to powerful contender in her own right we have witnessed over seven seasons—has seen her fleet destroyed. She must win without help from the sea or recourse to it for escape. Once again, she will want for a fleet.

NOTES

1. David Benioff and D. B. Weiss, "The Door," season 6, episode 5, dir. Jack Bender, *Game of Thrones*, aired May 22, 2016, on HBO.
2. David Benioff and D. B. Weiss, "The Queen's Justice," season 7, episode 3, dir. Mark Mylod, *Game of Thrones*, aired July 30, 2017, on HBO.

14

What the Walls of Westeros Teach Us about War and Warfare

JOHN SPENCER

Dragons, wildfire, Valyrian steel swords, bows and arrows, spears, and daggers—these are the weapons of warfare in the world of *Game of Thrones*. Some are fictional; others, very real and timeless. A good, sharp blade—be it a sword or multipurpose folding pocket knife—will always be a necessary piece of kit for warfighters. But there are also weapons that are often taken for granted but are vital, major tools of warfare—whether fictional or real-world. Among those that repeatedly shape the battlefields of the Seven Kingdoms, and influence the outcomes of battles, are walls—simple walls, whose importance in war and warfare is often forgotten.

The war that rages throughout *Games of Thrones* in many ways resembles warfare of the Middle Ages and onward. The battle scenes, tactics, and even outcomes look remarkably like many of the great battles of European history from the twelfth century well into the nineteenth. Characters like Robert Baratheon or Jon Snow might be likened to great warriors of that era, like Henry V of England, famous for his victories during the Hundred Years' War, including his dynamic defeat of the French in the 1415 Battle of Agincourt. There is much that modern strategists, warfighters, students of war, and a whole range of interested observers can take from the heroes and villains of both the Middle Ages and the Seven Kingdoms that apply to strategy, international relations, and politics. In particular, the ways in which walls have been used, throughout the bloody conflicts of both history and *Game of Thrones*, provide insights that help us better understand the real battlefields of today and anticipate the contours of those of the future.

Cities have formed the central focus of military campaigns throughout recorded history. Egyptians battled Hittites for control of cities along critical trade routes in the thirteenth century BC. Later, the leading city-states of ancient Greece stayed busy besieging, sacking, and destroying each other during the Peloponnesian War. Prior to defeating Napoleon at Waterloo, the Duke of Wellington waged siege warfare and attacked castles in the early 1800s during the Peninsular War, which would have closely resembled *Game of Thrones* battle scenes like the sieges of King's Landing or Riverrun. Capturing or destroying your enemy's cities, especially their capitals, was the quickest way to achieve victory in the ancient world.[1] Taking enemy cities and protecting your own—this was the art and science of warfare.

And this is the type of warfare that characterizes *Games of Thrones*. The castles and cities of Westeros (and Essos, across the Narrow Sea) share a key feature: they are surrounded by walls. In battle after battle, we watch as one army or another attempts to breach these walls to seize a castle or occupy a city. Want the Iron Throne? Build a massive army and lay siege to or attack the capital of the Seven Kingdoms—King's Landing. That was Daenerys Targaryen's single goal in season 1. Stannis Baratheon and Robb Stark each aimed to do the same, leveraging long-standing alliances, family loyalties, and oaths previously taken, all with the hope of ultimately building a force big enough to take King's Landing.

What stood awaiting each of them? The walls of King's Landing. Walls create fortifications that provide defensive positions of strength with which to repel attacks. They have served as the primary lines of protection for cities across history. The castles like we see in the Seven Kingdoms most resemble those first introduced in England by the Normans in 1066 after the Battle of Hastings.[2] Just as in *Game of Thrones*, for centuries castles and their towering walls protected the nobility, their loyal citizens, and their claims to power during the Middle Ages.

Walls are incredibly challenging obstacles for any would-be attackers to negotiate. From atop a castle wall, defenders can stand behind protected positions to launch waves of arrows at approaching forces, drop stones and oil to set ablaze on attackers, or attack largely defenseless fighters attempting to scale the walls. When defending from behind walls, an outnumbered army can overcome its numerical disadvantage. In 1683 an outnumbered force of approximately twenty thousand defended Vienna from its fortifications against an estimated seventy-five thousand Ottomans for two months, until reinforcements saved them.[3] That episode has echoes in Tyrion Lannister's actions at the Battle of the Blackwater, where he and a small force positioned at the single weakest part of King's Landing, the Mud Gate, held off a vastly larger army led by Stannis Baratheon, until they were saved by reinforcements from House Tyrell.

The Battle of the Blackwater provides a great example of what can happen when walls are too narrowly considered. Tyrion Lannister showed his lack of military training with his shallow defensive plan. The spot on the perimeter wall Tyrion wisely chose to be the point of battle should have been incorporated into a much broader defensive plan. A trained military practitioner would have developed a defense in depth, meaning a plan to attack (in what we term "kill zones") the incoming forces as far out and continuously as possible. The use of wildfire in the harbor was excellent, but that and a few archers was the extent of the defense until the attackers were trying to bust down the gate. Tyrion's forces had the time to construct obstacles forward of the gates—such as an abatis, where trees and branches are sharpened and faced toward the enemy—that the attackers would be forced to negotiate and that would allow defenders to continue their fire forward of the wall. Such obstacles protecting walls can still be seen at preserved battle sites like Fort Ticonderoga or Stony Point in New York.

Walls are boundaries—physical and also political. The Wall of *Games of Thrones* serves as a fortification, physical barrier, and political boundary separating Westeros from the wild areas to the north. The Wall was seven hundred feet tall, three hundred feet thick, and three hundred miles long, and it was said to be enchanted with strong, ancient magic to "protect men from what lies beyond," spanning from the Bay of Seals in the east to the Gorge in the west.[4] Protecting the people of Westeros from the Free Folk and the White Walkers, its simple purpose was to serve as the physical boundary between the North and the Seven Kingdoms.

The Wall is not unlike real boundary walls erected to demarcate borders and protect against invasion—from the Great Wall of China to Hadrian's Wall in northern England. The Great Wall of China—actually a series of many walls and fortifications constructed over two millennia—totals *more than thirteen thousand* miles in length. Originally conceived by Emperor Qin Shi Huang in the third century BC as a means of preventing incursions from barbarian nomads, the Wall has experienced fluctuations in its importance and effectiveness across time, but it remains standing after many centuries, a symbol of the seemingly timeless turn to wall building to protect against the menace of invasion.

According to George R. R. Martin, Hadrian's Wall provided the inspiration for the Wall in *Game of Thrones*. Erected by Roman legionnaires beginning in 122 AD, Hadrian's Wall extended seventy-three miles from coast to coast across the width of northern Britain.[5] It served "to separate the Romans from the barbarians."[6] Martin recalled visiting Hadrian's Wall, saying "I stood up there and I tried to imagine what it was like to be a Roman legionary, standing on this wall, looking at these distant hills. It was a very profound feeling. . . . We know that there were Scots beyond the hills, but they didn't know that. It could have been any kind of monster. It was the sense of this barrier against dark forces—it planted something in me."[7]

Walls also serve as political and administrative boundaries denoting ownership. The Wall in *Game of Thrones* separates the Seven Kingdoms from the land north of the Wall and the Free Folk, who live there. Such boundaries (whether physical walls or lines on a map) not only form the lines of war but can also be a cause of the fighting. The Free Folk didn't agree that the line traced by the Wall somehow decided what land was theirs and what was not. Nor do many people in the real world agree that lines on a map serve that same purpose. The redrawing of borders after World War I and World War II; during decolonization; and to some degree, after the fall of the Soviet Union have triggered generations of political, cultural, economic, and social change—sometimes good but often at the cost of many, many lives. Shifting loyalties of some of the lesser lords in *Games of Thrones* upend previously agreed boundaries, much like what can be seen today in places like eastern Ukraine, where pro-Russian sentiment among parts of the population partly underwrites the first effort to redraw European boundaries by force since World War II.[8]

And when these boundaries, whether historical or fictional, are marked by walls, they provide lessons that are important today, in war and for society.

Walls are only effective if there is a system of overwatch and their positions are properly manned. The Battle of Castle Black is a case in point, demonstrating how a guarded wall, properly manned, can help defeat a superior force. Jon Snow and just one hundred defenders of the Night's Watch beat a vastly superior army of Free Folk led by Mance Rayder. But without overwatch—meaning without defenders manning the wall—it is only a matter of time before an option is discovered to overcome the obstacle. Prior to the Battle of Castle Black, Jon Snow and a band of Free Folk were able to scale the Wall without detection, using ice axes and crude crampons to infiltrate northern Westeros, because most of the forts along the Wall were unmanned. What does this teach us? If you intend to build a wall to protect a border, don't just plan for the construction costs. Plan to pay for the costs of manning, surveilling, patrolling, and providing overwatch of it. The 224 tunnels unearthed along the U.S.-Mexico border between 1990 and 2016 show why.[9]

We only get a few glimpses in *Game of Thrones* of the type of fighting that evolved as city walls and castles improved in their protective qualities—siege warfare. The tactics of busting through city gates and castle walls improved with time. Early battering rams have been identified in ancient Egypt as early as 1900 BC, along with scaling ladders as early as 2400 BC.[10] A besieging force's tactics also included the option to just surround a city or castle and starve the defenders out. Vice versa, the inhabitants of a well-provisioned castle could opt to sit and wait for the attackers to run out of supplies. This was the tactic Ramsay Bolton thought he would employ after losing at the Battle of the Bastards—that is, until a giant demonstrated the same lesson real-world defenders intending to outlast a besieging force often learn when faced with advanced machinery like heavy artillery: with sufficient power, castle gates can come down in a few seconds.

The problem with the use of walls is that they only work if there is actually a formidable obstacle to effectively keep people in or out. There can be no holes, no vulnerabilities. Tyrion Lannister shows why, when he uses his knowledge of the sewers of Casterly Rock—something he obtained when his father assigned him the management of its sewers—to help Daenerys Targaryen capture the castle. Sewers are mundane, to say the least. But then again, so are walls themselves. And especially when it comes to fighting in cities, mastery of the mundane can tilt the balance decisively in one side's favor. Walled fortifications are not very effective—nor is defending against a siege—if people, weapons, and equipment can get in and out of them at will. With the growth of urban areas around the world, the ability to besiege a city has become more and more difficult. In 2016 the Iraqi military was only able to begin to take back control of the Iraqi city of Mosul from Islamic State fighters after they had effectively surrounded and isolated it with over one hundred thousand security forces.[11]

Walls are not solely defensive in nature; they can be used to attack, as well. In the 2008 battle for Sadr City, a densely populated neighborhood of eastern Baghdad, U.S. military forces (perhaps unknowingly) used siege warfare to defeat an uprising by an armed militia called Jaish al-Mahdi led by the fiery cleric Muqtada al-Sadr. For over thirty days during the height of the battle, soldiers used civilian cranes to emplace more than three thousand six-ton concrete barriers to create a three-mile wall that connected previously emplaced barriers and ultimately completely encircled Sadr City. The walls restricted the militia's ability to move freely in and out of Sadr City and were the main weapon that led to the end of the battle.

Ultimately in *Game of Thrones*, dragons negated much of the advantages of castles and defensive walls. Tywin Lannister said it best when he described the destruction of Harrenhal to Arya Stark. "Harrenhal was built to withstand an attack from the land," he told her. "A million men could've marched on these walls and a million men would've been repelled. But an attack from the air, with dragon fire . . . Harren and all his sons roasted alive within these walls. Aegon Targaryen changed the rules."[12] Dragons' real-world analogs—aircraft—certainly changed what cities must endure during war. But German bombing of London didn't compel a British surrender during World War II, and Hamas hasn't capitulated despite Israel's air supremacy over Gaza. What changed the rules in the real world in a way most like the effect dragons had in Westeros was not aircraft but gunpowder. Brought to Europe in the 1300s, gunpowder allowed besiegers to fire cannonballs that were able to smash through walls, and by the time of the Franco-Prussian War in the 1870s, rifled artillery could reduce most city fortifications from a range of nearly two miles.[13]

And yet humanity still turns to walls. From the battle for Sadr City to the Islamic State's building of defensive fortifications in Iraq and Syria, from plans for a wall on the U.S. southern border to European discussions on how to reinforce borders amid tensions over migration, walls still feature prominently in the world. And as long as walls are built, they will define the contours of war, peace, and security. We all would be wise to study the lessons of other walls—whether Hadrian's or Harrenhal's—in whatever games we play in the future.

NOTES

1. Louis A. DiMarco, *Concrete Hell: Urban Warfare from Stalingrad to Iraq* (Oxford, UK: Osprey Publishing, 2012), 19.

2. C. N. Trueman, "Castles," History Learning Site, March 5, 2015, https://www.historylearningsite .co.uk/medieval-england/castles/.

3. Lou DiMarco, "Attacking the Heart and Guts: Urban Operations through the Ages," in *Block by Block: The Challenges of Urban Operations*, ed. William G. Robertson (Fort Leavenworth KS: U.S. Army Command and General Staff College Press, 2003), 6.

4. Mega McCluskey, "The Wall on *Game of Thrones*: Breaking Down Its History and Magic," *Time*, August 24, 2017, http://time.com/4912209/game-of-thrones-wall-history-magic/.

5. McCluskey, "Wall on *Game of Thrones*."

6. Quoted in *Encyclopedia Britannica Online*, s.v. "Hadrian's Wall," by David J. Breeze, accessed November 23, 2011, https://www.britannica.com/topic/Hadrians-Wall.

7. McCluskey, "Wall on *Game of Thrones.*"

8. Anthony Faiola, "Russia Supporters in Eastern Ukraine Pose Challenges to Pro-Western Government," *Washington Post*, March 15, 2014, https://www.washingtonpost.com/world/europe/russia-supporters-in-eastern-ukraine-pose-challenges-to-pro-western-government/2014/03/14/be21eeec-ab77-11e3-b8ca-197ef3568958_story.html?utm_term=.80ac1f8c25e2.

9. Vanda Felbab-Brown, "The Wall: The Real Costs of a Barrier between the United States and Mexico," Brookings, August 2017, https://www.brookings.edu/essay/the-wall-the-real-costs-of-a-barrier-between-the-united-states-and-mexico/.

10. DiMarco, "Attacking the Heart and Guts," 17.

11. Margarita Konaev and John Spencer, "The Era of Urban Warfare Is Already Here," Foreign Policy Research Institute, March 21, 2018, https://www.fpri.org/article/2018/03/the-era-of-urban-warfare-is-already-here/.

12. David Benioff and D. B. Weiss, "A Man without Honor," season 2, episode 7, dir. David Nutter, *Game of Thrones*, aired May 13, 2012, on HBO.

13. DiMarco, *Concrete Hell*, 24.

PART 3

Combat and War

15

Siege Warfare in the Seven Kingdoms

LIONEL BEEHNER, BENEDETTA BERTI, AND MIKE JACKSON

"Sieges are dull."[1]

So says the Blackfish—Lord Brynden of House Tully, a formidable battle commander and younger brother of Hoster Tully—in season 6 of *Game of Thrones*. He is technically correct, albeit only in a narrow sense. Siege warfare, by design, can be high in casualties yet is rarely high in battlefield drama. Indirect combat is less theatrical than direct combat. Historically, sieges tend to drag on for several months, if not years. Yet in popular culture, whether in *Hamilton: The Musical* (Lafayette and Hamilton are almost giddy on stage—"Are you saying no sweat?"—at how easy the British capitulate at Yorktown) or *Game of Thrones*, representations of sieges too often take the form of armies confidently advancing. Think of Jaime Lannister's formidable forces besieging the stronghold of Riverrun; laying out a set of steep demands, leader to leader, on an extended drawbridge; getting rebuffed; and then advancing triumphantly with little resistance and easily penetrating the defenses, all while keeping casualties low. The only person who died in the recapture of Riverrun was, well, the Blackfish. Dull indeed.

Yet sieges throughout history have proved neither dull nor casualty free. These are battles noteworthy for their brutality. The Red Army took losses of 2,500 *per day* during the siege of Stalingrad.[2] A siege can also signify an inflection point in a long-standing civil war. The Peloponnesian War, for example, was arguably just a series of sieges. Siege warfare—in Boston, Quebec City, Yorktown, Vicksburg, and elsewhere—also played important roles in America's Revolutionary and Civil Wars. The Siege of Madrid was an important pivot point of the Spanish Civil War, and the 1954 siege of Dien Bien Phu precipitated the full removal of French forces from Vietnam as that country slid further into civil war. Jerusalem has found itself under siege at various times over the course of the twentieth century, as well as earlier throughout its history. Sieges can occur over areas of great importance to the operational or strategical level of the war, but they can also revolve around strategically marginal yet symbolically powerful places.

The Siege of Riverrun

So what lessons does the treatment of sieges in *Game of Thrones* hold for modern strategy? A review of the back-and-forth struggle for Riverrun within the context of how siege warfare evolved over the centuries offers valuable insight into the logic of sieges from both a strategic and an operational perspective. Riverrun, the de facto headquarters of Robb Stark during his failed northern rebellion (cut short by the Red Wedding), gets subsequently handed back to Lord Walder Frey, before Lord Brynden Tully retakes the garrison, using his insider knowledge of its local terrain and underground passageways. Lord Frey then orders his two sons, Lothar and Black Walder, to retake the castle, which they attempt to do, spectacularly unsuccessfully. Following the tenets of siege warfare, their troops dig ditches and erect watchtowers to isolate the stronghold.

Still, Riverrun proves formidable to penetrate by force. Nestled high above the Riverlands, the fortress of Riverrun is perched on an island encased in high walls. Though Jaime commands an army of some eight thousand battle-hardened soldiers, the Blackfish again rebuffs demands to surrender peacefully, claiming that his men are willing to die for Riverrun and that he has enough provisions to withstand a siege of at least two years. Upon his arrival to the outer banks of Riverrun, Jaime Lannister scolds Black Walder for his tactical incompetence and even strikes him. Bronn, Jaime's right-hand man, also notes Black Walder's shortcomings, adding, "Now that is a sorry attempt at a siege."[3] However, their difficulties, even with superior forces, actually reveal that a siege is as much a psychological exercise as it is a physical or material one. It is about conveying fortitude and endurance, hoping the other side cannot stomach a long, protracted battle. Riverrun was arguably of little importance to the larger balance of power in the Seven Kingdoms. Its capture was motivated more by revenge and score settling than by strategic necessity. This is analogous to Stalingrad in World War II, which has been described as "the city that Hitler had never planned to capture, and that Stalin had never intended to defend."[4] Despite its situation along the Volga, Stalingrad was not strategically important; however, taking the city was such a matter of pride to Hitler that it became one of the bloodiest battles of all time, with nearly 2 million military and civilian casualties.[5]

Ultimately Jaime Lannister and his forces recapture Riverrun, with little blood spilled. Yet the episode offers some lessons for modern war strategists, while providing a few cautionary notes. First, arguably, Riverrun offers little strategic value to the Lannisters. It is the symbolism that matters, as it signifies the return of a Stark-held garrison to Lannister hands. Second, rarely do sieges end with zero shots fired or zero casualties. Finally, the size of the besieging army and its credibility matter. Jaime Lannister has a reputation throughout the Seven Kingdoms for ruthlessness. The Black-fish's men surrender, well aware of the cruel fate that awaits them if they do not lay down their arms. When it comes to applying maximum pressure to lay siege to a city or castle, in many cases, the defense holds the tactical advantage, given its fortifications, knowledge of local terrain, and presumed ability to withstand a protracted assault. To break a modern siege, armies rely on brutal and often scorched-earth tactics. Had the Blackfish's men not surrendered, one imagines that Riverrun would have suffered a similar fate as Grozny in 2000, which fell to overwhelming Russian forces after immense bloodshed and leveling of the city, or Aleppo in 2016, which fell to Syrian forces, trapping roughly three hundred thousand civilians, after heavy bombing of infrastructure with Russian assistance.[6]

Background of Sieges

Historically, siege warfare predates medieval times. By its simplest definition, a siege is any attempt by an adversary to control access into and out of a town, neighborhood, or some terrain of significance to achieve a military or political objective. More importantly for the modern era, a siege is a type of indirect warfare that shifts the burden of war from armed combatants to unarmed noncombatants, aimed at achieving its objective by imposing cost on the civilian population while avoiding troop loss by the besieging army.

Popular notions of siege warfare tend to focus on a conventional army advancing in lines on some heavily fortified, Camelot-looking castle or breaching city walls or on the devastation of cities—London in 1940 or Stalingrad in 1942—by mass conventional armies and air power. For centuries, siege warfare was defined by indirect fire—before the advent of mortars, a trebuchet would lob projectiles to batter enemy fortifications.[7] During the Crusades and the Hundred Years' War, siege warfare also became associated with biological warfare, as diseased and putrefying carcasses of animals were catapulted into castle moats.[8]

In earlier battles, the defender was traditionally thought to hold the military advantage. Yet as technology advanced to favor the offense, the balance began to shift. With the advent of heavy artillery in the fifteenth century—big cannons capable of launching massive numbers of destructive projectiles against fortifications previously thought nearly impregnable—siege warfare would seem to become less relevant, with direct assault and immediate capitulation becoming a viable option. After all, siege warfare is often a fallback plan when seizing a city by overwhelming force is not a viable option, either given the relative power asymmetry or the offense-defense balance of the warring parties.[9] This partly explains why port cities were often besieged by a naval blockade, preventing aid from entering and inhabitants from fleeing. Even so, in the sixteenth century siege warfare continued to be a relevant military option, as innovations in artillery systems pioneered by the French army meant that castles and fortresses were no longer robust enough to protect soldiers armed with modern weaponry.[10] Whereas strong fortifications during medieval times favored the defense, siege warfare, enabled by greater infantry weapons from cheaper iron, ostensibly favored the offense, reinforcing the psychological aspect of sieges as the besieged could no longer feel secure within their stronghold.[11] Siege warfare in this period required the type of large-scale centralization of resources that would lay the groundwork for the bureaucracy of modern states. Over the next century, siege warfare was influenced by masters of siege artillery, men whose names may not be remembered in history but whose contributions to the evolution of warfare cannot be overstated, such as Sébastien Le Prestre de Vauban and Menno van Coehoorn.[12] Despite the siege warfare tactics favoring the offense that innovators such as these pioneered, there was also a broader decline in the importance of military engineering. The increased complexity of the terrain, notwithstanding the technology available, made it increasingly difficult for generals to conduct sieges themselves, pushing most officers away from the field.

During the eighteenth and nineteenth centuries, the dominant form of conventional warfare was one of marching armies in separate formations, concentrating them in a dense mass and converging on the enemy, piercing its defenses at a point of weakness. The bulk of offensives in *Game of Thrones* fit this description. Frontal assaults or dazzling maneuvers, this type of warfare was firepower intensive yet typically led to grinding wars of attrition. Think Grant's post-Vicksburg campaign in 1864. With rapid developments in military technology after the Industrial Revolution, the organization and tactics of warfare would also change. Improvements in artillery, faster transport (with the advent of the railroad), more rapid communications (like the telegraph), and trench defenses all incentivized armies to disperse.[13] Soldiers during this era also became more professionalized, educated, and disciplined.[14] The prevailing doctrine until the early twentieth century, according to British World War I military historian Jonathan Bailey, emphasized flank attack, envelopment, and annihilation.

By the early twentieth century, given the massive firepower at militaries' disposal, there was a mistaken belief that war would be short, decisive, and favorable toward the offense.[15] The modern era of conventional warfare has put a premium on time, intelligence, maneuver, and superior firepower. These elements also informed previous centuries of warfighting, but with the speed, size, and industrialization of twentieth-century armies, war was made more lethal. Embedded in this approach was a belief that war had to be decisive and swift. Hence, early battles in war were deemed more important. By World War I, however, a "cult of the offensive" would give way to the trench warfare of attrition.[16] When the knockout blow failed to end the war decisively, states found themselves unprepared economically, as stockpiles were exhausted and war fatigue among soldiers and citizens settled in. After World War I, with the advent of tank warfare and strategic bombing, war would appear to shift back in favor of the offense. Speed and surprise informed Germany's military doctrine prior to World War II. Of course, blitzkrieg famously gave way to siege warfare, in places like London, Leningrad, and Stalingrad.

Operational Objectives of Sieges Today

Sieges in modern wars, unlike their medieval or even twentieth-century predecessors, are not merely intended to seize key terrain. Like *Game of Thrones*' Riverrun, the city or area under siege is often of little strategic consequence. Instead, the main desired outcome of contemporary sieges tends to fall under three core operational objectives.[17] These objectives are not mutually exclusive and help explain why siege warfare has reemerged as a popular tactic for armies, whether Bashar al-Assad's or Jaime Lannister's, fighting wars in dense urban environments and seeking to avoid direct contact with the enemy to minimize casualties.

Siege in Pursuit of Seizure

The classical objective of siege warfare is to seize terrain or infrastructure—a city or town or even a block or a building of significance (e.g., an armory or a church)—from the enemy. In effect, sieges provide a way to slowly bleed an enemy into capitulation, while limiting direct hostilities and reducing one's own casualties. The object in dispute is the terrain, which can be either symbolic, strategic, or both. That is, this type of siege is most common in cities located along strategic supply routes or axes (e.g., the Siege of Madrid), those that hold symbolic value for the enemy (e.g., the Siege of Jerusalem), or both (e.g., the 2016 siege of Aleppo). Because vital terrain is at stake, the assumption is that the political and military value of the besieged areas is higher than in other types of sieges and that therefore the besieged should be more committed to preventing its capitulation to the enemy, thus prolonging the siege and making it more lethal for the besieged side's forces.

Siege to Compel a Political Agreement

A second objective of sieges in modern warfare is to compel the besieged side to capitulate in order to secure a political agreement. In these cases, the city under siege is not necessarily of strategic value. Rather, the aim is to inflict some level of punishment on the civilians or enemy combatants as a way of pressuring them to surrender. Put another way, the main intent is not to *seize* the city but rather to *coerce* the military opponent or its supporters to surrender—in effect, to compel the acceptance of a ceasefire. If the city is not what is important, we might expect the besieging side to be more likely to carry out indiscriminate violence against civilians or to level infrastructure that provides concealment. A case in point is the siege of Grozny (1999–2000).[18] Here the strategic logic behind the siege was to punish and coerce the civilian population, with the expectation that this would then pressure the fighters to surrender.[19] In certain cases, however, the besieging side will be aware of the perils of inflicting too many casualties too quickly, as this may trigger a military intervention by a third party on behalf of the besieged side, or it may complicate the prospects of forging a peaceful settlement once the guns go silent.

In Syria, for example, dozens of cities suffered through prolonged and repeated sieges between 2012 and 2017 that were resolved by so-called "reconciliation" deals. One example includes the brutal siege of Madaya, where a Syrian government and Hezbollah-backed siege started in June 2015 and led to a severe humanitarian crisis. With military checkpoints and antipersonnel landmines preventing goods from entering the besieged area and civilians from leaving, Syrians in Madaya were literally starved to death.

Siege to Isolate a Population

A third objective is to isolate the enemy and prevent it from reconstituting resources or fighting elsewhere. This type of siege is meant to seal off a population as a way to separate insurgents from the population and rob an insurgency of its local base of support. It is also a mechanism to freeze a conflict and refocus one side's military assets, which may be overstretched, along different fronts. In other words, the strategic terrain of the area under siege could be perceived as nonvital to the larger war, with the siege acting as a way to suspend fighting on one front in order to focus on another more vital campaign, all while denying both enemy fighters and civilian supporters the possibility of becoming involved in other military engagements. An advancing army will tend to employ this type of siege sequentially, ostensibly to create a kind of holding pattern aimed at not sustaining direct fire or incurring casualties, while preventing escalation. Often the city under siege will be a base of armaments or enemy fighters, so the siege can serve as a chokepoint to prevent arms and other supplies from reaching the enemy in other theaters of operation. This logic was applied by U.S. forces when laying siege to Sadr City, a Baghdad neighborhood and stronghold of the Shiite Jaysh al-Mahdi militia, in 2004.

The inverse logic of this is sieges' perverse function of ensuring the displacement and depopulation of key embattled areas. In the context of an insurgency, depopulation deprives the insurgents of human resources and demoralizes the rebellion while bringing the regime renewed manpower and international assistance. Just as importantly, these measures can contribute to the government's claim that it is legitimate since it still rules over the majority of the population. In numerous sieges, including those at Grozny and Aleppo, the besiegers at times purposefully allowed humanitarian corridors to let some of the entrapped noncombatants flee, as a way of further separating the population from the enemy while also strengthening the besieger's leverage, given its ability to open or close the gateway. We also saw evidence of this dynamic during the 1992–95 Siege of Sarajevo in Bosnia, which was known for its porousness.[20]

Anything but Dull

Game of Thrones treats sieges—drawbridge extended, demands exchanged, forces neatly poised to advance—a bit too simplistically for the modern era. The siege of popular imagination has given way to one reflecting the complexity of modern war and the terrain of modern cities. Today's urban centers are no longer just population settlements or groupings of buildings; rather, they act as organisms, complex systems vulnerable to much more than traditional military attacks (e.g., food insecurity), and are defined by increased density, informal economies, tight networks, and poor governance—all variables that could foster violence or instability.[21] These factors help explain the modern appeal of siege warfare.

In *Game of Thrones* we see an unsuccessful siege of Riverrun by the sons of Walder Frey and a successful one by Jaime Lannister. What we don't see in either example is the complexity of siege warfare in today's world—increasingly urban and characterized by rapid technological innovation and the diffusion of power once held exclusively by states.

At least in modern wars, the Blackfish was wrong—sieges are anything but dull.

NOTES

1. Bryan Cogman, "The Broken Man," season 6, episode 7, dir. Mark Mylod, *Game of Thrones*, aired June 5, 2016, on HBO.
2. Tony Taylor and Robert Guyver, eds., *History Wars and the Classroom: Global Perspectives* (Charlotte NC: Information Age Publishing, 2012).
3. Cogman, "Broken Man."
4. William Craig, *Enemy at the Gates: The Battle for Stalingrad* (Connecticut: Konecky and Konecky, 2004), 28.
5. Ian Johnson, "August 2017: Stalingrad at 75, the Turning Point of World War II in Europe," *Origins*, August 2017, https://origins.osu.edu/milestones/august-2017-stalingrad-75-turning -point-world-war-ii-europe.
6. Lionel M. Beehner, Benedetta Berti, and Michael T. Jackson, "Innovations in Warfare and Strategy: The Strategic Logic of Surges in Counterinsurgencies," *Parameters* 47, no. 2

(Summer 2017), https://ssi.armywarcollege.edu/pubs/parameters/issues/Summer_2017
/10_BeehnerBertiJackson_StrategicLogicOfSiegesInCounterinsurgencies.pdf.

7. Jonathan B. A. Bailey, "The First World War and the Birth of Modern Warfare," in *The Dynamics of Military Revolution, 1300–2050*, ed. MacGregor Knox and Williamson Murray (New York: Cambridge University Press, 2006).

8. Andrew McKillop, "Strategy, Military Tactics, and Weapons: Asymmetric War and the New Geopolitics," *21st Century Wire*, January 26, 2014, https://21stcenturywire.com/2014/01/26 /history-arrives-late-asymmetric-war-and-the-new-geopolitik/.

9. Max Boot, *War Made New: Technology, Warfare, and the Course of History, 1500 to Today* (New York: Penguin, 2006), 84.

10. Christopher Duffy, *Siege Warfare: The Fortress in the Early Modern World 1494–1660* (London: Routledge, 2013).

11. Stephen Van Evera, "Offense, Defense, and the Causes of War," *International Security* 22, no. 4 (1998): 5–43.

12. Duffy, *Siege Warfare*.

13. Barry R. Posen, "Nationalism, the Mass Army, and Military Power," *International Security* 18, no. 2 (1993): 80–124.

14. Posen, "Nationalism."

15. Van Evera, "Offense, Defense, and the Causes of War."

16. Van Evera, "Offense, Defense, and the Causes of War."

17. While a case can be made that destroying the enemy's forces may be a fourth function, in the modern era this logic is less applicable, despite a few exceptions, or operationally effective.

18. Timothy L. Thomas, "The Battle of Grozny: Deadly Classroom for Urban Combat," *Parameters* 29, no. 2 (Summer 1999): 87–102.

19. Alexander B. Downes, *Targeting Civilians in War* (Ithaca NY: Cornell University Press, 2011).

20. Peter Andreas, *Blue Helmets and Black Markets: The Business of Survival in the Siege of Sarajevo* (Ithaca NY: Cornell University Press, 2008).

21. Andreas, *Blue Helmets and Black Markets*.

16

Dragons, Dothraki, and Achieving Victory in Battle

MICK COOK

The use of strategic strike capabilities—in particular, joint fires from the air, land, or sea—should create opportunities for the achievement of campaign objectives. Often, commanders will need to integrate strategic strikes by joint-fires units with action taken by maneuver forces to exploit these opportunities. In *Game of Thrones* nobody was more adept at creating and exploiting these opportunities at the tactical, operational, and strategic levels of war than Daenerys Targaryen. Her enemies, by contrast, were not.

Before exploring these greatly divergent capabilities of Daenerys and her adversaries, it's worth noting that "joint fires," "maneuver," and "campaign objectives" are not nearly as conceptually complex as their dry, doctrinal labels suggest. "Joint fires" refers to the capability to bring firepower to bear from multiple forces operating in multiple domains (and often aimed at targets in a different domain)—airplanes dropping bombs on ships, ships launching missiles at soldiers on land, and soldiers firing antiaircraft weaponry at airplanes, for example. "Maneuver" is simpler yet; it's just moving forces around on the battlefield. Combine the two—fire and maneuver—more effectively than your enemy, and you have a formula for battlefield victory. Those battles combine to form a campaign. Win enough and you achieve your goals—your campaign objectives.

Back to Daenerys. During the Second Siege of Meereen, the fleet of the Wise Masters, the nobility who rule the slave cities of Yunkai and Astapor, bombarded the besieged city of Meereen from the sea. The destruction caused by these sea-based fire units is impressive but ineffective. The reason it is ineffective is that it fails to apply some of the most basic targeting principles in the application of fires. These principles include focusing the fires on achieving the most advantageous results, understanding the effects needed to achieve campaign objectives, and approaching the targeting of the enemy in a systematic manner to ensure that the highest-priority targets are effectively dealt with.[1] Unfortunately for the sailors on the fire ships and their slave-trading overlords, Daenerys did not fail to apply these principles when she unleashed her three dragons on the besieging ships.

The purpose of the Second Siege of Meereen, from the perspective of the besiegers, was to reclaim the city and humiliate Daenerys, undermining her model of a slave-free city. It is important to remember these objectives when analyzing the use of their military forces, particularly the sea-based joint-fire support. Understanding the objective of an operation or campaign is key to formulating a strategy to achieve those objectives. The Wise Masters decided to besiege the city of Meereen most likely because it would achieve their objectives with the least amount of risk and cost to their forces. This was a step toward adhering to a principle of joint operations, the economy of force.[2] They achieve this economy by primarily using their sea-based fire support to maintain the tactical pressure on Daenerys's forces within the city. They are, therefore, reliant on the destructive and psychological effects of such tactics as the main avenues to achieve their objectives. However, the employment of fires at an operational or campaign level needs to be coordinated to ensure that it meets the commander's objectives. Such coordination is achieved by adhering to principles and processes designed to maximize the effect of each engagement. The targeting of the city of Meereen by the fleet of the Wise Masters lacked coordination and failed to maximize those effects that would support the achievement of the campaign objectives.

The bombardment of the city of Meereen by the sea-based fire support of the fleet of the Wise Masters was undoubtedly destructive. It also appeared to create a significant amount of psychological stress on the citizens of the city, including those in charge. Tyrion Lannister was visibly rattled with each explosion of a projectile bursting on the walls of the Great Pyramid. In fact, Daenerys signals that she intends the break the siege immediately after one such explosion interrupts a discussion between herself and the droll dwarf. From all appearances, the use of sea-based fire support to bombard the city worked to achieve the objectives of the Wise Masters. Their campaign plan seems to have fit; however, Daenerys's failure to surrender during the agreed parlay and her subsequent counterattack with air-based fire units revealed the flaws in how the Wise Masters employed their fires. The failure to ensure that the tactics were suitable to meet the operational campaign objectives was a failure of strategy at all levels.

The Wise Masters were clear in their objectives: retake Meereen and humiliate the Mother of Dragons. They had, in strategy terms, defined their "ends." They were also clear in deciding which tactics to employ with which forces; sea-based fires were to create destruction, apply psychological pressure, and blockade the port, while the Sons of the Harpy prevented land access to the city. Again, in strategy terms, they had decided which "ways" they would employ their "means" to achieve the previously mentioned "ends." This strategy employed standard forces using predictable tactics in siege warfare (i.e., block entry and exit points and bombard the enemy until they surrender). But in the case of the Second Siege of Meereen, this basic strategy was not good enough. The Wise Masters failed to adapt their tactics (their "ways") to meet the situation and achieve their objectives (their "ends"). The most significant failure in this strategy was their poor target selection and lack of coordination for their sea-based fires, without question their most potent weapon.

Target selection is quite critical in achieving the objectives of the campaign or operation. It determines which targets should be attacked in which way to achieve a specific effect that supports the achievement of the campaign objective. Simply put, good target selection will create the opportunities that can be exploited to achieve the campaign objectives. The target selection for the fire units within the fleet of the Wise Masters appeared to be entirely random. There is no apparent link between the targets selected and the effects needed to achieve the campaign objectives. In targeting terms, they did not conduct a target appreciation to determine whether the targets they were engaging would contribute to the achievement of their objectives and support the strategy to oust Stormborn from Meereen.

It is clear from the arcs of fire that most of the catapults on the fire ships were engaging different targets. Many of these appeared to be soft targets of opportunity, such as markets and residential areas. It is true that some of the fire was focused on the defensive towers and other such fortifications of the besieged city; however, there does not appear to have been a concentration of firepower sufficient to destroy the fortifications and provide further tactical opportunities. The failure to provide further tactical opportunities indicates that the commanders of the Wise Masters' campaign did not clearly understand the role that their fire units could play in enabling the forces to achieve the campaign objectives.

The purpose of fires at the strategic, operational, and tactical levels of war is to create opportunities to achieve the campaign objectives.[3] These opportunities could be an opening for maneuver forces to take decisive action or create leverage for diplomatic negotiations. It is clear from the expectations of the Wise Masters during the parlay that they believed their tactics had created such diplomatic leverage. They failed, and in this failure, they gave their enemy a chance to demonstrate what good target selection and fires integration with maneuver can achieve.

Daenerys Stormborn, her dragons, and her maneuver forces could quickly and decisively achieve her campaign objectives, defeat the Wise Masters, and lift the siege because she understood how to employ her fires. During the surrender negotiations, the ones where the Wise Masters incorrectly believed they had achieved a military advantage that translated into political leverage, Daenerys Stormborn mounts one of her dragons and attacks the sea-based fire units in the enemy fleet. At the same moment, the Dothraki warriors and other mercenaries attack the besieging land forces of the Sons of the Harpy at the gates of Meereen. This coordinated assault by fire and maneuver created a dilemma for the Wise Masters, who were soon to be summarily executed and did not live long enough to dwell on their folly.

The destruction of the sea-based fire units by the dragons demonstrates a sound target appreciation by Daenerys and her generals. The main threat to the city was the fire ships. They were the only military force that could significantly damage the fortifications and create an access point for the besieging forces. By destroying the sea-based fire units, Daenerys was targeting the primary offensive capability of her enemy. She could have used the dragons to destroy the dismounted Sons of the Harpy troops that were besieging the land approaches to Meereen. She could have also used the dragons to target the command and control by destroying the flagships of the fleet. She could have done either of these but didn't. She had accurately assessed that the Sons of the Harpy would be little match for her mounted Dothraki and mercenary forces. The plan to execute the leaders of the Wise Masters at the parlay made the need to destroy the flagships redundant. The destruction of the enemy's main fires unit was the best use of Daenerys's most potent strategic strike capability, her air-based fire units.

The dragons offered Daenerys more than shock and awe when launched into a battle. Their use as a strategic strike capability by her ancestor Aegon the Conqueror was well known. Each time such a reliable, flexible, and destructive capability was used by Aegon during his conquest of Westeros, a message was sent to those who would stand against him. This message wasn't simply that he had dragons. It was that he could strike his enemies from the air at will, regardless of their own forces' dispositions. A dragon's fire burns those defending the walls of a castle as easily as it does foot soldiers on the field of battle. These lessons learned by Aegon were applied by Daenerys three hundred years later at the Second Siege of Meereen. She understood that her dragons were an air-based strategic strike capability. That is why she used them against the sea-based fires units, her enemy's main offensive capability. Once the sea-based fires units were destroyed, the Wise Masters would not have had anything within their arsenal to create the opportunities needed to achieve their campaign objectives. Daenerys, on the other hand, had learned a valuable lesson in how her strategic strike capability could be used to create opportunities for her maneuver forces to achieve her objectives. She also learned that a good target appreciation and selection can reduce the risk and cost of the achievement of those objectives. Both are lessons she would apply when she took the field against the Lannister army in Westeros.

When Daenerys's Dothraki horde charged the disciplined Lannister army and their bannermen, they did it with aerial fire support. Learning from her experience in Meereen, Daenerys unleashed her dragon on the front lines of the Lannister forces moments before her assaulting force crashed through their lines. The firestorm created by the close air support reduced the ad hoc defenses of the Lannister forces and sowed panic among the soldiers who were not prepared for such a strike. The following route by Daenerys's ground forces, even after their aerial support was neutralized by an antiair weapon, demonstrates the importance of coordinating fires and maneuver forces to create opportunities to achieve the campaign objectives.

The strategy and tactics employed by Daenerys, particularly her target selection, appreciation, and prioritization, highlighted the benefits of integrating fires and maneuver to achieve campaign objectives. Daenerys and her generals adapted their tactics to maximize the impact of their forces. Land-based fires such as catapults and trebuchets would not have effectively supported the lightning charge of the Dothraki against the hastily defended Lannister army train. Likewise, mounting similar fire support on the walls of Meereen and attempting to target the mobile fire ships of the Wise Masters would also have yielded limited results. The air-based joint fires provided by the dragons shaped the tactics available to Daenerys to achieve her objectives. If Daenerys had not adapted her tactics to meet the capabilities at her disposal, she would likely have been unable to achieve victory in the two battles as quickly as she did.

The experience of Stormborn and her foes in the use of successful and unsuccessful application of joint fires to achieve their campaign objectives is often mirrored in modern conflict. The invasion of Iraq was enabled through joint-fires strikes at the strategic, operational, and tactical levels as the fight advanced to Baghdad.[4] This included the engagement of strategic-level targets, such as command-and-control nodes, as well as targeting the field force of Saddam Hussein's Republican Guard in the close fight. The campaign in the Libyan civil war that toppled Muammar Qaddafi's regime is another example of joint fires, particularly air-based fires, engaging key targets to provide ground forces, the rebels, conditions to achieve their campaign objectives.[5] The counterinsurgency operations in Iraq and Afghanistan are also good examples of joint fires being used to support forces defending patrol bases against mortar and rocket attacks by insurgents. In each of the modern examples above, the use of joint fires was linked to providing opportunities for ground forces or to creating political leverage. Not all of them, like the Wise Masters, were successful.

Both Daenerys and her enemies throughout Slaver's Bay and Westeros had joint-fires capabilities, whether they were land, sea, or air based. However, Daenerys was the one to utilize her joint-fires capabilities in a manner that created the opportunities to achieve her campaign objectives. She could adapt her tactics to meet both the situation and the capabilities at her disposal. She, in strategic terms, was able to employ her "means" in "ways" that achieved her "ends." In her case, her means were mobile land forces and air-based fire support. Some may argue that her success was due to the exclusivity of her access to air-based fires; however, during her battle with the Lannister forces, it was clear that her dragons were not invulnerable to antiair weapons. In fact, her enemies did not see the dragons as enough of a threat to deter them from engaging her forces; therefore, one must conclude that it was not the fact that she had dragons that ensured her victory but rather her integration of their offensive capabilities into her forces.

NOTES

1. Joint Targeting School, *Joint Targeting School Student Guide* (Dam Neck VA: U.S. Joint Chiefs of Staff, March 2017), 26–28, http://www.jcs.mil/Portals/36/Documents/Doctrine/training /jts/jts_studentguide.pdf?ver=2017-12-29-171316-067.

2. Joint Chiefs of Staff, *Joint Operations*, joint publication 3-0 (Arlington County VA: U.S. Department of Defense, January 17, 2017), A-2, https://www.hsdl.org/?abstract&did=798700.

3. Joint Chiefs of Staff, *Joint Planning*, joint publication 5-0 (Arlington County VA: U.S. Department of Defense, June 16, 2017), III-9, http://www.jcs.mil/Portals/36/Documents/Doctrine/pubs/jp5_0_20171606.pdf.

4. J. Jacobs et al., *Enhancing Fires and Maneuver Capability through Greater Air-Ground Joint Interdependence* (Santa Monica CA: Rand, 2009), 21.

5. Karl P. Mueller, ed., *Precision and Purpose: Airpower in the Libyan Civil War* (Santa Monica CA: Rand, 2015), 376.

17

The Wildlings at the Wall

When Climate Drives Conflict

J. DANIEL BATT

The land beyond the Wall was no friend. It gave no boon. No gifts. No forgiveness. Those alive had earned it. Beyond the seven-hundred-foot-high, three-hundred-mile-long monolith erected by Bran the Builder, each moment was secured with determination.

Yet the land had not been unnecessarily cruel. It was simply ambivalent. A desolate expanse that gave sustenance to those who earned it and swift death for those who hadn't. Its mercy was in that swiftness. Life or instant death.

For eight thousand years, that binary had been the constant.

The Stark's banner words were now truer than in the long seasons of the past. *Winter is coming.* True winter. The promise of the millennia was delivered with a sharp change in the temperature and the arrival of the Others—a migrant force that removed the mercy of a swift death.

It is in the shadow of those words that we first enter *Game of Thrones.* Rangers, heading out from the Wall, encounter evidence of a migratory population stirred from their former homes by the change in climate. That first violent encounter sets the tone of the conflict.

The Long Night of Westeros has all the markings of climate change: the temperature changes; animal life begins to migrate; and on their heels, the human inhabitants follow after. Lord Commander Mormont reports, "The cold winds are rising, Snow. Beyond the Wall, the shadows lengthen. Cotter Pyke writes of vast herds of elk, streaming south and east toward the sea, and mammoths as well."[1] After the encounters with the Others, the flood of the wildlings south was often met with violence, mirroring climate-sparked migration conflict in our world. Half the recorded climate-refugee migrations resulted in violent encounters, some erupting in massive death tolls.[2] The wildlings and Jon Snow's subsequent response as the lord commander can both reflect and potentially guide our actions in our current and future refugee crises.

Yet the change in climate that the long winter would bring was not the first. The retold memories of that first still drifted into bedtime stories such as the one Old Nan told Bran Stark as he lay in bed:

> What do you know about fear? Fear is for the winter when the snows fall a hundred feet deep. Fear is for the Long Night when the sun hides for years. Where children are born and live and die, all in darkness. . . . Thousands of years ago, there came a night that lasted a generation. Kings froze to death in their castles, same as the shepherds in their huts; and women smothered their babies rather than see them starve, and wept, and felt the tears freeze on their cheeks. . . . In that darkness the White Walkers came for the first time.[3]

The Others rode on the cusp of that winter—their home far, far to the north. While the wildling migration was the first to be recognized by the Night's Watch, the Others were the first to migrate in response to the changing climate.

Why did the Others move south? We know nothing of their home, their resources, their economy or way of life. Nor do we know the chicken or the egg dilemma of Westeros: Do the Others bring the Long Night, or does the Long Night bring the Others? All that is certain is that with the sharp change in climate, their violent forces migrate south, pushing the Free Folk ahead of them, sparking conflict.

The wildlings could be defined as climate refugees, a term first ascribed in our world to those fleeing the flooded urban areas of New Orleans after Hurricane Katrina.[4] The description of those wildling refugees mirrors images of climate refugees we've seen in recent years coming out of Syria, Rwanda, and the Sudan: "Wordless, they formed up in lines behind the wagons. There were three women for every man, many with children—pale skinny things clutching at their skirts . . . men on crude crutches, men with empty sleeves and missing hands, men with one eye or half a face, a legless man carried between two friends."[5] These are descriptions that could be heard coming out of several border zones today.

An initial tool to add to our predictive tool belt is to look at disasters through a vulnerability lens.[6] With predictions of further severe environmental change in our future, determining which populations are most at risk for migration and potentially violent encounters is critical to ultimately defining future hot spots of conflict. Climate change often affects less developed populations far harder than developed areas. And when impacted, developed nations have resources to respond quicker and better to these challenges. Winter was coming for all of Westeros, but the delayed development of the loosely knit nation beyond the Wall was hit the hardest and the earliest. Their margin of sustainability was the thinnest, and when that eroded, along with the pressure of the primary migration of the Others, they were forced to flee and became refugees.

The strength of the climate disaster is often inconsequential; the moment of flight is in direct relation to how strong it is relative to the ability of people to withstand it. "A sparsely populated region with freshwater reservoirs, for example, will suffer relatively less from a drought than a densely populated region without reservoirs."[7] The factors weighing on the decision to migrate (and *decision* is used loosely, as it assumes choice when more often the migration can be seen as forced—thus the decision is less individual and rests with the group as a whole) include the destruction of resources, from land to livestock to agriculture; governmental regulations; current threat of violence; and more. "Individuals decide to migrate if the net benefit from migrating is larger than that from not migrating."[8]

Simultaneously, we need to understand the path from climate change to potential conflict. However, that task is far more difficult; the climate change–migration–conflict nexus is simultaneously simple and complex. A chain reaction starts from climate change and proceeds down multiple paths, triggering migration and, potentially, conflict. The chain reaction, though, isn't always linear. The existential challenges triggered by climate change are many: resource loss, habitation loss, pressure from outside groups, disease, and grouping changes. Any one of these can lead toward migration of refugees fleeing the locale. Often, a unique recipe of factors forces migration.[9]

Compounding the challenge of prediction and response is that the path of flight isn't necessarily initially toward resource-rich areas. Consider the wildlings fleeing the north—their migration took them up against the Wall and a land full of strife, working on rationing resources prior to the refugees' arrival. Countries on the brink of disaster can find refugees at their borders, and the precariously limited resources become exhausted, forcing their own citizens to become refugees.

Whether the chain reaction results in conflict isn't guaranteed. Conflict arises from a recipe unique to each encounter and "requires associating expected environmental changes with topographical features, dependence on the environment for livelihood, weather patterns, resource availability, population density, order structures, and sociopolitical fault lines."[10] Half the time, climate migrations do not result in conflict. In *Political Geography,* Rafael Reuveny's table of the climate change–migration–conflict nexus highlights over thirty-eight distinct climate change–induced migrations in the last half century,[11] nineteen of which led to conflict. Half the climate migrations resulted in violence. The 1990s saw 1.7 million refugees from Rwanda due to scarcity of arable land and water, land degradation, and deforestation, resulting in a lack of food, civil war, and underdevelopment. Conflict erupted in the destination area due to ethnic tension, ultimately growing into genocide.

Westeros's wildling migration can be explored on this same table; thousands of the Free Folk fled south due to the environmental push factors of extreme weather, temperature change, resource shortage, and food scarcity (as hunting herds moved south also), as well as the additional push factor of the migration of the Others. Conflict erupted along the border with antagonistic border forces, further accelerated by ethnic tension and distrust. With two distinct violent factions on both sides, a large majority of the wildlings were injured or killed in their journey south. Lord Commander Jon Snow moved to create refugee settlements within his own lands, removing the wildlings from the theater of conflict, initially.

In our present world, a similar nexus can be seen in northern Africa. The countries of Nigeria, South Sudan, Somalia, and Yemen have 20 million lives at risk of famine due to reliance of food imports and subsistence agriculture, both uniquely vulnerable to climate change.[12] The outside factors include reduced-capacity governments, rapid population growth, and already-present violent conflict due to terrorist efforts. "The mass exodus of people out of South Sudan is quickly making it the world's fastest growing refugee crisis with 1.6 million people displaced in surrounding regions."

And why is this happening? What are the environmental push factors of this displacement? "Over the past forty years, the desert in northern Sudan has moved 100 kilometres towards the once fertile south."[13] Nearly 40 percent of the country's forests have been eliminated, with 1.3 percent disappearing each year. This lack of grazing land impacts the nomadic herdsmen first, forcing them to move their livestock to still-fertile pastures. However, the arrival of the herds brings them into direct conflict with the farmers who still need that land for agriculture. As soil erosion increases, these conflicts have grown more intense. The lack of rainfall has displaced over eighty thousand starving people internally in Sudan. The nationwide fighting began when the government intervened militarily, escalating border conflict into violence.[14]

Nature doesn't always bear the blame itself. Humans can directly create environmental factors that are catalysts for migration conflict. Unlike the conditions beyond the Wall, poor governance accelerated the Syrian unrest.[15] The environmental push factors of water scarcity were mixed with outside push factors of governmental regulations. As water grew scarce and droughts more frequent, President Bashar al-Assad increased agricultural production and thus expanded the need for irrigation. Water, already in short supply, was exhausted.

As rural economies shifted toward ramped-up agricultural production, the very resource to maintain that was declining. The rural workers ramped up work and subsequently, when that work quickly halted, had nothing to rely on across the region as far as industry. Failed policy produced a disastrous recipe that was only exacerbated by severe climate change.

Jon Snow, beyond being the main character of Martin's epic, can be an example of great strategic leadership in the face of environmental migration. Our governments today face the same challenge Lord Snow did: what to do with the massing refugees at our borders? The Syrian refugee crisis is currently being grappled with by the majority of first-world nations. The crowds of displaced individuals at the borders take priority, often far before engaging the influences that forced the migrations.

The fast and quick answer, and the one most often turned to, is what several of Snow's advisors guided him to—bar the gates and keep them on the other side of the Wall. This is similar to the insistence echoed in the modern-day United States to "Build the wall." That instinctual first reaction to keep refugees on the other side of a wall is not new rhetoric in our world—governments often turn to that decision. A significant campaign focus of President Donald Trump was on the building of a wall along our southern border, citing both Mexican immigrants and the potential threat of terrorists. The insinuation was that those entering the United States would bring potential violent conflict to citizens' relatively safe worlds.

The haunting images from early 2018 of children separated from their asylum-seeking parents at the border remind us of another option: imprison the refugee. This becomes an alternative to recognizing the refugee as an asylum seeker and thus needing the resources of the receiving population. As it is today, efforts to rationally consider ways to assist the refugees—and by doing so, eliminate or halt conflicts—are often met with resistance.

Jon Snow's approach was development oriented and aligns with the conclusion of the UNHCR (the UN Refugee Agency) that "alternative-to-camp" solutions, basically allowing the refugees to live in host communities, create resilience within the refugees and provides for greater success in future "resettlement, integration, or return."[16] Snow's acceptance of the wildling refugees deescalated the constant and increasing conflicts along the border of the Wall.

Yet his efforts to allow the wildlings through the Wall, providing them land to settle, in the hopes of raising a force against the army of the Others on their heels, are met with opposition. His detractors postulated the same arguments that arise in today's refugee debates. Bowen Marsh responds with fear: "Once past the Wall, the wildlings will have thrice our numbers."[17] Snow reminds him that numbers alone do not equal an invading force. In a review of climate change–migration conflict, refugee groups do not often incite conflict.[18]

The reaction of the receiving people is an identical potential catalyst for conflict. Marsh then raises the question of financing: "And this food will be paid for . . . how, if I may ask?" Stannis's wife, Queen Selyse, ignores all these concerns and concludes, "Let them die."[19] The U.S. president himself affirmed, "The United States will not be a migrant camp and it will not be a refugee holding facility, it won't be. You look at what's happening in Europe, you look at what's happening in other places, we can't allow that to happen to the United States, not on my watch."[20]

This is a debate that will be repeated often in the next century. Our world is on the edge of a long summer that could potentially be just as terrible as Westeros's long winter. Just as they experienced the Long Night once before, the great warming we are on the precipice of has impacted our world before.[21] The increasing population and the thin margins of sustainability put our world at far more risk of environmental disaster due to rising temperatures. With climate change, migrations naturally follow. "When temperatures in the source country deviated from a moderate optimum around 20 degrees Celsius that is best for agriculture, asylum applications increased. Thus, the net forecast is for asylum applications to increase as global temperatures rise."[22] The Center for Climate and Security points to twelve distinct locales "where climate change could stress global security, possibly igniting conflicts around the world."[23]

Our own governments wrestle with this issue now. Which is the greater threat: the climate refugees or the climate change that forced them out? The failure to see the threat pushing the initial wave to our borders makes us all that more vulnerable to that threat. The lands of Westeros are willfully ignorant of the Others driving the wildlings to the Wall, seeing only the fleeing masses as a threat to their already-thin resources. Despite the clamor of environmental activists and scientists, many today appear willfully ignorant of the long-term threat of climate change. The current U.S. administration's efforts to ramp up border-control efforts— including building of our own "Wall," while simultaneously pulling out of the Paris Agreement, an international series of accords prescribing committed action to climate change, and calling reports of global warming a hoax—is ignorance in the same vein as the comfortable citizens of Westeros ignoring the impending danger of the Others. In the very year that recorded the second-warmest temperatures across the planet on record,[24] Trump tweeted, "Perhaps we could use a little bit of that good old Global Warming that our Country, but not other countries, was going to pay TRILLIONS OF DOLLARS to protect against."[25]

The long summer is upon us. Record temperatures are hit year after year. And there is no Wall able to hold back the rising temperatures, the coming drought, rising ocean waters, depleted resources, food scarcity, and other potential extenuating issues. The first wave of refugees fleeing out of Syria is only the first of many mass migrations. Remembering Old Nan's words—the Long Night treated king and servant the same—is key to surviving the coming storm. In a worldwide environmental change, even developed nations are at risk of their populations being forced to migrate. We might find ourselves fleeing north, being counted as refugees waiting outside someone else's Wall.

Hopefully, there will be someone like Jon Snow on the other side, fighting to let us in and silencing those who have concluded, "Let them die."

NOTES

1. George R. R. Martin, *A Game of Thrones*, bk. 1 of *A Song of Ice and Fire* (1996; repr., New York: Bantam Books, 2011), 654.

2. Rafael Reuveny, "Climate Change–Induced Migration and Violent Conflict," *Political Geography* 26 (2007): 658.

3. David Benioff and D. B. Weiss, "Lord Snow," season 1, episode 3, dir. Brian Kirk, *Game of Thrones*, aired May 1, 2011, on HBO.

4. Harald Welzer, *Climate Wars* (Malden MA: Polity Press, 2012), 25.

5. George R. R. Martin, *A Dance with Dragons*, bk. 5 of *A Song of Ice and Fire* (New York: Bantam Books, 2011), 296.

6. Leon Hermans, "Climate Change, Water Stress, Conflict and Migration: Taking Stock of Current Insights through a Vulnerability Lens," in *Climate Change, Water Stress, Conflict and Migration* (Paris: UNESCO, 2012), 23, http://www.hydrology.nl/images/docs/ihp/nl/2011 .09.21/Climate_change_water_conflict_migration.pdf.

7. Reuveny, "Climate Change–Induced Migration and Violent Conflict," 661.

8. Reuveny, "Climate Change–Induced Migration and Violent Conflict," 658.

9. Welzer, *Climate Wars*, 113.

10. Reuveny, "Climate Change–Induced Migration and Violent Conflict," 658.

11. Reuveny, "Climate Change–Induced Migration and Violent Conflict," 663.

12. J. Jordan Burns, "Preventing the World's Next Refugee Crisis: Famine, Conflict, and Climate Change in Nigeria, South Sudan, Somalia, and Yemen," *American Security Project*, May 2017, https://www.americansecurityproject.org/wp-content/uploads/2017/05/Ref-0202 -Preventing-the-Worlds-Next-Refugee-Crisis.pdf.

13. Welzer, *Climate Wars*, 11.

14. Welzer, *Climate Wars*, 63.

15. Colin P. Kelly et al., "Climate Change in the Fertile Crescent and Implications of the Recent Syrian Drought," *PNAS* 112, no. 11 (March 17, 2015), http://www.pnas.org/cgi/doi/10.1073 /pnas.1421533112.

16. Office of Internal Oversight Services, *Evaluation of the Office of the United Nations High Commissioner for Refugees* (Geneva, Switzerland: United Nations High Commissioner for Refugees, March 18, 2015), http://www.unhcr.org/5568170d9.html.

17. Martin, *Dance with Dragons*, 661.

18. Andrew Shaver and Yang-Yang Zhou, "Reexamining the Effect of Refugees on Civil Conflict: A Global Subnational Analysis," presented at ISA 2014 and APSA 2015, https://papers.ssrn .com/sol3/papers.cfm?abstract_id=3107830.

19. Martin, *Dance with Dragons*, 781, 985.

20. Betsy Klein, "Trump: 'The US Will Not Be a Migrant Camp,'" CNN, June 18, 2018, https://www.cnn.com/politics/live-news/immigration-border-children-separation/h _356506d56793bd211fd74eed9ab58b14.

21. Brian Fagan, *The Great Warming: Climate Change and the Rise of Civilization* (New York: Bloomsbury Press, 2008).

22. Anouch Missirian and Wolfram Schlenker, "Asylum Applications Respond to Temperature Fluctuations," *Science* 358, no. 6370 (2017): 1610.

23. Adam Aton, "Once Again, Climate Change Cited as Trigger for Conflict," *Scientific American*, June 9, 2017, https://www.scientificamerican.com/article/once-again-climate-change-cited-as-trigger-for-war/.

24. Jason Samenow, "The First Half of 2017 Was the Planet's Second-Warmest on Record," *Washington Post*, July 18, 2017, https://www.washingtonpost.com/news/capital-weather-gang/wp/2017/07/18/the-first-half-of-2017-was-the-planets-second-warmest-on-record/?utm_term=.a50944fb6a18.

25. Donald Trump, @realDonaldTrump. "In the East, it could be the COLDEST New Year's Eve on record. Perhaps we could use a little bit of that good old Global Warming that our Country, but not other countries, was going to pay TRILLIONS OF DOLLARS to protect against. Bundle up!" Twitter, December 28, 2017, 5:01 p.m.; emphasis original.

18

Shock and Chaos

Psychological Weapons of War in Westeros and Our World

GREGORY S. DROBNY

Characters drive stories. From *The Iliad* to *The Lord of the Rings,* classic tales resonate most deeply with us when we can relate to the individuals portrayed in them.

It is for this reason that good novelists are often considered better psychologists than those who have doctorates and professionally operate in that field. To build characters from tabula rasa and turn them into something that thousands—maybe even millions—of people can relate to, love, or despise requires an insight into the human condition that transcends the norm.

Interestingly, many of the great military leaders throughout history possessed a similar trait. They understood, at a deeper level than most, what made their soldiers tick—what motivated them, how they related to one another, and what it took to get them to do extraordinary things in the worst circumstances.

Popular, fictional stories offer a tremendous platform for gaining that needed insight, if for no other reason than the fact that they are popular—meaning, they resonate with a great number of people and therefore depict something many of us can relate to. Getting hung up on the fictional aspect of these tales would lose sight of the potential therein.

Consider the introduction of the dragons onto the battlefield in *Game of Thrones*. What happened to those on the opposing side? Confusion. Panic. Terror.

It is easy for those of us who spend a great deal of time in a pragmatic, utilitarian mode of thought to miss the lesson here. The dragon is not just a mythical, fire-breathing beast—it is the introduction of a *chaos monster*. It represents the unknown, the unfamiliar; "Aegon Targaryen changed the rules," as Tywin Lannister succinctly put it. "That's why every child alive still knows his name—three hundred years after his death."[1]

This is, of course, exactly what commanders search for to use against the enemy—a weapon of war of which the opposing forces are completely unaware that can provide an unbalanced advantage. But it is also what must be guarded against in case the enemy introduces their own chaos monster. The best way to begin to do that is to build an army that can *psychologically* handle such a thing. Physical fortifications and equipment are crucial, to be sure; but they are all for naught if the actors utilizing them are frozen or too afraid to function in response to the unknown.

How would your warriors respond to chaos? How would they react if they encountered a previously unforeseen and unknown threat on the field of battle?

In short, how well do you know your army? The more intimately a commander understands the fighters, the easier it is to answer the questions regarding the mysteries of the unknown.[2]

In season 3 of *Game of Thrones*, Daenerys acquires an army referred to as the Unsullied. These warriors are considered some of the fiercest in the world, because they are trained from birth to fight and because, as eunuchs, they have been robbed of all sexual desires and thus their energies are solely devoted to martial prowess. Without girlfriends, wives, or children, their loyalties rest solely with each other and their leader.

The temptation for many kings, presidents, and commanders throughout the centuries was to take this concept literally and to the extreme. From ancient Sparta to Nazi Germany, leaders were convinced that if they could develop a fighting force full of men who were devoted fully and completely, from birth, to the army itself, then they would essentially be unstoppable. They would, in essence, be a military of robots whose singular purpose consisted of crushing the leader's enemies—or dying gloriously while trying.

That approach, however, misses the bigger lesson, while being simultaneously ignorant of history. Both the Spartans of old and the Nazi *ubermensch* soldiers of the twentieth century were effectively kicked into the dustbin of history by citizen soldiers—Theban farmers against the former and young men from Allied countries against the latter, most of whom had grown up working in factories, on ranches, and on farms and would return to doing the same at the close of the war.[3] Men who had been handcrafted from young ages to be nothing but warriors and then assembled with the greatest of care to be cold, efficient killers were all undone on the field of battle by nonprofessional soldiers pulled from the ranks of the common worker.

Why, then, does the archetype of the Unsullied hold such appeal? Well over two thousand years separate the Spartans and the Wehrmacht, after all; clearly, this is an ideal sought after across numerous times and cultures, despite its notable failures.

It resonates because it ultimately speaks to our timeless connection to war and, at an even deeper level, internal conflict. These concepts, despite sounding esoteric in nature, are crucially important to understand, lest the aforementioned mistakes are repeated.

The Unsullied are special for two primary reasons that go well beyond their emasculated physical structure or their training from birth. They are unique first because of their loyalty and second because of their being set apart from the rest.

Loyalty is, at first glance, one of those terms that seems obvious, yet it is more elusive than most of us would allow. We can define it with a dictionary, but experiences in the real world show us how quickly that becomes less black and white. Were the American colonists of the eighteenth century technically supposed to be loyal to the King of England—and if so, when did that obligation stop? Should Jaime Lannister be loyal to his sister, or should it be the other way around? Who is obligated to whom is a decidedly muddy topic with a long history in philosophical inquiry.[4]

Do you know whom your people are loyal to? Do you know the answer to that question beyond a shadow of a doubt?

This is the first quality that makes the Unsullied truly special—there is no uncertainty regarding their loyalty. We know without question to whom they are beholden, and that is a trait that speaks to our deepest perceptions of humanity. We seek loyalty even when we do not realize it, and that is reflected in our music, literature, and movies.[5]

Military commanders know how important loyalty is, to be sure; this is a desired quality expressed by everyone dating from Sun Tzu to the present day. But how, exactly, it is fostered is not nearly as simple as we would like to think. Is it bred into someone? Do they have it by nature of where they were born? The legions of men throughout time who have either deserted or been forced into battle at the point of a sword or barrel of a gun would suggest that one is not necessarily loyal to Country X simply because it is his or her natural homeland.

We know intuitively that people will be more loyal to the country of their birth, no doubt. But we also know that it only goes so far. The story line of *Game of Thrones* offers numerous examples of what we know to be true in this regard. If treated poorly enough, even one's own family does not command loyalty, let alone a particular house they live under. Tyrion, after numerous attempts by his sister to take his life, eventually pledges himself to the very individual who poses the biggest threat to his family. Samwell Tarly abandons his mother and father when he refuses to meet the latter's demands. The Hound walks away from his sworn position if for no other reason than being tired of putting up with a pretentious leader who doesn't deserve being protected.

And therein lies the lesson. While loyalty is a tricky thing to foster, perhaps, we have very solid ideas about what erodes it, and that is why these character developments in *Game of Thrones* resonate with us. We see good people leaving bad ones because they are loyal to *what is right* rather than to a specific person, house, land, or family. This makes sense to us because it is what we want to see ourselves as doing.

We latch on to characters when we witness them acting out what we know we *should* do in a given situation if we were in it. As individuals, we see ourselves beholden to a code that exists a priori to any particular entity, so when we see those in stories who follow a similar code in an extreme manner, we vicariously follow.

This ever-changing dynamic of loyalty is a continuing theme in *Game of Thrones* and undergirds a great deal of both the individual stories and the overarching narrative. How does the plot change if loyalties do not shift prior to the Red Wedding? Where does House Lannister go if Tyrion chooses not to kill his father? How would Theon Greyjoy's story have altered the bigger events if he had stayed with House Stark?

The lessons here for a military commander are plentiful. If one chooses to assume the loyalty of subordinates without actually knowing them, there is a risk of losing that faithfulness to completely unforeseen factors—unforeseen because of ignorance stemming from arrogance. Remember, chaos monsters are not just dragons.

Loyalty ultimately stems from an individual's heart and where its passions lie. Money, sex, power, a noble cause, a code, brotherhood—some motivations are bad and some are good, but they greatly impact how warriors choose to spend their energies. The archetype portrayed by the Unsullied in *Game of Thrones*, then, is one who's loyalties are *focused*—the ideal warrior mindset.

The second quality making them special is, in fact, their specialness—their *other*ness. When a unit or group sees themselves as being set apart from the rest, it enables a certain style of groupthink—something that is normally looked down on but has its upsides in the martial setting.[6]

For a unit to do extraordinary things on the field of battle, they need to be *cohesive*. In order to be cohesive, the group must, as obvious as it seems, see itself as a group, one that is different from others. The in-group and out-group concepts of social psychology are nowhere more prescient than on the field of battle, and any commander who wants to be successful should understand this at a deep level.[7]

How to grasp this psychological advantage with any particular group is, of course, the art of leadership and an ever-changing dynamic that has a great deal to do with social norms of any given society at any given time in history. The best way to motivate a group of warriors and enable them to see their otherness is, after all, somewhat different for a General David Petraeus than it was for Charles Martel stopping Islamic forces from taking over Western Europe in the eighth century or Genghis Khan commanding a lightning-quick cavalry to conquer most of Eurasia in the twelfth.

This is exactly where our relationship to stories becomes so invaluable. We watch or read something like *Game of Thrones* and are able to see the fundamental aspects of human nature that transcend particular times and cultures.

The lesson we take from the otherness of the Unsullied is not to literally gather a group of babies, castrate them, and train them from birth in order to separate them from everyone else and enable their unique nature as ruthless fighters. As described above, that has not had the best results in the past. Rather, the example set forth shows our innate desire to be different while remaining part of an in-group—an inherent need within ourselves to fight alongside those of like mind without sacrificing the individuality that sets us apart from out-groups.

We see this in the Night's Watch, as well. A brotherhood dedicated to a centuries-old cause, set apart from the whole of society, is completely unique and yet bound by a code into a cohesive unit. The leader who can best exploit this balance with a particular group will succeed, whereas the one who cannot . . . won't.[8] John Snow understood it, whereas Alliser Thorne got sidetracked with petty obsessions about *his* power over the power of the group.

It is here, then, that we return with full force to the central question and even expand it: How well do you know your army, and how much does it matter?

Gathering intelligence on enemy forces has always been an integral component of waging war. Commanders often fail, however, to recognize how important this very same concept is with their own men. Understanding the culture of their army—to include cultures within cultures, subgroups of already-existing in-groups—is often passed over in favor of grand strategies developed at war colleges and the latest and greatest technologically advanced weapon systems. Stannis Baratheon siding with a witch rather than a trusted advisor who understood his military comes immediately to mind.

Grand, epic tales that resonate with millions of people help us do exactly this—understand the underlying themes of culture and human nature and how they play out in infinitely complex scenarios. We cannot sit down and war-game every possible situation involving cultural and ideological shifts in a group that led to an alteration of loyalties, but we can take part in stories that do so, especially when they do it well.

Game of Thrones offers us that very opportunity. Through absorbing story lines and character developments that attract the masses, we gain insights into the human condition. For military commanders to ignore this opportunity is to turn their backs on one of the most important aspects of leadership—*knowing* their army. The Unsullied and the Night's Watch enable a viewer to vicariously experience what loyalty means at a deeper level than just "support" or "allegiance," if we understand the underlying theme; we can gain insight into otherness by looking past the superficial into transcending, archetypal models. Our modern special operations forces are certainly not castrated from birth, but they are individuals who are willing to put their bodies through torturous processes—multiple times—in order to be the best. The U.S. Army's Rangers and Special Forces, the U.S. Navy's SEALs, the Marine Corp's MARSOC, and the U.S. Air Force's Pararescue Jumpers and Combat Controllers are decidedly neither eunuchs nor celibate, but they embody the archetypal models of the Unsullied and the Night's Watch, voluntarily punishing their physical nature in order to be stronger and setting themselves apart from the remainder of the military in a distinct otherness.

Similarly, the shifting of individuals in this story, in relation to these very same concepts, grants us insights into how certain personality types behave in different situations. If we pay careful enough attention to those around us, we can see where these traits manifest in those under our care and thereby learn valuable lessons *before* issues spin out of control.

Commanders who truly know their army have a distinct advantage over those who do not. The methodology for gaining that understanding is, of course, somewhat dependent on numerous factors that can only be ascertained within a situational context, but there are fundamental aspects to human behavior that exist beyond societal changes. Popular stories are a magnificent way of understanding these foundational principles—they are popular because they resonate so deeply with our innermost desires, fears, and ambitions.

An army is drawn from a particular population, and it is in a commander's best interest to understand that population as much as possible.[9] In *Game of Thrones* we see the dichotomous nature of our own society—at once wanting desperately to be involved with the in-group in something with a purpose and yet revolting against anything that steals our personal identity.

Commanders who learn from these insights and balance that tightrope of discipline, loyalty, and individual creativity become true leaders, for they are in a superior position to meet the chaos monsters that come their way. As great as it is to have solid strategy, that strategy is still enacted by human beings, along with all their complexity. And at its core, *Game of Thrones* is an epic story about that very thing—the intricacies of individual-to-group dynamics and how they play out in the most horrendous circumstances.

How well do you know your army? This is just another way of asking how well you understand the human condition—a journey that has, most often throughout history, been conveyed through storytelling. So to know the stories of humanity is to know ourselves, the first step in knowing the face of interpersonal conflict, which is to say human interaction in all walks of life, from the battlefield to the business meeting.

NOTES

1. David Benioff and D. B. Weiss, "A Man without Honor," season 2, episode 7, dir. David Nutter, *Game of Thrones*, aired May 13, 2012, on HBO.

2. See Victor Davis Hanson, *The Soul of Battle: From Ancient Times to the Present Day, How Three Great Liberators Vanquished Tyranny* (New York: Free Press, 1999).

3. See Hanson, *Soul of the Battle*; Stephen E. Ambrose, *Citizen Soldiers: From the Beaches of Normandy to the Surrender of Germany* (Premier Digital Publishing, 1997).

4. For a great place to begin further inquiry into this subject, see Richard Dagger and David Lefkowitz, "Political Obligation," in *Stanford Encyclopedia of Philosophy*, Fall 2014 ed., ed.

Edward N. Zalta, article published April 17, 2007, last updated August 7, 2014, https://plato.stanford.edu/entries/political-obligation/.

5. *The Odyssey*, by Homer, and the 2001 movie *Black Hawk Down*, written by Ken Nolan and directed by Ridley Scott, offer prescient examples of loyalty.

6. The phalanx of ancient Greece and Rome, contra popular movie descriptions, relied on the cohesiveness of a unit; if they broke ranks or tried to fight individually, they lost.

7. See Feng Fu et al., "The Evolution of In-Group Favoritism," *Scientific Reports* 2, no. 460 (2012), https://doi.org/10.1038/srep00460.

8. See Pete Blaber, *The Mission, The Men, and Me: Lessons From A Former Delta Commander* (New York: Penguin, 2008).

9. See again *The Soul of Battle* by Victor Davis Hanson for tremendous insights into how leaders like Generals Sherman and Patton understood—and exploited—this concept better than most. They believed that armies have souls and that in order to enable them to succeed, a leader needs to understand that soul—what makes it tick and what makes it special.

19

How to Fight the Lannister Armies

JOSHUA D. POWERS AND JONATHAN BOTT

My lord,

You do not know me by name, but I have fought beside you in battle on countless occasions over the past twenty years. It is no secret that our army is in dire condition following the defeat outside of Highgarden. Such conditions warrant extraordinary reactions, hence a letter from a common foot soldier to a man of your standing.

I served as a regimental commander on the fateful day outside Highgarden—the day when the majority of your field army was destroyed with little effort by the Dothraki horde and a young queen with only one of three dragons. Only a handful of us escaped that day. Those who did escape implore you to heed our warning: we cannot continue to fight the same way and expect to be successful. This humble letter proposes a new way to think about how we employ the force to face a multitude of emerging threats.

The strategy we employed at Highgarden, as in all battles of old, focused on numbers, dominant technological advantages, and rapid tempo to defeat our enemies on the field of battle. Countless adversaries have watched our splendor over the past decades, carefully studying our strengths and experimenting with asymmetric approaches to mitigate them. Years ago a ten-thousand-man army was enough to succeed on any field of battle. The times have changed, and our advantage has decreased in relation to our enemies.

I propose a new approach to warfare to face these threats. This new approach focuses on mission command, employing a network of forces, and maximizing multidomain maneuver, carefully utilized to exploit emergent enemy weaknesses.[1] To be successful, we must embrace the very advantages these adversaries have adopted. I fear that continuing without at least considering this proposal will leave the army vulnerable to decisive defeat as Westeros slides into unruled chaos.

My lord, our field army must enable subordinate initiative within your overarching campaign vision. I know that this sounds far-fetched, but how can we survive against forces without central control if we lack the ability to adapt to conditions as they develop? Empowering field leaders to act is not a simple task, my lord. It requires us to deeply consider what we are truly fighting for.

What does our army fight for? From your perspective, we fight to retain Lannister control of the Iron Throne. But that is not what we fight for, my lord. We bear allegiance to you, but at the individual level, we fight to retain the Westerosi way of life. We are men like the Tarlys. I have heard the tale of how the young queen sentenced Randyll and Dickon to death for refusing to bend the knee before her.[2] These men swore allegiance to you and your family, but they burned standing up to an invading queen with a savage and foreign army at her back. They are an example of what we fight for. We fight for freedom against such a horde, freedom for our families and the Westerosi way of life. Let that be our rallying cry. Let us unite around the example the Tarlys set.

Let us, in fact, look to the example Daenerys Targaryen provides. Daenerys is of a common lineage to our traditional allies, but her approach is not the same. Daenerys unites a loose confederation of the Dothraki horde and the Unsullied legions and even affiliates with Jon Snow's forces in the North. What tool does Daenerys use to unite this disparate team? I would argue that her power in this campaign is not about what she controls but rather her employment of a centralized purpose to enable decentralized actions by subordinate commanders.

"Trust begets trust."[3] Prior to her return, the young queen traveled the realms, spreading her vision and uniting the force she wields today. She built trust through shared hardship and bloodshed, all for the common purpose of freedom and equality. Such trust is not automatic, my lord, but rather a relationship developed over time between commanders.[4]

With trust as a foundation, Daenerys developed and distributed a common purpose for the disparate force.[5] Before conquering Meereen, Daenerys delivered her vision to a captive audience of lords and the slaves that they would soon lose control of. In this address, Daenerys presented the lords as the enemy of the slaves, providers of only sorrow and suffering. Daenerys offered an alternative, the option of freedom and pursuit of freedom for other enslaved people.[6] This clear and common vision became the basis for her current campaign in Westeros. Her operations still focus on "breaking chains," while reducing the hardship and suffering of common people. This is a strong narrative to oppose, especially when coupled with dragons' fire.

The young queen's strategy expands on this purpose to frame operations in Westeros. Daenerys deliberately withholds her most effective weapons, dragons, against our clearest vulnerability, King's Landing. Instead, the young queen's strategy focuses on isolating the capital and denying it resources.[7] She maximizes Westerosi force employment around the capital to reinforce this narrative, with foreign forces operating in the periphery.[8] There are rumors that you and Queen Cersei have met with the young queen and negotiated an agreement to defend against the wight army to the north.[9] Even this negotiation relates to her strategic design, focusing on reducing the suffering of Westerosi commoners. I can only imagine how this collective defense will build support, should you agree to it.

Returning to trust, the young queen now maximizes the trust in those subordinate commanders who have chosen to bend the knee, allowing them latitude to act within her intent.[10] Those who refuse to bend the knee, who refuse to act within her intent, are incinerated with dragon fire in very public ways. Given this latitude, her army thrives in ambiguity and chaos as they are empowered to act within the framework she has established.

My lord, our forces are not structured to counter such a force, one that rapidly changes tactics in the field with little or no central control. Even the Unsullied legion acts with autonomy and the ability to shift tactics on the battlefield, dependent on the situation.[11] We have but one large field army. Although the envy of all Westeros, your army operates through your command alone. It has no independent components. The Iron Fleet has no connection to the field army. Newly developed weapons such as Qyburn's scorpion and its potential uses are not well known.

An excellent example lies in the employment of Qyburn's scorpion outside Highgarden. I lie awake at night dreaming of ways my infantry could have maneuvered in concert with that beautiful weapon. We could have served as bait in an ambush, drawing the dragon close and then unleashing the bolt on its exposed underbelly. But why, my lord, did we not have the luxury of experimentation and synthesis with this wonderful machine? Because we did not know it existed until the first shot was fired on the beast. My lord, our forces will continue to fail if we cannot work together to expose the weaknesses of such opponents and rapidly exploit these fleeting windows of opportunity.

Our forces are dependent on your presence on the battlefield to integrate and fight. At the Second Siege of Riverrun, you deftly assigned Frey's forces to a perimeter defense and used your own trained men for important siege works.[12] Today we have a decisive advantage at sea, yet Euron Greyjoy operates his fleet absent of coordination. Without you on the field of battle, our forces have no common operating concept.

Though centralization seemingly increases security and accountability, we have reached a point where this method is no longer tenable. The usurper's dragons and expedient forces threaten us whenever we coalesce.[13] Therefore, our forces must decentralize to a point of parity with our adversaries.[14] Fostering disciplined independence will result in necessarily creative, innovative, or even outlandish ideas. This creativity, not sluggish central command from a position high above the field of battle, will win the day.

Knowledge must spread from foot soldier to commander, incorporating the best ideas, though they may emerge at the fringes of the force.[15]

Daenerys's strategy maximizes a network of forces and includes flexibility based on her available means to accomplish certain goals.[16] Her network increases in power and extends options with the addition of new armies.[17] She adjusts her operational goals based on the potential of creating relationships with additional allies. Look at her most recent negotiations with Jon Snow, the false king in the North. Daenerys is willing to accept his objectives against the wight army, tying this effort back to her overarching narrative of freedom and breaking chains. She utilizes a guiding coalition, the commanders of her networked forces, to delineate relative strengths and weaknesses and then develop an appropriate maneuver strategy to the operational problem.[18]

There are stories of Daenerys recruiting houses and discussing strategy with them on Dragonstone.[19] The queen does not depend solely on traditional methods of recruiting through transaction. Her diversification gains numerous perspectives and advice.[20] As she did with her Dothraki horde at the battle outside Highgarden, she gives her allies the chance to engage challenges from the start rather than relegating them to supporting functions.[21] All have heard of her freeing the slaves of Meereen and becoming the Breaker of Chains. Her actions become a recruitment story, known throughout the realm.

My lord, our army's legacy of success is blockading the changes needed to win against Daenerys's adaptable, multifaceted force. For years, we have struck down our enemies through superior numbers, better training, and premium technology. No other force on this side of the Narrow Sea is equipped as well as yours. Even the vaunted Knights of the Vale would fall to our numerical superiority combined with the armor and weapons on which you spare no expense. The superb training of your field army is second to no other Westerosi force. Your soldiers remained disciplined, executing your commands, even in the face of unfathomable threats like that damnable dragon.[22] The years of training that created this discipline cannot be wasted on further engagements without a sound operational approach against such a formidable foe.

Our tradition of besting peer competitors is being upended by the unpredictable, multifaceted maneuver of our enemy. This campaign requires more than defeating armies in the field and defending strongpoints like Casterly Rock. Our approach must improve battlefield innovation to overcome a variety of capabilities. Although her potential numbers were blunted by our efforts against Dorn and Highgarden, Daenerys has disciplined, traditional Unsullied legions.[23] She has fast, maneuverable, yet negligibly armored Dothraki hordes. She has a nascent sea power utilizing stolen slaver ships and traitorous Iron Islanders. And then, of course, there are the dragons, but who could forget their ability to control the air and rapidly change the dynamic on the field of battle?

As Daenerys increases these varied capabilities, the traditional Lannister army must avoid stasis and evolve our military theories. Our operations have often deconflicted rather than integrated operations. At the Siege of Casterly Rock, our forces fatefully attempted a strongpoint defense, without even the consideration of employing maritime forces. Your strategy of moving the bulk of our force against Highgarden, while baiting our enemy with our home, resulted in a genius tactical victory.[24] However, Casterly Rock was quickly defeated by adaptive maneuvers. Daenerys's forces probed for a weakness, employing both maritime and land forces, and then rapidly flooded Casterly Rock, rather than fighting up the walls and sustaining more significant losses. The castle defenders depended on traditional walled defense rather than a planned multilayered operation with the Iron Fleet. We must face the Unsullied, not in open combat, but where they are weaker, such as in transition to their sought battle. In our own battle at Highgarden, the strength of your soldiers' discipline could creatively combine with Qyburn's scorpion technology, using our retreating infantry as a baited ambush to draw in the damnable dragon. Instead of meeting the Dothraki in the open, we must set the battle conditions to face them in a confined space, as the Knights of the Vale have defended their home for centuries. Our military cannot depend on continuous domain superiority and must become resilient while temporarily ceding superiority in any singular domain. We can only be successful with mutual understanding and experimentation.

Technology is only a portion of strategy. As a panacea, technology is inadequate. Technology will change fast enough that eventually even the wealthy Lannisters will not be able to purchase a feasible solution.[25] Proliferation of technology and an enemy that constantly adapts their fighting style by incorporating new expertise, such as adding Dothraki horsemen and Iron Island mariners, create situations that require variable solution sets. Technology adaptation will outpace large-scale technology acquisition. Technology must be combined with trained people and appropriate tactics. We must develop patterns of mind that create flexible theorizing and battlefield reorientation.[26]

The question is not how to defeat the Dothraki horde or the Unsullied legions; rather, the appropriate question is, How do we train and equip to innovate in the face of whatever force Daenerys, or a future competitor, sends toward us?[27] We must know ourselves and our enemy for consistent success in battle.[28] There may come a day when we integrate even more domains of warfare, such as the tales from the North of people who can see through animal eyes.[29] Although our capabilities do not include this ability, or dragons, and we cannot control what force we face, we can control how we understand the capabilities, limitations, and maneuver options of our own forces. Regimental commanders with widened understanding improve their problem assessment and ability to create options in the presence of emergent opportunities. It helps us think differently when facing nontraditional enemies. Just as the dragons opened an opportunity in our defensive line for the Dothraki, multidomain operations represent change by developing an integrated approach to create and exploit windows of opportunity across heavily contested domains.[30]

My lord, I most humbly implore you to consider these points. Our force is at a crossroads. What got us here—superior numbers, superior technology, and superior training—will not win the day on the future battlefield. We must become a nimble fighting force, decentralized during battle with an understanding of your intent while exploiting our enemies' weaknesses, and we must maneuver in multiple domains to create opportunities for glory. I concede that the changes proposed in this letter will not be easy, but drastic times call for drastic measures. My men trust you, Ser Jaime Lannister. We trust your prowess as a warrior through countless years of shared hardship on the field of battle. Do you trust us, my lord? I fear that continuing down our current path will lead to the demise of our force and our way of life. Trust, empowerment, and agility as a fighting force will win the day. The choice is yours, my lord.

NOTES

1. The U.S. Army defines mission command as "the exercise of authority and direction by the commander using mission orders to enable disciplined initiative within the commander's intent to empower agile and adaptive leaders in the conduct of unified land operations"; Headquarters, Department of the Army, *Mission Command*, Army Doctrine Reference Publication 6-0 (Washington DC: Government Printing Office, 2014), Glossary-2, hereafter ADRP 6-0. Although there is no current joint doctrinal definition of domain, Dr. Jeffrey Reilly defines it as "a critical sphere of operational influence whose control provides the foundation for freedom of action." Multidomain operations involve the simultaneous exploitation of asymmetric advantages across domains to achieve the freedom of action required by the mission. Multidomain maneuver, in or through one or more domains, sets the conditions to exploit a window of opportunity in another domain. Jeffrey M. Reilly, "Multidomain Operations," *Air and Space Power Journal* 30, no. 1 (Spring 2016): 71.

2. Dave Hill, "Eastwatch," season 7, episode 5, dir. Matt Shakman, *Game of Thrones*, aired August 13, 2017, on HBO.

3. Ori Brafman and Rod A. Beckstrom, *The Starfish and the Spider: The Unstoppable Power of Leaderless Organizations* (New York: Portfolio, 2006), 168.

4. The U.S. Army includes trust as a guiding principle of mission command. Commanders build mutual trust through daily interactions. Senior commanders trust subordinates to execute actions with overarching intent. Subordinates trust these leaders to provide sound guidance, enable action, and accept prudent risk to accomplish the mission. ADRP 6-0, 2-1.

5. Creating shared understanding, another guiding principle of mission command, focuses on building a common picture of the operation's purpose, problems the organization will face, and the approaches available to solve these problems. ADRP 6-0, 2-2.

6. David Benioff and D. B. Weiss, "Breaker of Chains," season 4, episode 3, dir. Alex Graves, *Game of Thrones*, aired April 20, 2014, on HBO.

7. Brian Cogman, "Stormborn," season 7, episode 2, dir. Mark Mylod, *Game of Thrones*, aired July 23, 2017, on HBO. This letter is dated after the events of season 7, episode 5, and before Daenerys and Jon Snow attempt a grand bargain with Cersei.

8. Cogman, "Stormborn."

9. David Benioff and D. B. Weiss, "The Dragon and the Wolf," season 7, episode 7, dir. Jeremy Podeswa, *Game of Thrones*, aired August 27, 2017, on HBO.

10. Success on the future battlefield will require empowering leaders who understand their commander's intent and can adapt rapidly when facing emergent principles. ADRP 6-0, 2-4.

11. David Benioff and D. B. Weiss, "The Queen's Justice," season 7, episode 3, dir. Mark Mylod, *Game of Thrones*, aired July 30, 2017, on HBO.

12. David Benioff and D. B. Weiss, "Oathbreaker," season 6, episode 3, dir. Daniel Sackheim, *Game of Thrones*, aired May 8, 2016, on HBO.

13. Brafman and Beckstrom, *Starfish and the Spider*, 195.

14. Brafman and Beckstrom, *Starfish and the Spider*, 189.

15. Brafman and Beckstrom, *Starfish and the Spider*, 203.

16. Stanley McChrystal, Tatum Collins, David Silverman, and Chris Fussell, *Team of Teams: New Rules for Engagement for a Complex World* (New York: Portfolio, 2015).

17. Brafman and Beckstrom, *Starfish and the Spider*, 201–8.

18. John P. Kotter, *Leading Change* (Boston: Harvard Business Review Press, 2012).

19. Cogman, "Stormborn"; Colin S. Gray, *Perspectives on Strategy* (Oxford: Oxford University Press, 2013), 2. Gray provides a simple and useful definition of strategy as "the direction and use made of means by chosen way in order to achieve desired ends."

20. Lawrence Freedman, *Strategy: A History* (Oxford: Oxford University Press, 2013), 554–55. Freedman observed that benefitting from the experiences of all members trumps depending solely on senior management.

21. Benioff and Weiss, "Queen's Justice."

22. Benioff and Weiss, "Queen's Justice."

23. David Benioff and D. B. Weiss, "Dragonstone," season 7, episode 1, dir. Jeremy Podeswa, *Game of Thrones*, aired July 16, 2017, on HBO.

24. In the summer of 1796, General Napoleon Bonaparte lifted his siege of Mantua in order to bate the arriving Austrian forces to follow. Napoleon utilized his troops' faster march to ensnare and defeat four subsequent columns of Feldmarschall Dagobert Sigmund von Wurmser's Austrian army. See David Chandler, *The Campaigns of Napoleon* (New York: Macmillan, 1966).

25. Gordon E. Moore, "Cramming More Components onto Integrated Circuits," *Electronics* 38, no. 8 (April 1965): 114–17. Gordon Moore observed that the number of transistors on integrated circuits doubles approximately every two years. This exponential technological improvement is known as Moore's Law.

26. Frans P. B. Osinga, *Science, Strategy and War: The Strategic Theory of John Boyd* (London: Routledge, 2007), 117, 123. See John Boyd's decision cycle of observe, orient, decide, act.

27. "Getting the questions right is the first step to finding the correct answers." See Hew Strachan, *The Direction of War: Contemporary Strategy in Historical Perspective* (Cambridge: Cambridge University Press, 2013), 97.

28. Sun-tzu, *The Art of War*, trans. Samuel B. Griffith (Oxford, UK: Clarendon Press, 1964).

29. This can equate to everything in modern combat being used as a sensor or potential intel collection and exploitation in the cyber-domain.

30. Jonathan Bott, John Gallagher, Jake Huber, and Josh Powers, "Multi-Domain Battle: Tactical Implications," *Over the Horizon: Multi-Domain Operations and Strategy*, August 28, 2017, https://othjournal.com/2017/08/28/multi-domain-battle-tactical-implications/.

20

Becoming No One

Human Intelligence in the Seven Kingdoms

ANDREA N. GOLDSTEIN

Qyburn shows tender care to a street child who is healing from a minor injury and then asks about the boy's family. The move is motivated not by genuine concern at all—Qyburn may not have an empathetic bone in his body—but rather by a desire to build rapport with a child spy who had previously worked for Varys during his time as Master of Whisperers (a fantastic name that the United States and its allied forces should strongly consider adopting for the J-2, the director of intelligence, and for the J-2X, the director of counterintelligence and human intelligence). The child says in response to Qyburn's questions, "He called us his little birds. He gave us sweets."[1]

The street children who comprised Varys's spy network had very simple motivation that Varys and later Qyburn exploited: to be seen, to be cared for, and to earn an incentive that could not be earned otherwise—in this case, candy. Qyburn presents the "little birds" with sweets, which they eagerly consume, and asks that if their friends are in need of help or sweets, they come to him: "All I ask in exchange are whispers." He then introduces the gargantuan undead Ser Gregor and says, "His friends are my friends," a visual warning to the children not to betray him.[2]

Whom do you trust with your secrets? Who is invisible to you? While using street children would not be considered ethical or legal for the United States' human intelligence collection efforts, the example is a good one in reminding us of how people may be motivated to become intelligence sources or agents. Furthermore, it's a reminder to ourselves that a good counterintelligence plan is to know that the enemy is always listening and that it may be in the form of people whom we least expect.

Doctrinally defined, human intelligence "is a category of intelligence derived from information collected and provided by human sources," while counterintelligence has a more narrow focus and targets those entities that are targeting friendly forces and information.[3] Readers and viewers of the *Game of Thrones* series are presented with a number of forms of human intelligence and counterintelligence methods, including running source operations, interrogations, and liaison operations.[4] Many of the methods employed throughout the Seven Kingdoms are morally and ethically dubious and might not even be considered legal in a U.S. context—for example, Septa Unella depriving Cersei of water while demanding that she "confess" and Cersei "wineboarding" Unella clearly violate the Geneva Conventions. However, they do provide an interesting insight into considerations of human behavior, motivations, and interaction.

We are not totally aware of who comprises Varys's and Petyr "Littlefinger" Baelish's source networks or how they are recruited. However, it is clear from Varys's "little birds"—who both include street children as well as many adults and live beyond King's Landing—and from Littlefinger's prostitutes that these networks are marginalized people whose agency is invisible to the people they are informing on.

The social constructions of gender affect how an individual interacts with the world and how the world interacts with that person. According to NATO's directive on implementation of a gender perspective into military operations, gender "refers to the social attributes associated with being male and female learned through socialization and determines a person's position and value in a given context."[5] It affects who has power and how they wield it and who is rendered invisible. An effective counterintelligence and human intelligence strategy is conscious of those dynamics and will take them into account in enhancing situational awareness, operational effectiveness, and achieving mission success—whether the end state is defeating the Night King and White Walkers or sitting on the Iron Throne as ruler of the Seven Kingdoms.

If human intelligence is about exploiting social relations in order to gather intelligence from human sources and "gender pertains to the construction of relationships between male and female, and the attendant power dynamics found within these relationships,"[6] then it follows that any good human intelligence and counterintelligence strategy will deliberately consider the gender of the source handler and source, interrogator and detainee, as well as the additional effects of the intersections of other identities, such as class, culture, race, and religion.

The Faceless Men of Braavos apply these considerations when selecting the face they will wear before carrying out their assassinations. Wearing the disguise of someone else's face gives one the ability to become someone who might be considered invisible or unthreatening in any given context. Like many human intelligence professionals who present a character that will best endear themselves to a potential source, the Faceless Men become "no one," a blank canvas who can appear sincere and convincing in becoming anyone he or she needs to be to accomplish the mission. In her assassination campaign, Arya chooses faces that will give her placement and access to her targets, from a serving woman to Walder Frey.

While human intelligence operations pertain to collecting information about an enemy, counterintelligence operations set out to deny the enemy the ability to do so. Specifically, counterintelligence comprises "information gathered and activities conducted to protect against espionage, other intelligence activities, sabotage, or assassinations conducted by or on behalf of foreign governments or elements thereof, foreign organizations, or foreign persons, or international terrorist activities."[7]

While they lack a number of technical capabilities present in modern warfare, counterintelligence operations are rife in Westeros. For example, Varys recruits the prostitute Ros to spy on Littlefinger. This is an excellent example of a double agent operation; part of Ros's duties of working in Littlefinger's brothel was to gather information on her clients. After witnessing the death of one of Robert Baratheon's illegitimate children in the brothel, Ros confides in Littlefinger. Rather than trying to retain her trust, he tells hers a story that contains a thinly veiled threat, implying both complicity and lack of care. Ros becomes convinced that Littlefinger is not interested in her safety and feels that working with Varys is more in her interest. This is a valuable lesson on managing source loyalty and how sources can turn against you after you betray their trust. And it's also a reminder of why certain establishments are off-limits to military personnel.

And finally, what of the interrogations in *Game of Thrones*? Most of them appear to be sadistic torture sessions, in which the detainee will say anything to abate the pain. Interrogation is defined as "the process of questioning a source to obtain the maximum amount of usable information. The goal of any interrogation is to obtain reliable information in a lawful manner, in a minimum amount of time."[8] In Westeros and beyond in the *Game of Thrones* universe, there hardly appears to be any kind of legal framework surrounding interrogation, and interrogation appears to serve little point other than to prove who has power over another. Even Cersei observes this when she has turned the tables on Septa Unella, after enduring humiliation and torture at her hands. As she pours wine on Unella's face, Cersei accuses the septa of being unconcerned with her atonement and says, "Confess! You did it because you liked it!"[9]

This is not to say that examples of more nuanced interrogation techniques do not exist in *Game of Thrones*. In season 3, Theon endures repeated torture at the Dreadfort, unaware of where he is. After having his fingernails torn out and his foot impaled, he still has not confessed anything of meaningful value—only just enough to try to get the pain to stop. A mysterious man (whom the audience knows is Ramsay Snow but Theon does not) claims to have been sent by Theon's sister, Yara, to free him; helps smuggle him out; and even shoots down would-be captors who are in hot pursuit. In the moment just before Theon thinks he is about to be free, he confesses everything to Ramsay, whom he thinks he can trust: that he betrayed the

Starks; that he regrets it; that it was all to please his father; and that the Stark children, whom he had pretended to kill, are still alive. The very next moment, he finds himself back in the very cell he thought he had escaped. Ramsay created the illusion of an actual incentive (the reward of freedom, rather than a respite from pain) for Theon, and Theon only confesses when he feels safe. If there are any lessons to be learned from the depiction of interrogation in *Game of Thrones*, it's that torture doesn't work, but earning the trust of and building rapport with a detainee *does*.

The Master or Mistress of Whisperers (or J-2) and their ilk in *Game of Thrones* have a number of resources at their disposal for human intelligence, counterintelligence, and interrogation operations. However, due to the lack of other methods, cuing or redundancy of multiple collection methods often means operations have to be planned on single-source intelligence or simply on good historical analysis. It's unclear how we can categorize Bran Stark's ability to see the past, hack into the body of another person, mind meld with the Night King, or be a human UAV (unmanned aerial vehicle) to track White Walker troop movements, but it is certainly an intelligence collection method.

This means there is practically zero awareness of the maritime domain, which might explain the intelligence failure to predict that Euron Greyjoy, arguably the greatest mariner in the kingdom, would attack Daenerys's fleet and kidnap Yara. Even so, human sources would know when his ships left port, what the wind speeds were, and how far he might have traveled in the time since he left King's Landing. Furthermore, knowledge of his deceptive nature might have improved situational awareness and potentially mitigated risk.

While the human intelligence operations in *Game of Thrones* are often morally and ethically questionable, this does reveal a few key truths about these kinds of activities in any time, place, or season. First, even with the best intentions, masterful manipulation of other people is key to success— build trust and rapport; understand a source's motivations; and create an incentive for them to feel as if you, as their handler, are the vehicle to get what they want, whether it's candy or the Iron Throne. Second, gaining and keeping someone's trust is far more effective as a motivator than threatening or actually inflicting harm. Third, always assume the other side is working against you, being mindful of whom you trust with your secrets while knowing that "invisible" people may be the greatest counterintelligence threats. And maybe keep out of the brothels in King's Landing.

NOTES

1. David Benioff and D. B. Weiss, "Oathbreaker," season 6, episode 3, dir. Daniel Sackheim, *Game of Thrones*, aired May 8, 2016, on HBO.

2. Benioff and Weiss, "Oathbreaker."

3. U.S. Joint Chiefs of Staff, *Joint Intelligence*, Joint Publication 2-0 (Arlington VA: U.S. Department of Defense, October 22, 2013), B-4, http://www.jcs.mil/Portals/36/Documents/Doctrine/pubs/jp2_0.pdf.

4. U.S. Joint Chiefs of Staff, *Joint Intelligence*.

5. Hugues Delort-Laval and Graham Stacey, *Integrating UNSCR 1325 and Gender Perspective into the NATO Command Structure*, Bi-strategic Command Directive 40-1 (Brussels, Belgium: NATO, 2017).

6. Gunhild Hoogensen and Svein Vigeland Rottem, "Gender Identity and the Subject of Security," *Security Dialogue* 35 (2004): 163.

7. U.S. Marine Corps, *Counterintelligence*, Marine Corps Warfighting Publication 2-14 (Quantico VA: U.S. Marine Corps, January 31, 2015).

8. Headquarters, Department of the Army, *Human Intelligence Collector Operations*, Army Field Manual 2-22.3 (34-52) (Arlington VA: U.S Department of Defense, September 2006), 1-6, 1-7.

9. David Benioff and D. B. Weiss, "The Winds of Winter," season 6, episode 10, dir. Miguel Sapochnik, *Game of Thrones*, aired June 26, 2016, on HBO.

21

The Battle of the Bastards and the Importance of the Reserve

JESS WARD

They think I'm stupid. They think I don't know of their whispering in the corners of the courtyard and down the alleys that this will be the "Battle of the Bastards." They think they are clever. Well, Father thought he was clever too. He tried to replace me with the son of the fat whore, Lady Walder. He didn't think any more of me than any great lord would think of a daughter. He thought only to strengthen his house through a marriage with Sansa Stark. They all eventually learn, and these soldiers will be no different. Their laughter will turn to screams as I peel the skin from their muscles and use their bodies to fatten my hounds. But first, I need them. I need their numbers against the bastard Jon Snow.

Ramsay looked up from the table he was standing at as his thoughts broke away. He looked around at the bannermen and soldiers gathered in the great hall of Winterfell around the long table that had been covered to resemble the pending battlefield to their north. He had gathered his men here to commence battle plans. Like his father, Ramsay was a man of detail, precision, and control. Unlike his father, Ramsay had a bias for action that had thus far served him well.

"Men, sit. Lord Karstark to my right, Lord Umber to my left." Ramsay knew exactly how he wanted this battle to unfold and did not want to leave any doubt that he had complete control after the parlay that had taken place earlier in the morning with John Snow and his advisors.

Ramsay began laying out his plan. "This will be a three-phase battle with a preliminary phase." Ramsey stood up from his seat and, reaching behind him, pulled out the dagger that he had sheathed there. He reached across the table and, using the tip of the dagger as a pointer, pointed at each of the six symbols of the burning man that resembled his great house.

"These will be my phase lines for the battle. These will be marked on the ground by flayed and burning men launched into the air on stakes. The men chosen for the honor of marking my battlefield will be the traitor's reconnaissance party that was found by my hounds in the woods a week ago." Ramsay resumed his seat at the head of the table, placing his dagger next to him as an unconscious show of strength.

"The preliminary phase will center on psychological warfare against the bastard traitor Jon Snow and his army of wildlings. I will personally plan and control this phase, as I think we can all agree that I am the best man for the task," Ramsay said with a sneer. "Phase 1 will be the deployment of our archers, which will be triggered by the charge of the undisciplined wildling army. The archers will aim between phase lines 1 and 2. The main effort of the archers will be to degrade the enemy forces to set the conditions for the deployment of cavalry. Although the archers will be commanded down the line by senior officers, they will fire on my command alone."

Ramsay knew that aside from having a clear advantage of six thousand men and horses bred for war, discipline would win this battle. "Once I have finished with the archers, they will return to Winterfell to protect the castle from any counterattack." This was a tactic he had learned from his father. Use as much force as necessary to win, but don't forget what you're trying to protect in the meantime.

"Phase 2 will be the cavalry charge. This will be triggered once Snow's forward line of troops pass the phase 1 line. The main effort of the cavalry will once again be the attrition of the wildling army in the main assault. The cavalry will be led by Lord Karstark." Ramsay tilted his head to his left. Although he did not look directly at the man while doing so, he saw

Harold Karstark's posture straighten at the mention of his name and the realization that he would be the first into battle.

"The final phase will be the deployment of my infantry. This will be triggered by either the death or forced dismount of two-thirds of the cavalry. The main effort of the infantry will be to exploit the battle. I will be splitting the infantry into thirds. One-third will be utilized as the dismounted attacking force; two-thirds will be utilized as my reserve. The reserve will be led by Lord Umber."

Ramsay could feel the air in the great hall shift as he announced this, as he knew it would. He knew that his more loyal bannermen, like Lord Karstark, would loathe the thought of Smalljon Umber, a man who would not even bend the knee, being in command of two-thirds of the fighting force, as well as having a greater chance of outliving him should his own forces do their job in killing the traitor's army before the reserve were ever required. Ramsey raised his gaze and observed his bannermen, looking each in the eye, daring them to say with their tongues what they were screaming from their hearts. None did so.

"You have until nightfall to conduct your own appreciation of the battle and back brief me on your plans." This was merely a gesture to his men to make them believe they were in any way stakeholders in the battle to come. Ramsey slowly rose from his seat and started to walk toward the door before thinking better of it. "Lord Umber," Ramsey called back to the table, "accompany me to inspect the troops." Lord Umber, a large man by any account, rose to his full height. Although Ramsay was astute in reading the body language of his men to predict their motives, Smalljon Umber was still somewhat of a mystery.

As they left the great hall and walked down the passageways that led to the courtyard, Ramsay walked in silence. This silence gave Lord Umber the uneasy feeling of not knowing what the Warden of the North was thinking. Ramsay was most comfortable in silence.

"Do you know why I chose you to lead my reserve?" Ramsay asked, without looking at the man to whom he spoke.

"I suppose you don't trust me to take the lead charge," replied Umber.

The answer surprised Ramsay, who thought that Smalljon inherently understood the prestige of being in command of the reserve force. "Only an idiot would make that assessment. Are you an idiot, Lord Umber?"

The larger man stopped dead in his tracks and rested his hand on the hilt of the sword hanging from his side. "Only an idiot would question my honor in battle by giving me command of the force most likely to walk away from battle unscathed and then piss in my face by telling me it's a pleasure to do so."

Lord Umber was becoming agitated, and Ramsay knew that once this mood began, it was hard to talk him down again. He continued to walk, knowing that Lord Umber would follow, knowing also that giving space to the man's rising anger would be the only way to dissipate it.

"The reserve is one of the most important elements on the battlefield. It allows me flexibility with the way my other forces are utilized. The commander of that force is also given great freedom. You may be used in a flanking attack, a counterattack, to block a withdrawal route, to capture and kill the wilding encampment after the battle, to conduct the battlefield clearance, to protect the main assault from a counterattack, or, should the bastard be so clever, to withdraw and defend Winterfell from an attack by another force." Ramsay had now reached the top of the stairs overlooking the courtyard, which was currently full of officers practicing their sword drills away from the soldiers, whom he knew were doing the same in the large camps established to the south of Winterfell's walls.

He stopped and turned toward Lord Umber, who was two steps below him and thus equal in height to Ramsay. Ramsay looked him directly in the eye. "I need a commander whom I can trust. I need a commander who, when the time comes, can rally his troops and stain the lands of the North with traitors' blood. I need a commander who has self-discipline and can, when ordered to do so, win me a decisive victory."

Lord Umber's face flushed a light pink as he remembered the rush that came with killing men. He opened his mouth to speak, but Ramsay turned his back and continued to walk before he got the chance to do so.

"I assume from your distaste of the position that you have never done the task before, nor witnessed a commander use his reserve force properly, so let me explain how this will work," Ramsay said, in a tone similar to a father explaining to his son why sweetened water was bad for his teeth. "I will give you several tasks that you are to be prepared to conduct. Each task will have a set trigger that will align with my intent and will give you the freedom to maneuver your infantry forces around the battle space to best meet my intent."

Both men were now standing next to the balustrade above the courtyard, neither leaning against it, as they absently watched the officers below.

"The bastard Snow will have a reserve; however, he will put his undisciplined but most combat-hardened right hand, Ser Davos, in charge of the force. It will not be large, as his main force is small, and he will see his best chance in winning as triggering my attack first and then committing the bulk of his wildling army in the main offensive, hoping that their passion to fight will create some shock action. He will therefore back himself into committing his reserve in the main fight when our main attack undoubtedly begins to overrun him."

Smalljon was silent a moment as he took this information in.

"And how do you suppose he will make us attack first?" he finally asked, without looking up from the courtyard.

"Well, it doesn't matter," Ramsay replied, the corners of his mouth turning upward slightly without his control. "I have one thing that the bastard doesn't have—a disregard for other people's lives, and in this case, the life of his brother."

Ramsay knew that his bannermen found his tactics disgusting. They all understood that while the Stark boy lived, Lord Bolton's claim as Warden of the North would always be questioned. He must therefore kill the boy, but they thought there was no honor in making a show of it.

"So, if it doesn't matter what Snow is going to try to do, why are we even talking about it?" Lord Umber was starting to get frustrated at having his intelligence questioned, just as Ramsay's frustrations were rising at having to explain himself, a tedious task he had always hated, as he believed it undermined his command.

He took a long, deliberate breath in to display his frustration. "You will work off of triggers. These are points in the battle that, should they occur, will determine what action you take in order to meet my intent. By understanding what the bastard will do and how the battle will play out, you will be more observant of the signs leading up to one of those triggers. When Ser Davos inevitably commits his reserve force in a counterattack in the battle, that will trigger an action from your force."[1]

As Ramsay spoke, he realized that he may not have chosen the best man for the job, but he was too stubborn to change his mind now, after the uproar he had undoubtedly started in the great hall. Ramsay mentally resigned himself to the idea that he would need to be alongside Lord Umber to direct him to the best course of action on the ground.

Ramsay knew that he would need to spend some more time explaining this to the proud Lord Umber and even, despite his mood, be patient with the man.

Ramsay once again took out the dagger, which he had earlier resheathed upon leaving the great hall, and began to etch the pending battlefield into the balustrade.

"I will give you a set of tasks you are to be prepared to conduct later. However, if the battle goes the way I have planned it and the bastard is the man he showed himself to be in our little meeting this morning, he will attack first. It will be clumsy, it will be unplanned, and it will confuse his soldiers, who don't seem the type to be creative enough to be flexible when a plan changes." He stood back from the railing to allow Smalljon Umber to see.

"Now, as I have already said, a reserve, to be effective, should be of a credible enough size and composition to allow the overall commander freedom of action on the battlefield. In some instances, the composition of the force should replicate the main force, which in this case would mean placing archers and cavalry in the reserve as well as infantry.

"However, noting the size of the battlefield, the fact that our scouts have already witnessed Snow's army digging trenches on his flanks, and the fact that we have comparatively a much larger force, I would prefer my archers and cavalry to be in the main attack, thereby creating attrition and possibly defeating them altogether. I see their reserve being utilized as a counterattack force. Should this occur, I would most likely call on my reserves to conduct a pincer with shields and spears."

As he spoke, Ramsay started carving out the tactical action.

"Thereby, as you can see, a noose is created. This is one of the many ways a reserve can be used to reinforce success. Once the wildings have been defeated and the bastard has been captured, my remaining force will be grouped and then split up again to conduct battlefield clearance, to raid the wildling encampment, and a third element as another reserve to which I will dictate further tasks they are to be prepared to conduct."

Ramsay looked up at the large man, hoping that the lesson had sunk in. The importance of a reserve force, deliberate consideration to its size and composition, its different uses, the freedom of movement that the force provides the commander, and how it is controlled on the ground were all vital aspects for him to understand. This was not merely a timeless lesson in tactics—this was a lesson in command.

"Do you understand now why I would put you in charge of my reserves?" Ramsay asked, watching Umber intently.

"I will join the others," Smalljon simply replied, not a man to admit his shortcomings or thank a man for pointing them out to him.

As Smalljon Umber lumbered away, Ramsay returned his gaze to the soldiers below him. *I really do wonder if the hounds will eat John Snow's eyes first.*

NOTES

1. Australian Army, *Operations*, Land Warfare Doctrine 3-0 (2018), https://www.army.gov.au/sites/g/files/net1846/f/lwd_3-0_operations_full.pdf; Australian Defence Force, *Command and Control*, Australian Defence Doctrine Publication 00.1 (Canberra ACT: Defence Publishing Service, 2009), http://www.defence.gov.au/adfwc/Documents/DoctrineLibrary/ADDP/ADDP_00_1_Command_and_Control.pdf; Australian Army, *The Fundamentals of Land Power*, Land Warfare Doctrine 1 (2017), https://www.army.gov.au/sites/g/files/net1846/f/lwd_1_the_fundamentals_of_land_power_full_july_2017.pdf; Australian Army, *Formation Tactics*, Land Warfare Doctrine 3-0-3 (2016), https://www.army.gov.au/sites/g/files/net1846/f/lwd_3-0-3_formation_tactics.pdf; David C. Callahan, "Retention and Employment of Tactical Reserves" (master's thesis, U.S. Army Command and General Staff College, 2002).

PART 4

Strategy and War

22

The Myth of the Accidental Strategist

STEVE LEONARD

Early in the sixth season of *Game of Thrones*, Tyrion Lannister is holding counsel with Missandei, Varys, and Grey Worm in Meereen. With the Dragon Queen, Daenerys Targaryen, missing since escaping the Sons of the Harpy in Daznak's Pit, the four are discussing the progressive decline of her dragons Rhaegal and Viserion, chained in captivity beneath the Great Pyramid. Their conversation is significant, as it underscores the transformation of Tyrion from a comically drunken, lascivious rascal to a trusted confidant and adviser.

> MISSANDEI: They are not eating. They haven't touched any food since Queen Daenerys left.
>
> TYRION LANNISTER: Daenerys is the Dragon Queen. Can't very well let the dragons starve. That's obvious.
>
> GREY WORM: The dragon does not want to eat. How do you force him to eat?
>
> TYRION LANNISTER: Dragons do not do well in captivity.
>
> MISSANDEI: How do you know this?
>
> TYRION LANNISTER: That's what I do. I drink, and I know things.[1]

The youngest son of Lord Tywin Lannister, the powerful patriarch of House Lannister, Tyrion lives a seemingly cursed life. His mother, Joanna Lannister, did not survive his birth, a death for which both his father and sister, Cersei Lannister, blame him. He also suffers from dwarfism, a condition for which he endures persistent prejudice and persecution. Derisively referred to as "the Imp," "Halfman," and "the Demon Monkey," Tyrion is widely known for two unique and somewhat endearing characteristics: his insatiable taste for prostitutes and his uncanny ability to consume alcohol. His family has little respect for him, as do those with whom he associates.

Tyrion's lesser qualities, however, are more than mitigated by a substantial intellect, keen observational skills, and a deeply cynical perspective. While the rest of House Lannister is busy plotting and scheming to retain their tenuous grasp on the Iron Throne, Tyrion is watching, learning, and—without fail—drinking. All the while, those around him continue on, oblivious to the quiet evolution of the accidental strategist.

The Bastard Prince

In the fictional world of *Game of Thrones*, Tyrion Lannister is a Westerosi Niccolò Machiavelli: diplomat, philosopher, political realist. Machiavelli, who served in a variety of influential positions in the Florentine Republic of Renaissance Italy, was an astute observer of the brutal political realities of his time. While in service to the Republic of Florence, Machiavelli bore witness to unrelenting political deceit, deviousness, and unscrupulousness. His treatise on the realpolitik of the era, *The Prince*, remains relevant today as much for its timeless treatment of political immorality as for the subtle brilliance of the author himself.[2]

Much like Tyrion, Machiavelli enjoyed a rich and full life. While credited with being the father of modern political science and a military theorist of some repute, Machiavelli also found time to write poetry, satire, and even carnival songs. In these lesser-known works, he exhibits a wry sense of humor and biting wit honed through years of serving as "the Hand" to Florentine political elites. Even while assembling the ideas that would one day form *The Art of War*, Machiavelli was busying himself with "L'asino d'oro" ("The Golden Ass"), a satirical poem in which the author finds love with a beautiful herdswoman surrounded by the beasts of the enchantress Circe.[3] An irony, perhaps, that was not lost on George R. R. Martin.

In a world steeped in political intrigue, Tyrion is Machiavelli—easily overlooked by the princes around him, deeply intelligent, and quietly observant. In *Game of Thrones* the Italian poet-philosopher is not just a literary prototype for Tyrion; he is channeled through "the Dwarf of Casterly Rock." Even as we are introduced to Tyrion as the drunken castoff of House Lannister in the first episode, we get a glimpse into the character's future during a brief, but significant, exchange with Jon Snow:

> TYRION LANNISTER: Let me give you some advice, bastard. Never forget what you are. The rest of the world will not. Wear it like armor, and it can never be used to hurt you.
>
> JON SNOW: What the hell do you know about being a bastard?
>
> TYRION LANNISTER: All dwarves are bastards in their fathers' eyes.[4]

No two characters in *Game of Thrones* are as deeply connected. Both men are the "bastards" of their respective houses, and both men fight to earn the respect they have been denied for so long. Even as their paths take them in widely different directions for much of the series, they are reunited as the fantasy epic approaches crescendo. In whatever direction fate takes the two, it will take them together.

True to character, Tyrion walks away from the encounter, pulling a last drink from his ubiquitous wineskin.

The Unlikely Sage

Throughout *Game of Thrones* Tyrion dispenses Machiavellian wisdom. In every episode, his words are often noteworthy and inevitably memorable, ranging from the prophetic ("The Northerners will never forget") to the seemingly absurd ("In my experience, eloquent men are right every bit as often as imbeciles").[5] His counsel foreshadows the risks of ill-conceived plans ("It's hard to put a leash on a dog once you've put a crown on its head") and provides important perspective on life ("And a mind needs books like a sword needs a whetstone").[6] His advice can be simultaneously colloquial, comical, and controversial.

In Tyrion Lannister, Martin's choice of sage is at the same time unprecedented and profound. In *The Lord of the Rings* J. R. R. Tolkien channels wisdom through either Gandalf, the aged wizard, or the elves, who convey insight from a time before man. In the *Foundation* series, Isaac Asimov draws on mathematics professor Hari Seldon, who uses "psychohistory" to guide mankind through millennia of chaos. In each volume of *Tarzan of the Apes*, Edgar Rice Burroughs uses his archetype hero as a conduit for the hard-fought lessons of the jungle. Martin, however, chooses the least likely character to deliver the most important knowledge.

As with any sage, Martin bestows on Tyrion a powerful medium through which to channel his rare insight into the world around him. Gandalf had his staff, Hari Seldon his mind, and Tarzan his strength. Tyrion has alcohol, and an abundance of it. From the outset of the series, Tyrion the philosopher casts wisdom from the depths of a wineskin. Whether extolling the virtues of alcohol to Jon Snow ("Everything's better with some wine in the belly") or bemoaning his vice to Podrick Payne ("It's not easy being drunk all the time. If it were easy, everyone would do it"), Tyrion wields his drink with the power and conviction of a great wizard's staff.[7]

While such a choice might seem ironic on the surface, Martin's thinking is ever-so-subtly revealed as the initial season unfolds. In the fourth episode, "Cripples, Bastards, and Broken Things," the series offers what is probably the most significant clue about Martin's vision for the diminutive sage, when Tyrion gives the crippled Bran Stark his design for a saddle that will allow the boy to ride a horse upright:

> BRAN STARK: Will I really be able to ride?
>
> TYRION LANNISTER: You will. On horseback, you will be as tall as any of them.
>
> ROBB STARK: Is this some kind of trick? Why do you want to help him?
>
> TYRION LANNISTER: I have a tender spot in my heart for cripples, bastards, and broken things.[8]

In Tyrion, Martin finds a "tender spot" that strikes at the heart. While most fantasy epics leverage characters of lesser stature (dwarves or hobbits, for example) as comedic relief, Tyrion represents a sympathetic figure, a familial black sheep not by choice but by birth. Like Jon Snow, Tyrion has lived his life as an outcast in his own family; unlike Jon Snow, Tyrion provides a unique vessel to serve as Martin's sage, one as unusual as it is improbable.

Martin's sage drinks, and he knows things.

The Influential Hand

In the season 2 episode "What Is Dead May Never Die," Varys plays the role of prophet in a discussion with Tyrion, sharing with him a riddle that shrewdly defines the influence—and power—of a strategic adviser, the right hand to the throne:

LORD VARYS: Power is a curious thing, my lord. Are you fond of riddles?

TYRION LANNISTER: Why? Am I about to hear one?

LORD VARYS: Three great men sit in a room: a king, a priest, and a rich man. Between them stands a common sellsword. Each great man bids the sellsword kill the other two. Who lives? Who dies?

TYRION LANNISTER: Depends on the sellsword.

LORD VARYS: Does it? He has neither crown, nor gold, nor favor with the gods.

TYRION LANNISTER: He has a sword, the power of life and death.

LORD VARYS: But if it's swordsmen who rule, why do we pretend kings hold all the power? When Ned Stark lost his head, who was truly responsible? Joffrey? The executioner? Or something else?

TYRION LANNISTER: I've decided I don't like riddles.

LORD VARYS: Power resides where men believe it resides. It's a trick. A shadow on the wall. And a very small man can cast a very large shadow.[9]

Power *is* a very curious thing, and so is influence. Machiavelli's *The Prince* was not published until 1532, five years after his death, yet it stands today as one of the most influential treatises on realpolitik. Prussian military theorist Carl von Clausewitz died before finishing his masterpiece analysis of political-military strategy, *On War*. After his death in 1831, his wife, Marie von Brühl, edited and published the unfinished, and now classic, work. Major General Fox Conner of the U.S. Army, who personally and deftly mentored George C. Marshall, Dwight D. Eisenhower, and George S. Patton—three of the most impactful military officers of the twentieth century—throughout the course of their careers, ordered his papers and journals burned upon his death in 1951.[10] Were it not for the personal recollections of those he mentored, his profound impact on World War II might never have been revealed.

Each of these men exerted a tremendous amount of influence during their lives, but that influence went largely unnoticed until long after their deaths. They were quietly observant and deeply reflective, possessing a singular, transcendent wisdom. Tyrion is cast in this mold, emerging from the brothels of Westeros to assume a crucial role as Hand to Daenerys Targaryen. As the Dragon Queen's most trusted adviser, Tyrion's wisdom has never been more prophetic ("The world you want to build doesn't get built all at once, probably not in a single lifetime") or timely ("Sometimes, nothing is the hardest thing to do").[11] His counsel offers both restraint ("If that's the type of queen you want to be, how are you different from all the other tyrants that came before you?") and perspective ("Children are not their fathers, luckily for all of us").[12]

A very small man *can* cast a very large shadow. Martin's transformation of Tyrion comes full circle by the seventh season of *Game of Thrones*. Tyrion is able to bring Jon Snow—now the King in the North—together with Daenerys, forge alliances with the Starks and Greyjoys, and negotiate a ceasefire with the Lannisters. Even as the White Walkers descend on the Seven Kingdoms, his relatively quiet, humble influence guides Daenerys at a crucial time for her, the Seven Kingdoms, and Westeros.

The Accidental Strategist

In *Game of Thrones* the transformation of Tyrion Lannister appears almost as happenstance, a fortunate turn of circumstance. Nothing could be further from the truth.

History is replete with examples of influential strategists; men like Machiavelli and Clausewitz serve as two prominent cases. But many others came before, and still more have come since. The lessons of Sun Tzu and Thucydides resonate from antiquity; the works of B. H. Liddell Hart and John Boyd do the same in a more contemporary sense. Modern navies owe much to Alfred Thayer Mahan and Julian Corbett, and air power might not be what it is today without the influential efforts of Giulio Douhet and Billy Mitchell. Rarely were these influential figures great captains of battle, but men and women who, when afforded the opportunity, rose to the occasion and forged a timeless legacy that shaped the knowledge and understanding of future generations.

What separates these figures from those who aspire to but never attain such influence is quite simple: intellect, opportunity, and conviction. Remarkable mental acuity and perceptiveness are the hallmarks of a strategist; only the best among them are afforded the opportunity to serve in positions of significant influence. These men and women were among a rare breed of strategists who possess the conviction to cast an enduring legacy in their wake, to capture the lessons of their vicarious learning for those who follow.

In *Game of Thrones* Tyrion's ascent is presented as happenstance, a trick of fate, an accident. But it is no accident. He is Martin's Machiavelli—the voice of reason in a sea of chaos. A trusted confidant and adviser as adept at offering sage counsel as he would be penning a scandalous limerick. The astute strategist who serves wisdom from the depths of a wineskin. At the same time both ordinary and extraordinary. Easily overlooked but impossible to ignore. At its core, *Game of Thrones* is a grand Machiavellian epic, and Martin's fantasy tale would be incomplete without his own Niccolò Machiavelli at center stage. And for that, he has Tyrion Lannister—a seasoned intellect and wily opportunist intent on preserving his place in history, as well as history itself.

There are no accidental strategists.

NOTES

1. Dave Hill, "Home," season 6, episode 2, dir. Jeremy Podeswa, *Game of Thrones*, aired May 1, 2016, on HBO.
2. Niccolò Machiavelli, *The Prince*, trans. Harvey C. Mansfield Jr. (Chicago: University of Chicago Press, 1985).

3. Machiavelli's version was a period retelling of Apuleius's "The Golden Ass." The poem uses the animals as an allegorical device to explore human characteristics such as bravery, cruelty, violence, conceit, and greed. In Greek mythology, Circe is a goddess of magic often cast as a nymph or sorceress.

4. David Benioff and D. B. Weiss, "Winter Is Coming," season 1, episode 1, dir. Tim Van Patten, *Game of Thrones*, aired April 17, 2011, on HBO.

5. David Benioff and D. B. Weiss, "Mhysa," season 3, episode 10, dir. David Nutter, *Game of Thrones*, aired June 9, 2013, on HBO; David Benioff and D. B. Weiss, "Dance of Dragons," season 5, episode 9, dir. David Nutter, *Game of Thrones*, aired June 7, 2015, on HBO.

6. David Benioff and D. B. Weiss, "A Man without Honor," season 2, episode 7, dir. David Nutter, *Game of Thrones*, aired May 13, 2012, on HBO; David Benioff and D. B. Weiss, "The Kingsroad," season 1, episode 2, dir. Tim Van Patten, *Game of Thrones*, aired April 24, 2011, on HBO.

7. Benioff and Weiss, "Kingsroad"; Benioff and Weiss, "Mhysa."

8. Bryan Cogman, "Cripples, Bastards, and Broken Things," season 1, episode 4, dir. Brian Kirk, *Game of Thrones*, aired May 8, 2011, on HBO.

9. Bryan Cogman, "What Is Dead May Never Die," season 2, episode 3, dir. Alik Sakharov, *Game of Thrones*, aired April 15, 2012, on HBO.

10. Edward Cox, *Grey Eminence: Fox Conner and the Art of Mentorship* (Stillwater OK: New Forums Press, 2011).

11. David Benioff and D. B. Weiss, "Beyond the Wall," season 7, episode 6, dir. Alan Taylor, *Game of Thrones*, aired August 20, 2017, on HBO.

12. Benioff and Weiss, "Beyond the Wall"; David Benioff and D. B. Weiss, "The Queen's Justice," season 7, episode 3, dir. Mark Mylod, *Game of Thrones*, aired August 20, 2017, on HBO.

23

Why the Westerosi Can't Win Wars

CHUCK BIES

In order to use battle to bring an enemy to heel, the losses have to matter. In Westeros the losses not only do not matter, but they do not threaten power structures. Therefore, the tactical level of war in Westeros is divorced from the strategic level of war. Dead peasants and sellswords matter little in the game of thrones. For battles to matter, they must be a part of a coherent operational and strategic approach that hits the enemy where it hurts and destroys either their will or means to continue fighting. The only leader that seemed to intuitively understand this was Tywin Lannister, and though "The Rains of Castamere" survived him, the lesson that it taught did not.

> TYRION: "Rain fire on them from above" . . . you're quoting father, aren't you?
>
> CERSEI: Why not? He has a good mind for strategy, doesn't he?
>
> TYRION: Call it tactics, not strategy, but yes, he does have a good mind for it. The best mind some would say.[1]

During the above brother-sister discussion prior to the Battle of the Blackwater, Tyrion was exactly right. In Westeros even the greatest military minds lacked an understanding of what tactics, operations, and strategy are, let alone how they must be employed in concert to achieve victory in the game of thrones. This is not just a matter of nuance or semantics; it is also the reason why warfare in Westeros is seemingly endless and endemic.

To ensure common understanding, it's worthwhile to explain what we mean by the different levels of warfare: the tactical, operational, and strategic levels of war. Executed correctly, there are linkages between the three that will all but guarantee the success of a war; one or two battles will all but guarantee success. Executed incorrectly and the balance sheet of battles won and lost loses relevance, and the conflict becomes an unproductive and costly grind.

The tactical level of war

- refers to actions on the ground, usually manifested in battles or engagements between forces;
- is doctrinally defined as "the level of war at which battles and engagements are planned and executed to achieve military objectives assigned to tactical units or task forces";[2]
- includes modern tactical unit echelons that range from squad up through division;
- covers a time horizon that ranges from seconds to days;
- is the lowest level in terms of scale and closest in terms of proximity;
- can be easily categorized as area and mobile defenses, penetrations, envelopments, frontal attacks, flank attacks, infiltrations, and turning movements.

The strategic level of war

- refers to the employment of a nation's or state's resources, including nonmilitary capabilities, to achieve national level objectives;
- is viewed in terms of ends, ways, and means at the national level;[3]
- covers a time horizon measured in months and years;
- includes three general categories referred to as strategies of attrition, exhaustion, and annihilation.[4]

In comparison, the operational level of war

- resides between tactics and strategy and defies categorization;
- is the planning of campaigns and a series of engagements (tactical actions) to achieve the strategic objective (national strategy);
- encompasses the events that lead up to, surround, and follow engagements;
- involves the sustainment and movement of formations, from battalions through armies;
- covers a time horizon that ranges from days to months.

Despite its imprecise nature, the operational level of war is essential to connecting the tactical level of war to the strategic level of war. A battle fought without the context of an overarching operational approach is just that—a battle. On its own, it will not yield the decisive results necessary to achieve the strategic objective. Similarly, a strategic framework, no matter how well constructed, will not translate to success if there is no operational approach to translate national-level means to the tactical level; the best strategy cannot assure victory on the battlefield without an operational approach to mass resources to support the tactical engagement.

History provides several examples of where commanders and leaders succeeded or failed to employ these levels of war in concert. One of the most striking examples of success is Napoleon Bonaparte's Ulm Campaign during the War of the Third Coalition from 1803–6. Over the course of the Ulm Campaign, Napoleon skillfully maneuvered his corps around the Austrian army led by General Karl Mack von Leiberich; he used small tactical engagements to fix portions of the Austrian host while he maneuvered his corps around the Austrian flanks. After a few weeks, Mack found himself isolated from allied support and was compelled to surrender his army. This knocked Austria out of the coalition as a credible opponent, enabling Bonaparte to focus his efforts against the rest of the coalition. To quote Napoleon, "I have destroyed the enemy merely by marches." A few months later, he annihilated the Russian army at Austerlitz, ending the coalition against him. This was a shining example of the operational level of war to achieve coherence between tactics and strategy.[5]

An example of where the operational level was neglected was World War I from 1914 to 1917. During this bloody four-year period, national strategies on both sides failed because the operational level of war was absent and tactics were able to trump strategy. Despite local successes, neither side possessed the strength to capitalize on those victories and achieve a breakthrough. The two sides were too evenly matched, and neither could exploit those local successes. The strategies employed by both sides—whether opening additional fronts or "bleeding France white" at Verdun, in the words of German general Erich von Falkenhayn—failed because neither side was able to expand success beyond the immediate battle, destroy the enemy or their will to continue fighting, or appreciably erode the enemy's resources.[6]

Strategy in Westeros

In Westeros few leaders and commanders truly grasp strategy. An example of this is during Tyrion Lannister's war council with Daenerys and her allies—the Martells of Sunspear, the Tyrells of Highgarden, and the rogue Greyjoy flotilla. Tyrion outlined a coherent strategy at this council: the Martells would attack the Stormlands from the south to pull Cersei's forces away from King's Landing, the Tyrells would attack King's Landing from the southwest to seize the capital, and Daenerys's army of Unsullied and Dothraki would seize Casterly Rock to neutralize the Lannister alliance's source of power.[7]

It quickly became apparent that few of the participants at the meeting were capable of thinking strategically and were focused at the tactical level of war. Yara Greyjoy focused on using dragons against King's Landing—a narrow and tactical approach that, as Daenerys pointed out, would result in her losing the support of the people and, therefore, the war. Daenerys had no intention of being the Queen of Ashes.

Lady Olenna and Lady Martell were focused on the combat between their armies and the Lannisters and failed to grasp how they fit into supporting and shaping the larger strategic and operational goals. They resented that their armies would be used for lengthy sieges while Daenerys's would not. The only two people in the room who seemed to understand the bigger picture were Tyrion and Daenerys. They not only had a clear visualization of their end, but they understood that their means could only be employed in specific ways. Though the Unsullied and dragons presented an overwhelming advantage, they could only be employed against armies in the field and away from the Seven Kingdoms' seat of power. They lacked the resources and allies to fight a war of either attrition or exhaustion. They had to dismantle Cersei's alliance piece by piece in order to stand a chance of winning, and to do so, they had to draw the Lannister armies into the field, where they could be annihilated. Though they succeeded in destroying a significant portion of the Lannister army, it was, ultimately, Daenerys's alliance that was dismantled.

What of the Lannisters? Their objective was to remain in control of the Iron Throne; their means for doing so were the Lannister army and diplomacy with key players. By season 7, the Lannisters had only two allies remaining, the Greyjoys and the Tarlies. Though they dispatched most of their enemies, they were surrounded by threats; the Starks to the north, the Martells and Tyrells to the south, and the Targaryens and the Iron Bank across the sea to the east. They managed to subdue the Tully threat from Riverrun, and the Arryns to the north remain a wild card. But most of their key allies, specifically the Boltons and the Freys, had been dispatched. By ruling the seas and holding a central position, their strategy was to use their opponents' inability to concentrate against them to take on their opponents in series. They succeeded in destroying the Tyrells, but in the process, they lost their Tarly allies, Casterly Rock, most of their army, and most importantly the gold they needed to settle their debts with the Iron Bank. True, the Martells remained uncommitted, which resulted in the Lannisters' southern flank becoming more secure, but the Lannisters now face an increased risk of the Iron Bank hiring every mercenary company in Essos against them.

This illustrates why Daenerys and Tyrion, by the end of season 7, had failed and the war remained suspended in stalemate. Instead of focusing on isolating the Lannisters from their allies and annihilating both them and their allies in the field to set conditions to attain the Iron Throne, their strategy was to defeat the Lannisters so that they could seize King's Landing. They failed to appreciate that the strategic value of King's Landing is little more than a pile of rocks. Seizing the Iron Throne itself does not equate to seizing the power of the Iron Throne; the Targaryens, Baratheons, and Lannisters were able to rule the Iron Throne because they annihilated those who challenged their rule and subsequently assumed the Iron Throne, not because they had possession of it. Even after losing Casterly Rock, the Lannisters still retained the ability to effectively prosecute the offensive, as evidenced by their capturing Sunspear's leaders and sacking Highgarden.[8] The Lannisters removed the threats to their south, and their adversaries remained unable to concentrate against them. As long as the Lannister army survived, Cersei and Jaime would continue to rule. Though Tyrion and Daenerys's strategy was coherent, it was still flawed.

In comparison, Robb Stark's (earlier) war against the Iron Throne was doomed to failure. He won multiple battles against Tywin Lannister's alliance, but in the end, these battles didn't matter. Without being able to cut out what was then the Lannisters' true source of power, their allies and their money (which, according to Littlefinger, were little more than just numbers on paper), any victory over the Lions of Casterly Rock was temporary, since the Lannisters were able to hire new hosts to replace their losses in the field.

Tactical and Operational Warfare in Westeros

The lack of appreciation for war above the tactical level appears to be common throughout Westeros. Early on in the War of the Five Kings, we see Robb Stark admonish his uncle Edmure Tully after an engagement with Ser Gregor Clegane's army. Edmure Tully was focused on his victory over Clegane at the Battle of the Stone Mill; he saw Clegane's host, engaged it in a costly battle, and won. At the tactical level, this was a success.[9]

At the operational level, this success was pyrrhic. Robb intended to lure Clegane into an area where he could be fixed, isolated, and ultimately killed or captured along with his army. Battle with Clegane was a means to an end, not an end in itself. When Edmure prematurely engaged Clegane's army and defeated him, he compelled Clegane to retreat, unraveling Robb's plan to trap Clegane and either ransom or kill him. Edmure's failure to appreciate warfare above the tactical level was a costly setback for Robb Stark.

When battles have effects that extend beyond the tactical level out to the operational and strategic levels, they are known as decisive battles. This extends far beyond a simple rout or bloody engagement; decisive battles change governments, language, and history. The quintessential historical example of a decisive battle is the Battle of Hastings. William, the Duke of Normandy, invaded England to challenge King Harold's succession to the English throne and met Harold's Anglo-Saxon army at Hastings. Harold was killed late in the day during the battle, causing the Anglo-Saxon army to break and the Norman invaders to annihilate it during the pursuit. William, later crowned as the Conqueror, subdued remaining resistance in the vicinity of London before some of Harold's surviving loyalists fully capitulated, but the true victory had already been won at Hastings. Hastings had effects so far reaching that it put a Norman on the English throne and went so far as to change the English language for centuries to come.[10] Though the term "decisive" is used frequently, in history they are in fact rare.

If decisive battles are few and far between in reality, in Westeros there are even fewer. Prior to the events of the series, the only decisive battle of note was the Battle of the Trident, wherein Rhaegar Targaryen was killed by Robert Baratheon; it resulted in Robert Baratheon becoming the king of the Seven Kingdoms but did nothing to quell the violence, rebellion, and infighting endemic to Westeros. In the series, there are only two major battles that come close to being decisive: the Battle of the Blackwater and the Battle of the Bastards. However, even in these two battles, the tactical success failed to yield strategic and operational success.

In the Battle of the Blackwater, Stannis Baratheon besieged King's Landing with his army, using the pirate Salladhor Saan's fleet to transport his host to the city walls. Tyrion Lannister employed wildfire against the encroaching fleet and succeeded in destroying many ships but not enough to stop Stannis, who succeeded in reaching and breaching the city's walls. Only the timely arrival of Tywin Lannister at the head of a Lannister-Tyrell army saved the city from being sacked. His army broken and his fleet in shambles, Stannis was sent back to Dragonstone to recover. Stannis failed to take King's Landing and would never be able to attempt the feat again; instead, he turned northward to answer Jon Snow's call for aid. A Lannister king remained on the Iron Throne.[11]

On its surface, this seems decisive, but in truth it was not. Cersei Lannister and her progeny remained set upon by enemies, and the Seven Kingdoms remained engulfed in war. The Lannister alliance, though still strong, was eventually weakened as they were abandoned by Highgarden and Sunspear, the Vale under Petyr Baelish threw its support behind Jon Snow to destroy the Boltons, and Walder Frey was assassinated. Winning at King's Landing did nothing to secure peace for the Lannisters. An analog to a more modern conflict would be the Brusilov Offensive during the First World War—a catastrophic success for the Russians that ended a German onslaught and broke the Austro-Hungarian Army's back. Ultimately, Russia could not recover from its losses, and the cost of success set conditions for the Bolshevik Revolution.

Similarly, the Battle of the Bastards, fought between Jon Snow (born Aegon Targaryen) and Ramsay Bolton (born Ramsay Snow), did not do much to alter the strategic prospects of either Jon Snow or Westeros as a whole. True, the defeat of Ramsay Bolton effectively destroyed the Dreadfort as a power in the North and returned the Starks to Winterfell. But little changed to enhance Winterfell's strategic outlook; the North was unable to project its power southward against the Lannisters, more so than when Robb Stark remained alive. Instead of leading a campaign to avenge Eddard Stark and the North, even with the support of House Arryn, the best that Jon Snow could do is forge an alliance with Daenerys Targaryen to combat the undead hordes north of the Wall. The North remained at war with the Lannisters and no viable prospects of securing victory over them.[12]

Why Are There No Decisive Battles in Westeros?

In review, strategy is combining ends, ways, and means to achieve an objective. Throughout the War of the Five Kings, all of the combatants have employed similar strategies: create divisions within enemy alliances to weaken the main adversary and then use an army to fight the enemy's army in order to seize the enemy's castle. Assassination and arranged marriages are often used as tools to shape the diplomatic landscape to facilitate these military ways, and these tools are often creative. But ultimately, there is not much variety beyond sex, murder, and war.

This is important. A key element of a strategy to achieve a specific end is the way the means are used. In other words, when you change what you target with your means (the "ways"), then you are changing your strategy. In almost every case, the feuding lords use their armies to target other armies and military apparatus (fortresses, castles, etc.).

This begs the question of who or what was being targeted during the War of the Five Kings. What was the connection between Westerosi soldiers and their lord? This is the core problem of why, in Westeros, there were neither decisive battles nor lasting victories, because at its core there was no real allegiance at any level. The great nobles constantly shifted their alliances for their own benefit, and the houses themselves enjoyed no loyalty from the peoples who fell under their dominion. Targeting lords produced no effect on their people, and vice versa.

Much like in medieval Europe, Westerosi "soldiers," in most cases, just happened to live on the land owned by the lord. They fought because their feudal lord called them to fight. They fought for the false promises of adventure and glory. They fought for coin. They fought because they had no other prospects. Make no mistake, none of the "soldiers" who fought in this war were citizen-soldiers with a vested interest in their lord's success. One lord is the same as another; victory or defeat, their lot in life remained constant with the change of one banner to another. Modified to fit the screen and presented in season 6 by Brother Ray, the "Broken Man" speech from the books best explains the lack of connection between the soldiers, their lords, and their wars as a whole.[13]

Unlike the knights they served under, Westerosi "soldiers" lacked training. Training does more than just teach a soldier how to wield a weapon; it teaches them how to steel their resolve in the face of death. Training teaches soldiers to bury their fear to perform effectively, especially when they are so scared that their hands are shaking. Training teaches soldiers to stand their ground, especially when it means protecting their friend next to them. Westerosi soldiers had none of these things. The reward for success in battle and surviving and staying with the army was fighting in more battles. These soldiers had more incentives to desert and loot corpses for valuables than to pursue a defeated enemy.

This was the nature of battle in Westeros. The fighting continued until one side's morale broke and they fled, and the "winning" side was too exhausted and content to pursue their enemy's destruction. As a result, battles fought between Westerosi armies could not be decisive. Few armies were annihilated outright, the lords prosecuting the war did not lose their stomach for war, and there were always more men willing to fight.

None of this is to say that the lords of Westeros would have been better off targeting civilians as an element of their strategy. The people of Westeros suffered enough already, and no one wants to be the king or queen of ashes. Rather, the key point is that the leaders of Westeros generally failed to think beyond individual battles, and even Westeros's most brilliant military minds failed to grasp alternative strategies beyond simply engaging the enemy's power in combat. For battles to be decisive, they have to be nested within a larger campaign, and the ways and means must be appropriate for achieving the end. Operational art was either beyond understanding or too impractical to execute given the shortcomings of subordinate commanders.

There was no sense of citizenship, and both peer and peasant alike knew that loyalty would be mercurial. In comparison, in the modern era, wars are fought and peace is won with soldiers who are also citizens.[14] Originally articulated by Machiavelli in *The Art of War* as "civic virtu," when soldiers are intrinsically motivated rather than extrinsically, the state can expect them to fight harder and without as draconian measures of control. In return, the state must not waste their sacrifices and must offer them a measure of franchise during peacetime. Strategies that target these soldiers and seek decisive battle hold the potential for victory in the modern era because these soldiers are part of the state.

The key reason that strategies failed and combats meant little in Westeros is the soldiers employed to fight in them. War, as a tool of politics, was focused on killing people who did not matter to those prosecuting the wars. As Tyrion reminded Daenerys, "Killing and politics aren't always the same things."[15]

NOTES

1. David Benioff and D. B. Weiss, "A Man without Honor," season 2, episode 7, dir. David Nutter, *Game of Thrones*, aired May 13, 2012, on HBO.

2. Headquarters, Department of the Army, *Terms and Military Symbols*, Army Doctrine Reference Publication 1-02 (Washington DC: Government Printing Office, November 16, 2016).

3. Here, "ends" refers to the objective—the desired outcome, or the "what" of the strategy. "Ways" refers to the "how" of the strategy and how the strategy will achieve the desired ends. "Means" correlates to "with what" and refers to specific things, like armies, navies, and diplomatic and economic resources.

4. A strategy of attrition aims to erode the enemy's means to continue resistance until those means are reduced to the point that the enemy must capitulate. An exhaustion strategy, also referred to as a Fabian strategy, aims to reduce the enemy's resolve to continue fighting over time; whereas an attrition strategy targets means and resources, exhaustion seeks to sap will and morale. Strategies of annihilation seek to neutralize an enemy's means and will to resist in a short time frame, generally over the course of a single battle or campaign.

5. For a study of Napoleon Bonaparte and how he made war, there is simply no finer English study, or history book in general, than David Chandler's *The Campaigns of Napoleon* (New York: MacMillan Company, 1966). It went out of print many decades ago, so if you have the means to acquire it, this author recommends you do so immediately.

6. Erich von Falkenhayn, *General Headquarters, 1914–1916, and Its Critical Decisions* (London: Hutchinson, 1919), 286, https://archive.org/details/generalheadquart00falk.

7. Bryan Cogman, "Stormborn," season 7, episode 2, dir. Mark Mylod, *Game of Thrones*, aired July 23, 2017, on HBO.

8. In this sequence, even Jaime Lannister himself tells the soon-to-be-dead Lady Olenna Tyrell that "Casterly Rock isn't worth much anymore." David Benioff and D. B. Weiss, "The Queen's Justice," season 7, episode 3, dir. Mark Mylod, *Game of Thrones*, aired July 30, 2017, on HBO.

9. For the discussion between Robb Stark and Edmure Tully, see David Benioff and D. B. Weiss, "Walk of Punishment," season 3, episode 3, dir. David Benioff, *Game of Thrones*, aired April 14, 2013, on HBO.

10. The linguistic aftereffects of Hastings and the Norman rule of England are evident today in the culinary world. Livestock is so named after the English words: chicken, cow, pig, lamb. However, the food products from those animals take on their French origins: poultry (*poulet* is "chicken" in French), veal (*veau* is French for "calf"), pork (*porc* is "pig" in French), and mutton (*mouton* is French for "sheep"). The English took care of the animals, while their Norman lords enjoyed the culinary by-products of said animals.

11. This battle served as the centerpiece of George R. R. Martin, "Blackwater," season 2, episode 9, dir. Neil Marshall, *Game of Thrones*, aired May 27, 2012, on HBO.

12. This battle is the focus of David Benioff and D. B. Weiss, "Battle of the Bastards," season 6, episode 9, dir. Miguel Sapochnik, *Game of Thrones*, aired June 19, 2016, on HBO.

13. This speech can be found in George R. R. Martin, *A Feast for Crows* (New York: Bantam, 2005), 533. "They've heard the songs and stories, so they go off with eager hearts, dreaming of the wonders they will see, of the wealth and glory they will win. War seems a fine adventure, the greatest most of them will ever know. Then they get a taste of battle. For some, that one taste is enough to break them. Others go on for years, until they lose count of all the battles they have fought in, but even a man who has survived a hundred fights can break in his hundred-and-first. Brothers watch their brothers die, fathers lose their sons, friends see their friends trying to hold their entrails in after they've been gutted by an axe. They see the lord who led them there cut down, and some other lord shouts that they are his now. They take a wound, and when that's still half-healed they take another. There is never enough to eat, their shoes fall to pieces from the marching, their clothes are torn and rotting, and half of them are shitting in their breeches from drinking bad water. If they want new boots or a warmer cloak or maybe a rusted iron halfhelm, they need to take them from a corpse, and before long they are stealing from the living too, from the smallfolk whose lands they're fighting in, men very like the men they used to be. They slaughter their sheep and steal their chickens, and from there it's just a short step to carrying off their daughters too. And one day they look around and realize all their friends and kin are gone, that they are fighting beside strangers beneath a banner that they hardly recognize. They don't know where they are or how to get back home and the lord they're fighting for does not know their names."

14. I am purposely avoiding use of the term "citizen-soldier," because that term implies a lack of professionalism either in leadership or in soldiers. What is critical is that whether professional or amateur, soldiers bear a responsibility to the welfare of their regime.

15. David Benioff and D. B. Weiss, "Hardhome," season 5, episode 8, dir. Miguel Sapochnik, *Game of Thrones*, aired May 31, 2015, on HBO.

24

Strategic Storytelling in *Game of Thrones*

JAYM GATES

"I want YOU for U.S. Army / Enlist now!" the iconic poster declares, and just over one hundred years later, we still feel that atavistic pull, a straightening of spine, a surge of patriotic pride under those hawkish eyes and that bony finger. It's a visual we all know, one spread throughout media, history, and culture. It's propaganda. It's narrative. Sparse, lean, punched with color and a sharp message, it spares no frivolity in spreading its message.

The 1940s saw the rise of powerful propaganda in the United States. In 1941 Frank Capra began making films for the war effort. He was up against a masterpiece of the genre, Leni Riefenstahl's *Triumph of the Will*. "It scared the hell out of me," he said later, regarding the film. "It fired no gun ... but as a psychological weapon aimed at destroying the will to resist, it was just as lethal."[1]

Propaganda is a common concept, a powerful political tool in civilian and military spaces alike. But it is the result of a strategy, one that makes use of the human predilection for story, a framework to fit complex and often alienating ideas into a cohesive form, the power of narrative. If you Google the phrase "the power of narrative," thousands of results turn up, from courses offered by Harvard Business School to the use of antibiotics. Humankind has always used stories to relate to the world and to better understand it. It is, perhaps, no surprise that it is such a powerful tool for strategic use as well, as it is a form understood by every culture across history.[2]

What, then, is the difference between narrative, narrative strategy, and propaganda? Put simply, narrative is the big story. Narrative strategy is how that story may best be implemented for use. Propaganda is the specific communication and interpretation of that strategy.

According to the *Harvard Business Review*, "A strategic narrative is a special kind of story. It says who you are as a company. Where you've been, where you are, and where you are going. How you believe value is created and what you value in relationships. It explains why you exist and what makes you unique."[3] It goes on to discuss the importance of personalized interaction, a cohesive interpretation of the company's role and goals, and consistency.

Narrative is one of the oldest, and strongest, human strategies. The Egyptians spent incredible wealth on their narrative, building their greatness over generations.[4] The fear of Sparta was as potent a weapon as their swords, a mythology that has lasted to this day, despite the nation's size and short-lived supremacy. The Romans used narrative to bolster their expansions, and the story of the Huns spread terror farther than they ever rode, softening the enemy and changing military strategy even in their absence.[5]

Narrative strategy has many applications. It can be invisible, sowing fear and chaos within the enemy. It can give courage to an army or incite a rebellion. It can swing politics, culture, and academia. It creates a plot that can be followed even in times of high stress. Similar to physical training, it calls to the basic narratives that might as well be encoded in our DNA: honor, dignity, courage, responsibility, sacrifice, justice. If you look at stories like *Star Wars*, *Lord of the Rings*, *Captain America*, or *Game of Thrones*, they aren't new plots; they are stories told on an existing framework that has been reskinned over thousands of years. We've used those stories to illustrate important points of civil discourse, military strategy, government, morality, and the understanding of law.

It is easy, though, to look at something like *Game of Thrones* and ask how dragons, incest, and eunuchs can teach us anything about strategy. Based on the War of the Roses, *Game of Thrones* is a brilliant study of communication, loyalty, and propaganda in fictionalized form. We see conflicted loyalties, shifting moralities, dynamic battlefields, evolving technology (dragons are not so different from our own missiles, as another piece in this collection demonstrates), and narrative influence. Specifically, this piece illustrates how we see in *Game of Thrones* the power of myth and evolving narrative, particularly in the person of Daenerys Targaryen, a very young woman who finds herself mythologized to her known world and also thrust into the role of saving that world. Compared to all of that, being mother to a few dragons probably seemed simple.

Her saving grace was her status as a mythological being born of flame, the Mother of Dragons, liberator of slaves, defender of the people. It was a built-in narrative just waiting for proper usage, and she was the woman for the job.

Daenerys is one of the most adept users of narrative in *Game of Thrones*. From her early interactions with the Dothraki to the hatching of the dragons and, finally, to her great entrance to the meeting in season 7, she understands the power of visual propaganda. No matter how powerful you are, a woman on a fire-breathing, flying monster is going to at least make you pause so that she can get a word in edgewise.

Her development and deployment of the Unsullied is yet another brilliant use of narrative. She has rescued these hopeless slaves and given them a purpose. She is their mother, their hero, their guiding star.[6] If this sounds familiar, it is not unlike the mother and bride symbolism in classic Russian mythology, as well as more modern Communist symbolism.[7] They are fanatically loyal to her, and their faith in the narrative is what makes them powerful.

Looking back at modern military strategy, there are plenty of overlaps. The military of the United States is an army of choice. Soldiers are no longer drafted; they choose to join, often after years of knowing what path they wanted to take. Military lineages run in families, communities, and across cultural divides. Why? Because recruiters tell a story of heroism just around the corner. Grandpa tells a story of brotherhood and the bonds of war. The media tells a story of adventure and glory.

A narrative that can reach across cultural, lingual, generational, and geographic distances must be iconic, clear, and coherent. The tricky part is that the narrative needs to serve multiple purposes, including the offensive purpose of pressuring the enemy.

The American Historical Association sums it up clearly: "Today's war is four-dimensional. It is a combination of military, economic, political, and propaganda pressure against the enemy. An appeal to force alone is not regarded as enough, in the twentieth century, to win final and lasting victory. War is fought on all four fronts at once—the military front, the economic front, the political front, and the propaganda front."[8]

In a global battlefield, propaganda must be instantly understood by those who do not speak your language or share your cultural viewpoint, and so the development of a simple, iconic language becomes necessary. Most of us understand the visuals of Soviet iconography and the distinct style of Russian propaganda and can identify it as such. U.S. propaganda is no less distinctive but less foreign to the American mind, clearly—much of it carried through to World War II and Vietnam and has become a central component of our visual cultural identity. With the rise of social media and meme culture, military visual communication is more widespread and related to than ever, for better or for worse.

That saturation of narrative isn't confined to visuals. Movies, music, video games, science fiction, thrillers, TV, even clothing, the American obsession with all things military is filling the pockets of corporations and creators everywhere. After Iraq and the intensely nationalistic movement following 9/11, there is an almost mythical narrative surrounding soldiers and the military. The narrative of valor, honor, and duty has borne fruit across many levels of society. More than ever, we have a clear example of the evolution of a society that has been steeped in a narrative strategy over an extended period of time.

But the military is a little unique, because it's not a company or brand. It's a juggernaut on the American landscape, and its story is one that has been *lived* by millions in a way that no other story can be. That lived, shared experience gives it a cultural power that is unmatched on American soil by any other narrative. It's binding, a connection that weaves hundreds of thousands of disparate minds into a deadly force, one that feeds the narrative and is, in turn, fed *on* it.

But as mentioned earlier, it is all too easy for such a powerful tool to be used to destroy the cohesion and strength of its users. Miscommunication, misunderstanding, and lack of context can be deadly. For example, Greg Miller and Scott Higham described how some have "bridled at what they considered the unseemly spectacle of a U.S. government entity behaving like a social-media punk." They recorded counterterrorism consultant and former CIA case officer Patrick M. Skinner as saying, "They're trying to reach these kids, but it's backfiring. . . . It's like the grandparents yelling to the children, 'Get off my lawn.'"[9]

As our society becomes more digitized, we face a problem with more miscommunication through lack of context. Email, social media, and even visual and vocal communication programs do not give the nuance and connection of a face-to-face meeting. We are seeing a staggering rise in interpersonal conflicts across the internet, between religious and social groups, and within professional groups. It is far too easy to fire off a quick email, an angry tweet, or other communication that lacks nuance and forgets the audience that will be viewing it and the permanence of the form.

In *Game of Thrones* the endless miscommunications and conflicting narratives come to a head when Daenerys calls the houses together. You finally start seeing what they believe, what they have in conflict with each other, what they have in common with each other, and the misunderstandings. But for the first time, they see it too. It still isn't enough. It's been too long with the miscommunications of the past, with too many hereditary and cultural differences, and the communication breaks down quickly.

That narrative takes a sharp turn when one of the wights is released from its cage. Suddenly, there's no more misunderstanding; there's no "Maybe this is an intrigue," "Maybe this is another lie told by the Lannisters," "Maybe this is another lie told by the Targaryens." Suddenly, it's hard, cold reality.

The dragons and wights in *Game of Thrones* can easily map to superior air power and terrorist insurgents. Dragons present a foe that cannot really be planned for or defended against. Bringing one down will come at terrible cost, and the enemy not only has more where that came from but is likely to be *really unhappy about the loss*, which traditionally ends poorly for those who brought down the powerful weapon. But the dragons don't actually need to be present to destabilize and spread fear. The mere fact that they could show up is enough to leech courage from even a stouthearted force—again, story wielded as weapon.

The wights are a more complex example. Relentless, faceless, unstoppable, they are not unlike the shifting dangers our soldiers face as terrorism becomes less conveniently *other* and erupts more frequently at home. They are people we know, but they are unknown to us now.

The wights are also a convenient Other in another way. The most common tactic of military narrative is to paint the enemy as an alien force. The Japanese and Nazis were caricatures and jokes, the Romans fought tribes rumored to practice the blackest arts, science fiction portrays relentless waves of bug-like aliens. They speak a different language and call their god by another name, and to fight them effectively, the other side must believe that they are monstrous and heartless.

A common villain in a story where no one is really a hero, the wights make a convenient enemy to draw the houses together. But the fear and mysticism surrounding them prevents the living soldiers from understanding how to fight, and it is only when Daenerys and her allies bring fire that a new narrative is born.

It is a narrative we would be wise to heed. The battlefield is changing. The enemy is not what it once was. Technology is advancing faster than we can comprehend, climate change is stressing the human race at an unprecedented level, and Americans are being radicalized at a growing rate. Our dragons may be powerful, but as Daenerys learned, the enemy can get dragons too.

With the rise of globalization, the spread of "fake news," the power of social media, and the rise of new powers, war is no longer just armies clashing on a distant battlefield or terrorist attacks or even house-to-house guerrilla fighting. War is around us every day, from the memes we spread to the way we vote. We have more ability than ever to understand the powerful currents that move armies, but if we do not learn how those currents move, war will become part of our lives in a much less abstract way. As British general Gerald Templer said in February 1952, victory in war "lies not in pouring more soldiers into the jungle, but in the hearts and minds of the people."

In an era of cyberattacks, climate shifts, pandemics, homegrown terrorism, rapid technological advancement, cultural upheaval, war between nationalism and globalism, and strained resources, understanding the narrative strategies around us gives us a clearer understanding of what the world has become and will help us to forge a new strategy to face the future.

NOTES

1. Steve Rose, "The ISIS Propaganda War: A Hi-Tech Media Jihad," *Guardian*, October 7, 2014, https://www.theguardian.com/world/2014/oct/07/isis-media-machine-propaganda-war.

2. Aminatta Forna, "Selective Empathy: Stories and the Power of Narrative," *World Literature Today*, November 2017, https://www.worldliteraturetoday.org/2017/november/selective -empathy-stories-and-power-narrative-aminatta-forna.

3. Mark Bonchek, "How to Build a Strategic Narrative," *Harvard Business Review*, March 25, 2016, https://hbr.org/2016/03/how-to-build-a-strategic-narrative.

4. William Kelly Simpson, "Egyptian Sculpture and Two-Dimensional Representation as Propaganda," *Journal of Egyptian Archaeology* 68 (1982). "Messages emanating from the royal palace were intended to communicate well-defined statements about royal power and allegiance to the crown, while those from private individuals were meant to demonstrate high social status"; Ronald J. Leprohon, "Ideology and Propaganda," in *A Companion to Ancient Egyptian Art*, ed. Melinda K. Hartwig (Hoboken NJ: Wiley Blackwell, 2015), 309.

5. Nic Fields, *The Hun, Scourge of God AD 375–565* (Oxford, UK: Osprey Press, 2006).

6. Annie Shapiro, "Connections: Mother Symbolism in Russian Culture," in *The Motherland Calls*, accessed November 3, 2018, http://omeka.macalester.edu/courses/russ151/exhibits /show/love-thy-mother--symbolic-moth/connection.

7. Joanna Hubbs, *Mother Russia: The Feminine Myth in Russian Culture* (Bloomington: Indiana University Press, 1993), 302; Ellen Rutten, *Unattainable Bride Russia: Gendering Nation, State, and Intelligentsia in Russian Intellectual Culture* (Evanston IL: Northwestern University Press, 2010).

8. Ralph D. Casey, "War Propaganda," in *What Is Propaganda*, educational manual (EM-)2 (Arlington VA: War Department, 1944), available online at American Historical Society, accessed November 3, 2018, https://www.historians.org/about-aha-and-membership/aha -history-and-archives/gi-roundtable-series/pamphlets/em-2-what-is-propaganda-(1944) /war-propaganda.

9. Greg Miller and Scott Higham, "In a Propaganda War, the U.S. Tried to Play by the Enemy's Rules," *Washington Post*, May 8, 2015, https://www.washingtonpost.com/world/national -security/in-a-propaganda-war-us-tried-to-play-by-the-enemys-rules/2015/05/08/6eb6b732 -e52f-11e4-81ea-0649268f729e_story.html?utm_term=.0b7676453665.

25

Resources, War, and the Night King's Deadly Arithmetic

ANDREW A. HILL

"Strike hard who cares—shoot straight who can / The odds are on the cheaper man."[1]

Thus runs a verse of Rudyard Kipling's "Arithmetic on the Frontier," a poem that beautifully and starkly conveys an enduring characteristic of war—namely, that the ability to create military forces more rapidly and cheaply than one's adversaries is itself a powerful strategic advantage. Kipling's poem brutally concludes,

> With home-bred hordes the hillsides teem.
> The troopships bring us one by one,
> At vast expense of time and steam,
> To slay Afridis where they run.
> The "captives of our bow and spear"
> Are cheap, alas! as we are dear.

In this stanza, Kipling brilliantly captures the huge disadvantage in military force generation of the British, relative to their local opposition—in this case, Afridis of the Pashtun, but it could just as easily be the Taliban,

ISIS, Boko Haram, or even Chinese antiship missiles. Precious British troops arrive "one by one" and at "vast expense," while the Afridis literally sprout from the hills, endlessly supplying a resistance that can afford to lose men.

The painful consequences of a disadvantage in military force production is vividly illustrated in *Game of Thrones*, which features the "home-bred horde" to beat all hordes: the White Walkers' Army of the Dead (or wights), reanimated corpses under the command of the Night King, a spectral, blue-hued demon who was once a man. One of the series's most memorable scenes clearly demonstrates the cheapness of the wights. Near the conclusion of season 5, Jon Snow travels north of the Wall to visit Hardhome, the haven of the Free Folk, who have long been enemies of the Night's Watch, which Snow commands.[2] Seeking to form an alliance with the Free Folk and bring them to the safer side of the Wall in preparation for the zombie war Snow knows is coming, Snow convinces a minority of the Free Folk to trust him and follow him on the ships he brought. While the refugees are boarding the boats that will take them south, the Night King attacks Hardhome with a massive horde of wights. Hardhome's defenses are quickly overwhelmed. Only those already in the boats escape slaughter at the hands (or teeth) of the wights. Standing in the last boat to depart, Snow watches as the wights kill everyone left behind. Then the Night King emerges, striding through the mayhem and walking to the dock. Looking at Snow, the Night King raises his arms. Snow watches in appalled horror as thousands of dead Free Folk begin to jerk to life, rising from the earth as new members of the Night King's awful army.

Jon Snow understands the significance of the Night King's demonstration of the power to mobilize a population simply by willing it. Snow commands the Night's Watch, a professional military force. In fighting, an individual, ordinary wight does not rival a good ranger of the Night's Watch. But that sort of misses the point. Rangers are recruited—either by force or by choice—"one by one," to echo Kipling's phrase, from the various cities of Westeros, and their effectiveness is the result of years of discipline, training, and fighting. The Night King can create a wight in seconds. All he needs is the will to do it and a dead body. He has an abundance of the former, and the war against humanity will provide plenty of the latter. Collectively, the wights' sheer numbers and their mindless commitment to fight and kill pose a terrible threat to even the best-trained military force, and the Night King can produce them by the thousands simply by wishing it. Not only that, but every dead enemy of the Night King (even a dragon) is a potential recruit to his Army of the Dead. The "cheaper man" indeed.

Of course, zombie hordes are a fiction, as is all of *Game of Thrones*. It is, as yet, impossible to reanimate the dead and transform them into single-minded killing machines utterly obedient to the whims of some blue monster with a vendetta against humanity. Yet the mobilizing power of the Night King underscores an important aspect of strategy in war that has become all too obscure in American military thought—the ability of a society to produce military forces cheaper and faster than its adversaries. This is a pity, because in many respects the quick production of military force (usually infantry of some kind) is the oldest, simplest, and most reliable of all military strategies—"Git thar fustest with the mostest," in Nathan Bedford Forrest's (almost certainly apocryphal) words.

This problem is not new. For the military theorist Antoine-Henry Jomini, force generation was a minor detail of strategy. He wrote, "Strategy decides where to act; logistics brings troops to this point."[3] John Shy commented that for Jomini, armies appeared as "faceless masses, armed and fed in mysterious ways."[4] The historian Michael Howard lamented the effect of Clausewitz in leading military strategic thinkers to ignore logistical considerations.[5] Strategy, he argued, has operational, logistical, social, and technological dimensions.[6] Modern military strategic thought has tended to emphasize the first and last of these, with little attention to the middle two. Yet as Howard wrote, "No campaign can be understood, and no valid conclusions drawn from it, unless its logistical problems are studied as thoroughly as the course of operations."[7]

The Roman and Mongol Empires were largely built through innovations in force development, and the United States developed and exploited an advantage in force generation to its benefit in the three crucial wars of American history. Indeed, concerning the victory of the U.S. Civil War, for example, Michael Howard observed, "Fundamentally, the victory of the North was due not to the operational capabilities of its generals, but to its capacity to mobilize its superior industrial strength and manpower into armies which such leaders as Grant were able . . . to deploy in such strength as the operational skills of their adversaries were rendered almost irrelevant."[8] Put differently, in Clausewitz's arbitrarily precise formulation, "The skill of the greatest commanders may be counterbalanced by a two-to-one ratio in fighting forces."[9] This is a key point. The generation of force is not just a support to strategy; it *is* strategy. And we in the developed world ought to give it more thought.

Rome's rise was aided by the ability to produce military forces faster than they were consumed. Rome defeated Carthage in the First Punic War in large part because it could build and rebuild a navy. In the first five years of the war, Rome painstakingly learning how to build warships and conduct naval warfare against the much more experienced Carthaginians. Then, Rome lost three-quarters of its fleet—over 280 ships—in a storm in 255 BCE. Rebuilding its fleet, Rome suffered a similar disaster two years later.[10] Rebuilding its fleet yet again, in 249 BCE Rome suffered a significant naval defeat, shortly followed by the loss of over one hundred ships in another storm.[11]

More than a century later, the Roman consul Gaius Marius changed the course of Roman history by introducing what came to be known as the Marian military reforms. Prior to his innovations, in times of war, Roman citizens joining the army had to equip themselves at great expense. Furthermore, the majority of the Roman public was restricted to serving as unarmored skirmishers. Marius changed this, supplying conscripts with weapons and armor provided through the state. He also reorganized the legions to standardize and professionalize them. Although Marius turned service in the Roman legions into a career (as opposed to a wartime calling), he drastically lowered the barriers to entry into the military, "throwing open the legions to proletarians on terms of voluntary enlistment," in the words of historians M. Cary and H. H. Scullard.[12] With the system of force production designed by Marius, Rome conquered the Mediterranean world.

The Mongol example is even more instructive, for the Mongols came closer than any people in recorded history of mimicking the Night King's power of the spontaneous generation of military forces. If you imagine a Venn diagram in which two circles represent "qualities of an ordinary, adult male" and "qualities of a warrior," in Mongol society these circles overlapped almost completely. Other people have attempted to build effective military forces through the normal activities of citizens, from the longbowmen trained in the forests and marshes of Britain to the "embattled farmers," in the words of Ralph Waldo Emerson's "Concord Hymn" inscribed on the base of the Minute Man Statue at the site of the Battle of Concord.[13]

Yet the Mongols seem to have exceeded all in matching civilian life to the development of military capability. Mongols began training for military service early in life, and many of the skills they acquired in learning to be effective hunters on the Asian steppe were equally useful in preparing for war. As the historian Denis Sinor writes, "For the men of Inner Asia military service was a natural occupation. . . . Fighting was a precondition of survival."[14] Sinor continues, "The combination of inborn courage and discipline acquired through constant training accounts for the excellence of the Inner Asian warrior."[15]

The crucial war machine of the Mongols was the horse, which was also fully integrated into Mongol life and "the most formidable single factor of Inner Asian military power."[16] Sinor quotes the poet Sidonius Apollinaris, speaking of the Huns but equally applicable to the Mongols: "Scarce has the infant learned to stand without his mother's aid when a horse takes him on his back. You would think the man and beast were borne together, so firmly does the rider always stick to the horse."[17]

In the middle of the thirteenth century, the Franciscan John of Plano Carpini went on a mission to visit the Great Khan of the Mongols. John observed that Mongol men "hunt and practice archery, for they are all, big and little, excellent archers, and their children begin as soon as they are two or three years old to ride and manage horses and to gallop on them, and they are given bows to suit their stature and are taught to shoot."[18] Thus, Mongol man and Mongol warrior were almost synonymous, enabling the Mongols to generate military forces extremely rapidly. Furthermore, sustaining these forces required little of the mass of impedimenta that characterizes most other armies. Mongol warriors were astonishingly self-sustaining while on military campaign, living on a diet of dried meat and mare's milk.[19] The Mongols of the thirteenth century are the White Walkers of authentic history, for whom readiness for war and readiness for life were the same.

Building forces through rapid military expansion makes sense for the United States, a technologically advanced nation with tremendous natural, scientific, and industrial resources and geographic depth provided by two oceans and two friendly neighbors. Furthermore, with a population exceeding 300 million, few nations have a deeper reservoir of manpower. Given sufficient time, the United States can produce a military of immense size and capability.

Today, however, by both desire and design, the U.S. military generally focuses on maintaining a relatively small but highly effective force and ignores the significance and potential of rapid force generation. General Raymond Odierno, the former chief of staff of the U.S. Army, said in congressional testimony, "It takes approximately 30 months to generate a fully manned and trained Regular Army [Brigade Combat Team] once the Army decides to expand the force."[20] Thus, the modern U.S. Army needs two and a half *years* to create (in the case of an infantry brigade combat team) three infantry battalions and their support elements—about four thousand soldiers total. Why does it take so long? General Odierno cited the complex requirements of "policy decisions, dollars, Soldiers, infrastructure," and the nature of "today's highly technological, All-Volunteer Force" that is "much different than the industrial age armies of the past."[21]

In a nutshell, the U.S. Army's argument is that war is much more complex today, that it requires much more technological expertise, and that building this expertise requires a lot of time. This is highly suspect as both history and analysis. It oversimplifies the past and ignores an important characteristic of modern technology. Consider for a moment the thirty months the U.S. Army currently requires to build a brigade combat team. The United States was attacked at Pearl Harbor on December 7, 1941, drawing it into the Second

World War. Almost thirty months *to the day* later, on June 6, 1944, the U.S. Army and Navy led the largest amphibious invasion in history, employing almost seven thousand ships to land around 156,000 allied troops on the first day alone. One would have to be a tremendous egotist to think that such an operation was not extraordinarily complex and technological in the mere conception. Yet we are to believe that the U.S. Army today needs the same amount of time to create an infantry unit of four thousand soldiers.

Granted, from a global economic perspective, modern military service is fairly unique. Few occupational fields *outside* the military develop the human capital necessary to thrive in a combat environment. Militaries use unique technologies, and the work environment for combat units, with its requirements for physically courageous high-risk decision-making, high levels of mutual trust, willingness to sacrifice, deference to orders, and extremes of endurance in depraved conditions, is even more exceptional than the technology used in that environment. The U.S. Army, therefore, invests heavily in developing the ability of personnel to function in an environment that cannot be replicated outside the military. How can the U.S. Army reduce the required investment without lowering standards?

We can use technology to enhance the capabilities of the average person. This consists of investing in technologies that reduce the time it takes for new entrants to reach an effective level of military preparedness. Military modernization can be used to explain why creating civilian-soldiers is much harder than it used to be. A Sherman tank from the Second World War had more in common with heavy vehicles in the civilian world than an M1 Abrams tank does today. Fair enough. Yet other military technologies reduce the difficulty for an inexperienced, semi-intelligent trainee to achieve higher levels of competence. A well-designed rifle is just such a technology.

Game of Thrones also demonstrates another facet of the power of rapid force generation—winning the allegiance of opposing or neutral forces. The Night King's most capable opponent, Queen Daenerys Targaryen, conquers the cities of Slaver's Bay and builds the foundation of her invading army not through the power of her dragons but by converting the forces of her adversaries, be they the erstwhile masters of Slaver's Bay or the chiefs of Dothraki (George R. R. Martin's version of the Mongols). In fact, the *real* Mongols were similarly masters of transforming opposing forces into useful units under Mongol command. According to Jack Weatherford, the Mongols turned captive peasants into "an extension of their decimal organization of the military."[22] Captives performed menial but labor-intensive tasks such as getting food and water for the animals and soldiers and moving and operating siege engines. The Mongols also acquired highly capable engineering units by bringing defeated enemies under their banner. Weatherford explains, "More than merely using [siege] weapons, Genghis Khan acquired the engineering intelligence needed to create them. The Mongols eagerly rewarded engineers who defected to them and, after each battle, carefully selected engineers from among the captives and impressed them into Mongol service. . . . With each new battle and each conquest, [Genghis Khan's] war machinery grew in complexity and efficiency."[23]

The two greatest armies in George R. R. Martin's fantasy world are built by experts in force generation. The modern U.S. military should take a cue from this and focus on innovative approaches to building military forces.

The development of technologies that rapidly increase the lethality and military decision-making ability of relatively fit, intelligent Americans should be a major theme for U.S. Army modernization in the coming years. But it probably will be ignored, because modern, professional militaries want to preserve military competence as a special category of training and conduct. The more military effectiveness seems like the product of years of investment, the less likely the nation is to reduce standing military resources. The U.S. Army's lack of imagination in force generation is therefore predictable and lamentable.

Alas, the subtleties of government resource allocation give an army in peacetime little incentive to become good at building forces rapidly. Standing military forces are expensive, and unused military capacity is highly inefficient. Civilian leaders will therefore tend to demand constant justification for peacetime military forces. A military that is capable of swift expansion will tempt civilian leaders to give it fewer resources when it is not needed. Given these dynamics, it is hardly surprising that the U.S. Army is so lacking in creativity and innovation when it comes to expansion.

However, an explanation is not an excuse, and we need to do better. In a military expansion, the army is engaged in the production of soldiers. The raw material in this production process is the pool of manpower. The army takes human capital from this pool and invests time and energy into developing it into something fit for service in an operational unit. For the Mongols, the investment required was relatively modest. The modern U.S. Army, in contrast, sees the investment required as vast. Another writer on this topic asserts that all of that time is "essential for [soldiers] to develop reasonable expertise in increasingly difficult military skill sets" and that it is "required to develop even a modicum of expertise on the complex battlefield systems and network modalities of the 21st century."[24]

This emphasis on technology as a barrier to the rapid creation of military force ignores a crucial point—the pattern of technological innovation globally is to *reduce* barriers to entry for normal people to do sophisticated things that used to be the domain of professionals and experts. Software allows business owners to manage financial accounting without the aid of an accountant. We have technology today that can help an untutored person make smart tactical choices on a complex battlefield. On a more mundane level, modern military rifles can turn a slightly overweight, middle-aged, nonlethal academic into a much more lethal version of himself.[25]

The ability to build military forces quickly also makes other things in war less important. The Night King does not need to be a tactical genius to win a battle. In the same way, the United States did not rely on tactical brilliance or individual (i.e., platform-to-platform or soldier-to-soldier) superiority for its victories in the Civil War and World War II. In Greek mythology, Cadmus, the founder of Thebes, slays a dragon and then, following Athena's instructions, sows the dragon's teeth in the ground. To his astonishment, warriors began to grow from the teeth, rising out of the ground like so many stalks of corn.[26] In the Second World War, the United States reaped its own astonishing harvest from dragon's teeth. The military's total strength grew from 458,365 (all services) in 1940 to over 12 million in 1945, a twenty-six-fold increase.[27]

Conflict may not be the natural state of humanity, but it is a common occurrence and one that often surprises us, defying the expectations of even the most forward looking of military thinkers. An old adage asserts that "quantity has a quality all its own." It provides resilience against the shocks that are an inevitable part of war. A society with the power to create military forces faster and more cheaply than its adversaries has a significant advantage in war.

Which brings us back to the where we began. White Walkers (or Mongol warriors or ISIS fighters) are produced cheaply and quickly, while the Night's Watch (or the U.S. military) carries on building its forces, echoing Kipling, "one by one" and "at vast expense." We should be careful about that, because the "odds are on the cheaper man."

The U.S. military has lost one of its core strategic competencies—rapidly generating enormous numbers of soldiers, sailors, marines, and pilots through mobilization on a grand scale. This is not an argument for a peacetime draft. It is a call for innovation in how a nation builds military forces when those forces are needed. Unfortunately, instead of exploring how to prepare people and build equipment more rapidly in war, modern U.S. military leaders persist in a dubious, self-serving argument for maintaining the gold-plated military that the nation seems to need at all times, regardless of circumstances. This needs to change.

NOTES

1. Rudyard Kipling, "Arithmetic on the Frontier," in *Departmental Ditties and Other Verses* (London: Methuen, 1922), 95.

2. David Benioff and D. B. Weiss, "Hardhome," season 5, episode 8, dir. Miguel Sapochnik, *Game of Thrones*, aired May 31, 2015, on HBO.

3. Baron de Jomini, *The Art of War*, trans. G. H. Mendell and W. P. Craighill (Philadelphia PA: Lippincott, 1862), 69.

4. John Shy, "Jomini," in *Makers of Modern Strategy*, ed. Pater Paret (Princeton NJ: Princeton University Press, 1986), 160.

5. Michael Howard, "The Forgotten Dimensions of Strategy," *Foreign Affairs* 57, no. 5 (1979): 976.

6. Howard, "Forgotten Dimensions of Strategy," 978.

7. Howard, "Forgotten Dimensions of Strategy," 976.

8. Howard, "Forgotten Dimensions of Strategy," 977.

9. Carl von Clausewitz, *On War*, trans. Michael Howard and Peter Paret (Princeton NJ: Princeton University Press, 1976), 195, quoted in Lawrence Freedman, *Strategy: A History* (Oxford: Oxford University Press, 2013), 89.

10. Richard Miles, *Carthage Must Be Destroyed: The Rise and Fall of an Ancient Civilization* (New York: Viking, 2010), 189.

11. Miles, *Carthage Must Be Destroyed*, 192.

12. M. Cary and H. H. Scullard, *A History of Rome Down to the Reign of Constantine*, 3rd ed. (London: Palgrave, 1975), 219.

13. Clifford J. Rogers, "The Military Revolutions of the Hundred Years' War," *Journal of Military History* 57, no. 2 (1993): 241–78. According to Rogers, "England developed a pool of strong yeomen archers over decades of more-or-less constant warfare against the Scots and the Welsh—it is no coincidence that Cheshire archers, considered the best in England, came from the Welsh marches."

14. Denis Sinor, "The Inner Asian Warriors," *Journal of the American Oriental Society* 101, no. 2 (1981): 135.

15. Sinor, "Inner Asian Warriors," 137.

16. Sinor, "Inner Asian Warriors," 137.

17. Sinor, "Inner Asian Warriors," 139.

18. John of Plano Carpini, *The Mongol Mission*, ed. Christopher Dawson (London: Sheed and Ward, 1955), 18.

19. Jack Weatherford, *Genghis Khan and the Making of the Modern World* (New York: Crown, 2004), 86–88.

20. General Raymond Odierno, "Department of Defense Appropriations for Fiscal Year 2016," *U.S. Senate, Subcommittee of the Committee on Appropriations* (Washington DC: U.S. Government Publishing Office, March 11, 2015), 9.

21. Odierno, "Fiscal Year 2016," 9.

22. Weatherford, *Genghis Khan and the Making of the Modern World*, 92.

23. Weatherford, *Genghis Khan and the Making of the Modern World*, 94.

24. John Evans, *Getting It Right: Determining the Optimal Active Component End Strength of the All-Volunteer Army to Meet the Demands of the 21st Century* (Washington DC: Center for 21st Century Security and Intelligence, Brookings Institution, 2015), 21.

25. The author of this essay once had the opportunity to shoot a modified variant of the U.S. Marine Corps' M40 sniper rifle. With no instruction or practice, I bull's-eyed a target two inches wide at one hundred yards. After achieving this feat, I remarked (only half in jest), "Even a monkey could do that," and monkeys are cheap.

26. See Ovid, *Metamorphoses*, bk. 3.

27. Data from "Research Starters: US Military by the Numbers," National World War II Museum, accessed February 27, 2019, https://www.nationalww2museum.org/students-teachers/student-resources/research-starters/research-starters-us-military-numbers.

26

The Red Wedding and the Power of Norms

THERESA HITCHENS

Even for nonaficionados, the Red Wedding episode in book 3, *A Storm of Swords*, in George R. R. Martin's *Song of Fire and Ice* saga, and episode 9, "The Rains of Castelmere," in season 3 of the televised *Game of Thrones*, has become a notorious example of deadly political and military deception. The events that flow from that horrific, and extremely bloody, betrayal also elucidate how violations of norms can exact economic, political, and strategic costs.

The Red Wedding episode begins with Robb Stark, heir of House Stark and Winterfell and self-proclaimed King in the North, entering into a marriage pact with one of Lord Walder Frey's daughters in exchange for the allegiance of House Frey against the Iron Throne held by House Lannister in the War of the Five Kings. But Robb subsequently falls in love with another girl and reneges on that promise. In revenge for the marriage pact's breach, Lord Walder implements a plot (backed up by Lord Tywin Lannister and Lord Roose Bolton) to assassinate Robb. He invites Robb; Robb's mother, Catelyn; and Robb's loyal men-at-arms to the wedding of Robb's uncle Edmure Tully to Roslin Frey as a gesture of reconciliation. As the wedding feast winds down, Frey unleashes his own forces, who slaughter Robb, Catelyn, and most of the visiting Winterfell party.

The Red Wedding is an example of a violation of a societal "norm of behavior" writ large—in this case, the norm of hospitality that sets boundaries on the behavior of hosts and guests. Norms of behavior—both actions that are prescribed and those that are proscribed—not only are the underpinnings of civilizations dating back as far as known history but also serve as an important foundation for international relations and the development of international law in today's world. Norms not only can be implemented via "customary international law" or "soft law," but they can also be eventually translated into legally binding accords via international law and bilateral or multilateral treaties.[1]

The concept that hosts owe guests certain rights (and vice versa), including a guarantee of safety, dates back at least to the ancient Greeks, where the rules were known as *xenia* (guest-friendship) and were protected by the father of the gods himself, Zeus. Indeed, the Trojan War was a direct result of a violation of *xenia* by the Trojan prince, Paris, in abducting Menelaus's wife, thus ensuring Zeus's wrath and his championship of the Greek side.[2] In the pre-Viking Anglo-Saxon world, the rules of hospitality were widespread in custom at all levels of society, and in some cases, they were written into local laws,[3] showing how customs can be, and often are, eventually translated into legal instruments (although it should be said that "laws" in the fifth and sixth centuries were rather more fluid than today's Western concept of "legal" instruments). George R. R. Martin has noted that the Red Wedding concept was based on history, including the infamous 1692 Glencoe Massacre in Scotland—where Clan MacDonald was slaughtered by an army of Clan Campbell after the Campbell Captain asked for shelter from the winter weather on the pretense that the nearby fort was full.[4] The massacre was a violation of King James VI's 1587 edict, "Slaughter under Trust,"[5] designed to reduce wars among the Scottish clans by punishing those who tricked their clan enemies into a massacre by offering peaceful terms, and to this day the Claichag Inn in Glencoe sports a sign above the door denying entry to members of Clan Campbell.

While the concept of host-guest rights has lost much of its meaning in the modern Western world, the long-standing normative prohibitions against deception as a means of military strategy for killing or capturing enemies remain in place today—both via customary international law and via treaties. In particular, the Geneva Conventions define this sort of deception as "perfidy." Perfidy is defined in Additional Protocol I, Article 37(1) and Article 85(3)(f) as an act where one gains the enemy's confidence by promising protection under the laws of war, for the purposes of intending to kill, wound, or capture them.[6] In the Rome Statute of the International Criminal Court, perfidy is also a crime, though it is not as precisely formulated as it is in Additional Protocol I. The definition of perfidy in the Rome Statute, Article 8(2)(e)(ix), only criminalizes killing or wounding, not capturing.[7] In addition, the International Committee of the Red Cross has put together a website that examines perfidy in law and in customary international law by surveying national military manuals and laws, international practice, and legal opinion. For example, pretending to be Red Cross representatives to gain access to adversaries is considered perfidy and a crime.[8]

Treaties and laws can be enforced by various means—although international law requires states to provide enforcement—and generally spell out both consequences and enforcement measures within their terms. Norms, which are politically but not legally binding and thus by their nature "soft law," have neither prescribed enforcement terms nor specific methodologies to do so. Even when norms have been deemed "customary international law," enforcement of violations often does not occur, because states are generally unwilling to act unless their national interests are directly impugned.

In the *Game of Thrones* universe, the conspirators at first seem to only reap benefits from the violation of the "bread and salt" norm of hospitality.[9] House Lannister gets rid of its only real rival for the Iron Throne. Lord Tywin Lannister grants pardons, bestows titles to the houses of the perpetrators, and enacts marriages tying those houses to House Lannister for protection.

However, negative consequences of the Red Wedding ripple out across the rest of the saga, so much so that it totally undermines the stability of Westeros and the belief of the common people in the feudal system of the

Iron Throne and the great houses. It also underpins plotlines in each of books 3, 4, and 5. The distrust and disgust sowed by the Red Wedding is a foundational reason of a number of downfalls not just for House Frey but also for House Lannister that are portrayed in seasons 5 and 6 and in the books *A Feast for Crows* and *A Dance with Dragons*. Neither house can keep allies because of the Red Wedding, and indeed the incident fires the unending rebellion against the Iron Throne. While the Red Wedding ends the immediate threat to House Lannister's grip on the Iron Throne from House Stark, it shortly thereafter spurs several other lords and houses into broadening and deepening their military attacks. First, the collapse of Winterfell lures House Greyjoy to try to take over the North and further its bid for independence. It also piques Brynden Tully, Catelyn Stark's uncle also known as the Blackfish, to attack the Freys and take back his family seat of Riverrun. In *A Feast for Crows* (and episode 6 of season 6, "Blood of My Blood"), Jaime Lannister, one of the three siblings of House Lannister, is sent to help the Freys oust Tully. Jaime wants to end the standoff by offering the Blackfish a peace treaty but is warned by his aunt (who is married to one of the Freys) that this "won't work." She says, "Terms require trust. The Freys murdered guests beneath their roof." In the same book, Lord Rodrik Greyjoy sums up the overall situation in the Seven Kingdoms: "Crows will fight over a dead man's flesh and kill each other for his eyes. We had one king, then five. Now all I see are crows, squabbling over the corpse of Westeros."[10]

Specifically, it is the catalyst for the gruesome incident of the "Frey pies" in *A Dance of Dragons*, which suggests that Ser Wyman Manderly (a Stark loyalist from the North whose son was killed at the Red Wedding) serves Lord Walder three of his sons in a pie, and for the resurrection of Catelyn Stark in *A Storm of Swords* as Lady Stoneheart (who doesn't appear in the show) and her subsequent immortal quest for vengeance.[11] Finally, it is also part of the reason that the Sparrows religious sect are suspicious of Cersei Lannister (Tywin's daughter, whose son ends up on the Iron Throne) and an underpinning to her later arrest by the leader of the order, the High Septon, in *A Sword of Stones*.

Likewise, today, violation of norms also can, and has, come with costs—political, economic, and strategic. States often comply with norms precisely to avoid such potential costs, including political shaming and isolation or economic sanctions. Some violations, particularly those related to gross violations of human rights, also have seen state action to use military force to punish perpetrators.

In one example of the power of norms, in order to avoid political shaming, many states who are not parties to the 1997 Convention on the Prohibition of the Use, Stockpiling, Production and Transfer of Anti-Personnel Mines and on Their Destruction (known as the Ottawa Convention and stemming from norm setting by the International Campaign to Ban Landmines championed by Diana, Princess of Wales) have since decided to comply with the norms set by the treaty, refusing to use landmines and committing to voluntary efforts at destruction. Indeed, the United States (along with China and Russia, a nonsignatory of the Ottawa Convention) now bans the production and acquisition of antipersonnel landmines, as well as their use outside the Korean Peninsula.[12]

China's antisatellite (ASAT) weapons test of January 2007 is an example of how norms violation can lead to political censure and force a change of behavior. China's ASAT test violated not one but two standing norms agreed on by the international community. The first was the long-standing norm against explicit tests of ASATs. Prior to 2007 the last ASAT tests were conducted by the United States and the Soviet Union in the mid-1980s, which subsequently led to a gentleman's agreement between the two superpowers to discontinue such tests, due to concerns about their destabilizing effect on the nuclear balance and the negative effects for the space environment, because of the creation of debris, which poses risks to operational satellites due to possible collisions. That gentleman's agreement, in essence, created a norm that had not been violated by other countries up until the Chinese test. The second norm that the test violated was related to the issue of debris creation on orbit. Space debris—that is, pieces of junk emanating from launch, such as spent booster rockets; failure of satellites on orbit; or collisions with other on-orbit objects—has been internationally recognized since the 1990s as a threat to the space environment and the functioning of satellites. The Chinese ASAT test created nearly one thousand pieces of debris in a highly used orbit that could destroy active satellites.[13] Further, the test came in the midst of UN negotiations to develop a set of voluntary best practices for reducing the creation of space debris—negotiations in which China was a participant. To make matters worse, China had been chosen as the site of an April 2007 technical meeting supporting those negotiations. International outrage was immediate, and China was forced to back out of its plans to host the April meeting. Since that time, China has not conducted another debris-creating, or an explicit, ASAT test.

The 2013 use by Syria of chemical weapons against cities and civilians in its civil war is an example of when the threat of military force was brought to bear to uphold norms. The attacks were considered particularly egregious because they involved deliberate targeting of civilians in a noninternational conflict, something that is considered prohibited under customary international law. Furthermore, they violated the norm against the use of chemical weapons—despite the fact that Syria was, at the time, not a signatory of the 1993 Chemical Weapons Convention (CWC), which requires signatories to declare and destroy all chemical weapons stockpiles and production facilities. A UN investigation concluded in December 2013 that there were "reasonable grounds" to prove the use of sarin gas from Syrian Armed Forces stockpiles at several locations.[14] This resulted in enormous pressure—including economic sanctions—on Syrian leader Bashar al-Assad to adhere to the CWC and disarm. It also resulted in a threat by the Obama administration to respond with military force—a threat that was not, however, acted on after Russia proposed a diplomatic plan to dismantle Syrian weapons.[15] Following negotiations in late 2013, Syria adhered to the CWC, and inspectors from the Organization for the Prohibition of Chemical Weapons (OPCW) found that Syria had destroyed all weapons at its "declared" facilities. However, the investigators also stressed that they could not determine whether all Syria's chemical weapons were destroyed, due to suspicions that Assad hid the existence of some stockpiles. In 2014 and again in 2016, the Syrian government used chlorine gas in attacks on rebels in several cities—although the use of chlorine is banned by the CWC, its production is not.[16] However, it wasn't until April 2017, under the Trump administration, that a chemical weapons attack by the government on Khan Sheikhoun resulted in a missile strike by the United States.[17] In April 2018, as a result of three chlorine gas attacks in February, the United States, France, and the United Kingdom joined forces to launch yet more missile strikes on three weapons storage and research centers owned by the Syrian Armed Forces.[18]

Norms are a foundational element of international relations, as well as military practices. While norms are not always strictly upheld by the international community, violations often do come with negative political, economic, or strategic consequences. Even in the *Game of Thrones* universe, where seemingly "no good deed goes unpunished," the ramifications of the gross violation of societal norms exemplified by the Red Wedding came at costs over time to the perpetrators and to the stability of Westeros as a kingdom. Thus, states (whether fictional or real) should think twice before judging norms of behavior as easily discarded in pursuit of short-term aims, and they should beware of strategic thinking in which the ends justify the means.

NOTES

1. Customary international law is defined as international obligations arising from state practice. According to Article 38(1)(b) of the Statute of the International Court of Justice, customary law is one of the sources of international law. It can be shown by citing state practice, or *opinio juris*. An example is the prohibition on civilian attacks in noninternational armed conflicts (i.e., civil wars). See "Customary International Law," Legal Information Institute, accessed December 4, 2018, https://www.law.cornell.edu/wex/customary_international_law. Soft law is defined as rules that are neither strictly binding nor completely lacking legal significance. In international law, soft law refers to guidelines, policy declarations, or codes of conduct, but they are not directly enforceable. United Nations resolutions are a primary example of soft law. See "Soft Law and Legal Definition," U.S. Legal, accessed December 4, 2018, https://definitions.uslegal.com/s/soft-law/.

2. See "Hospitium," *A Dictionary of Greek and Roman Antiquities 1890*, ed. William Smith, William Wayte, and G. E. Marindin (London: John Murray, 1890), online at Perseus, http://www.perseus.tufts.edu/hopper/text?doc=Perseus:text:1999.04.0063:entry=hospitium-cn.

3. Tom Lambert, "Hospitality, Protection and Refuge in English Law," *Journal of Refugee Studies* 30, no. 2 (2017): 243–60, https://doi.org/10.1093/jrs/fev035.

4. Stacy Conradt, "The Real-Life Events That Inspired *Game of Thrones*' Red Wedding," *Week*, June 5, 2013, https://theweek.com/articles/463588/reallife-events-that-inspired-game-thrones-red-wedding.

5. "Slaughter under Trust," Clan Donald Heritage, accessed December 4, 2018, http://clandonald-heritage.com/slaughter-under-trust/.

6. Jonas Alastair Juhlin, "Rules of Deception" (research paper, Royal Danish Defence College, May 2015), http://www.fak.dk/publikationer/Documents/Rules%20of%20Deception.pdf?pdfdl=RulesofDeception. See also *Protocols Additional to the Geneva Conventions of 12 August 1949* (Geneva, Switzerland: International Committee of the Red Cross, May 2010), 30, 61, https://www.icrc.org/en/doc/assets/files/other/icrc_002_0321.pdf.

7. Juhlin, "Rules of Deception."

8. "Rule 65. Perfidy," International Committee of the Red Cross, Customary IHL Database, accessed December 4, 2018, https://ihl-databases.icrc.org/customary-ihl/eng/docs/v1_rul_rule65.

9. The "bread and salt" norm is mentioned by Robb Stark's mother, Catelyn, in *A Storm of Swords* just before the start of the Red Wedding; it stipulates that once a guest has eaten of "bread and salt" within a host's home, the host is bound to "do no harm." To this day, the concept of "breaking bread" with an enemy is a metaphor for a peaceful encounter. George R. R. Martin, *A Storm of Swords* (New York: Bantam Books, 2011), 671.

10. George R. R. Martin, *A Feast for Crows* (New York: Bantam Books, 2011), 714, 237.

11. George R. R. Martin, *A Dance with Dragons* (London: HarperCollins, 2011), 437. In the television series, it is Arya Stark who bakes the pies for Lord Walder; David Benioff and D. B. Weiss, "The Winds of Winter," season 6, episode 10, dir. Miguel Sapochnik, *Game of Thrones*, aired June 26, 2016, on HBO. In the novels so far, Lord Walder remains alive.

12. Daryl Kimball, "The Ottawa Convention at a Glance," Arms Control Association, January 2018, https://www.armscontrol.org/factsheets/ottawa.

13. Leonard David, "China's Anti-Satellite Test: A Worrisome Debris Cloud Circles Earth," Space .com, February 2, 2007, https://www.space.com/3415-china-anti-satellite-test-worrisome-debris-cloud-circles-earth.html.

14. UN Security Council, *United Nations Mission to Investigate Allegations of the Use of Chemical Weapons in the Syrian Arab Republic: Final Report*, A/68/663–S/2013/735, December 13, 2013, http://undocs.org/A/68/663.

15. "The Obama Administration on Syria, 2009–2017," Ballotpedia, accessed December 4, 2018, https://ballotpedia.org/The_Obama_administration_on_Syria,_2009-2017.

16. Colum Lynch, "To Assuage Russia, Obama Administration Backed Off Syria Chemical Weapons Plan," *Foreign Policy*, May 19, 2017, http://foreignpolicy.com/2017/05/19/to-assuage-russia-obama-administration-backed-off-syria-chemical-weapons-plan/.

17. Ashish Kumar Sen, "A Brief History of Chemical Weapons in Syria," Atlantic Council, April 9, 2108, http://www.atlanticcouncil.org/blogs/new-atlanticist/a-brief-history-of-chemical-weapons-in-syria.

18. Helen Cooper, Thomas Gibbons-Neff, and Ben Hubbard, "U.S., Britain and France Strike Syria over Suspected Chemical Weapons Attack," *New York Times*, April 13, 2018, https://www.nytimes.com/2018/04/13/world/middleeast/trump-strikes-syria-attack.html.

27

Daenerys Targaryen's Coalitions for War

MICK RYAN

At the beginning of season 7 of *Game of Thrones*, Daenerys Targaryen lands at Dragonstone island, as her dragons weave lazy circles in the air above. Daenerys drops to her knees in the wet beach sand and feels the solid earth of her native Westeros for the first time. Accompanied by her entourage of advisors, she enters and explores the deserted Dragonstone castle. Daenerys continues to the empty throne room, seeing the volcanic rock throne of House Targaryen. After pausing a moment, Daenerys strides past the throne and enters the Chamber of the Painted Table. She does so as a queen, khaleesi, Mother of Dragons, strategic commander, and coalition leader.

By this stage of the *Game of Thrones* story, she oversees powerful land, sea, and air (with her fire-breathing dragons) forces. She occupies a powerful and isolated fortress of Valyrian design. And she now possesses the only source of one of the only substances known to kill White Walkers—Dragonstone. These combined provide powerful incentives for other houses on Westeros to ally with her. As Daenerys looks at the Painted Table, she turns to her advisor Tyrion and states, "Shall we begin?" It has been quite a journey for the young queen.

A key story arc across all the seasons of the *Game of Thrones* saga has been the exiled descendant of the realm's deposed ruling dynasty, Daenerys, and her exploits in seeking a return to the Iron Throne. In the earliest days of this epic series, this was the crusade of her brother, Viserys. He had claimed the Iron Throne as King Viserys III in the wake of his father being killed in Robert's Rebellion. But he never sat on the Iron Throne. After Viserys is murdered by Khal Drago (by having molten gold poured over his head, no less), Daenerys makes the fateful decision to continue her brother's quest to seize back the Iron Throne for the Targaryen family.

The exploits of Daenerys cover multiple trials, relationships, coalitions, and continents, all to support her triumphant return to Westeros and accession to the Iron Throne. Her journey sees Daenerys assume new titles—khaleesi, queen, and Mother of Dragons—and results in her development as a commander, leader, and strategist. Above all, Daenerys develops a profound understanding of the requirement for coalition partners. By the conclusion of the seventh season, she possesses a superbly honed capacity to seek out potential allies, build mutually beneficial relationships, and apply the art of compromise in the quest of her strategic objective.

Before progressing in this examination of Daenerys's coalition-building skills, it is worth examining the difference between alliances and coalitions. These are not terms that are interchangeable. From a military perspective, alliances are formal arrangements for broad, long-term objectives and are often underpinned by formal treaties. A coalition, however, is a less formal agreement for common action between two or more entities (mainly nations but, for our purposes here, also houses, tribes, and ethnic groups).[1] For Daenerys Targaryen the majority of her security partnerships are coalitions—temporary relationships that sometimes come undone and sometimes provide significant advances in her pursuit of the Iron Throne. She has few true allies. Over the seven seasons of *Game of Thrones* it is only the Unsullied who could truly be defined as allies. This distinction between allies and coalition partners is important to remember.

This chapter examines the development of Daenerys Targaryen as a coalition builder. The narrative covers key steps in her development as a coalition builder, while examining the rationale for her seeking allies. This chapter also reviews her personal style and methods in soliciting and building these relationships. Finally, it examines lessons for coalition building that we might take away from the experiences of Daenerys Targaryen.

The recent U.S. National Defense Strategy noted that alliances and partnerships are *crucial to strategy, providing a durable, asymmetric strategic advantage that no competitor or rival can match.*[2] While Queen Daenerys, khaleesi and Mother of Dragons, may not have used these precise words, she was a fast learner when it came to seeking out and nurturing coalition partners. When we first meet her at the start of *Game of Thrones*, Daenerys is the subject of a trade between her brother (seeking an army) and Khal Drogo (seeking a wife). Despite this repugnant treatment by her brother and Drogo, she rapidly learns the ways of the Dothraki, through observation, empathy, and the advice of characters such as Jorah Mormont. She eventually gains the trust of the Dothraki by learning and respecting their ways, including wearing their clothes, learning their language, and even at one point eating a stallion's heart. She has learned the art of influence (a strategic skill in itself) and the value of gaining partners in achieving larger goals.

Her influence sees Khal Drogo eventually agreeing to move his forces, by ship, to Westeros to fight for the Iron Throne. But we soon observe that Daenerys's influence in sustaining this partnership with the Dothraki has its limits. With the death of Drogo following ritual combat and the stillbirth of their child, she is ostracized by the Dothraki. Her capacity to sustain influence with the Dothraki was based on her marriage to Drogo. She learns from this. It is a limitation that she will not allow to compromise her future efforts in alliance building to achieve her seizure of the Iron Throne.

At the end of the first season of *Game of Thrones*, we see Daenerys evolve her approach to leadership through a mix of personal inspiration and mysticism. The majority of the Dothraki have deserted her, leaving behind a small band of her supporters. She appeals to the remaining khalasar that they are free to go or follow her. And she appropriates the mysticism of fire and dragons (soon to be more than old myths) in demonstrating to this small band of followers that she is destined to ascend the Iron Throne.

It is her arrival in Astapor, in the Bay of Dragons, where Daenerys reveals a growing sophistication in coalition building. Accepting the advice of Jorah that she will need to build a greater source of strength to provide a foundation to eventually enlist the Dothraki in her cause, she trades a dragon for a small army of eight thousand Unsullied warriors. Using her new warriors, she captures Astapor. Demonstrating her growth as a leader, she then frees the Unsullied, who all elect to remain in her service. She then uses her new army, and a newly formed partnership with Daario, to capture the second key city in the Bay of Dragons, Yunkai, and eventually the largest city of Meereen.

Later, in season 6, we see Daenerys apply all she has learned to grow the size of her army through a new alliance with the Dothraki. While negotiations start poorly, she turned the tables on an assemblage of Dothraki leaders and burned them all alive. The remaining Dothraki pledge their allegiance to the Mother of Dragons, and she leads them back to Meereen. There she is challenged by the slave masters. Using dragons to burn the slave masters' ships, she negates the threat of the old masters of Meereen.

Not long after, Daenerys is approached by Yara and Theon Greyjoy to form a partnership. They offer to provide one hundred ships to Daenerys if she helps them defeat their uncle Euron Greyjoy. Dany accepts Yara's offer but demands that the Ironborn end all pillaging. The Ironborn agree to her terms; Daenerys and Yara Greyjoy make a pact to work together.

Daenerys Targaryan now commands a coalition that comprises mounted and dismounted land forces (the Dothraki and the Unsullied), an aerial support element (her dragons), and the means to transport her coalition force across the Narrow Sea to Westeros (the Greyjoy fleet). This represents the results of a multiyear effort on her behalf to bring together disparate forces from across Essos and, through compromise and guile, build a force that will enable her to fight for the Iron Throne in Westeros. The final episode of season 6 sees this coalition force led by Daenerys commence its move across the Narrow Sea to Westeros.

Her return to Westeros sees further expansion of her coalition. First, she forms a partnership with Ellaria Sand, who agrees to provide an army from House Martell for the conquest of Westeros. She also possesses a nascent relationship with House Tyrell, forged by Olenna Tyrell after the deaths of her son and grandchildren at King's Landing. The coalition is further expanded when Jon Snow is swayed to join Daenerys in the wake of her assistance to his mission north of the wall. This time, however, coalition partnerships are not secured with threats or armed force but with her personal negotiations with the principals: Jon Snow, Ellaria Sand, and Olenna Tyrell. While her maritime forces suffer a defeat at the hands of Euron Greyjoy and Ellaria is captured, the forces of the khaleesi's coalition are poised and ready for the conquest of the Iron Throne.

But as we depart season 7, for the first time in her quest for the Iron Throne, Daenerys must place this goal on hold. While the perfidious Cersei is the most obvious obstacle to her assuming the Iron Throne, the threat of White Walkers moving south of the Wall is a more compelling and existential threat to her goals—and to Westeros. The Army of the Dead represents the most dangerous obstacle to everything she has strived for. To defeat it will demand that she apply everything she has learned in strategy, command, and coalition management.

The Daenerys Method of Coalition Building

Over the seven seasons of *Game of Thrones*, the Mother of Dragons builds a deep appreciation of the need for coalitions to achieve her goals. Applying her own experiences and the advice of trusted advisers such as Jorah and Tyrion, she develops a sophisticated view of coalitions as a key "ways" in achieving her strategic "ends" of gaining the Iron Throne. The first part of this chapter has reviewed her dawning appreciation of the importance of building and sustaining alliances. As this narrative describes, it was a learning process built on failure and success over many years. Using her experiences, the khaleesi develops her own method of building and sustaining coalitions. This "Daenerys method" has several components.

First, Daenerys always retains a focus on her overall strategic objective of regaining the Iron Throne. She never deviates from this end state. This provides her with a unifying purpose for coalition formation and sustainment.

It also allows her to offer incentives to the leaders of different groups should their endeavor be successful and should she be able to claim leadership of Westeros and its spoils.

Second, Daenerys learns to apply various approaches to coalition building. There is no "one size fits all" to building an effective coalition army. She uses compassion with the Unsullied and with the slaves of Meereen. She exploits marriage to partner with the noble families of Meereen and avoid a conflict that would distract her from preparing for the conquest of Westeros. She applies other inducements with the Dothraki, the Greyjoys, House Tyrell, and Jon Snow in the conquest of Westeros in later seasons. This demonstrates a growing shrewdness in how she differentiates incentives for different coalition partners.

Finally, she demonstrates a streak of ruthlessness in forming coalitions. As she matures in her strategic decision-making, Daenerys essentially embraces a "join me or die" approach. This was used against Dothraki leaders at the Khalifa Vezhven and against the slave masters at Meereen during their revolt against her rule. In both instances, it was a choice between alliance and fire; both resulted in the incineration of her adversaries. Toward the end of season 7, we once again witness this approach when Daenerys has the dragon Drogon roast Randyll and Dickon Tarly when they refuse to ally with her after the Battle of the Goldroad. While this ruthlessness is somewhat ameliorated through the advice of Tyrion Lannister, it remains an instinctive stance for Daenerys and something we are likely to witness in future.

Lessons from Khaleesi's Coalitions

While *Game of Thrones* exists in the fantasy world, it nonetheless offers the contemporary strategic leader useful lessons on coalition formation and sustainment. The building of coalitions is almost as old as warfare itself. The twentieth and early twenty-first centuries have seen multiple occasions where the benefits of building coalitions can be demonstrated. The First and Second World Wars, the Cold War, and first Gulf War are good examples.[3] What might be the lessons from *Game of Thrones* and the coalition building of Queen Daenerys?

First, coalitions allow for the achievement of strategic objectives that individual actors or nations may not otherwise possess the means to achieve. When national resources from multiple nations can be pooled toward an individually unachievable goal, collective action is highly desirable. When we first meet Daenerys at the start of *Game of Thrones*, she possesses little more than her name and an aspiration to return to Westeros with her brother. She learns that as her aspirations grow, so too must she grow the means to achieve these aspirations. Only through coalition building, and the maintenance of increasingly larger coalitions, can she do this.

Second, friction within coalitions may be as significant as that between the coalition and its adversaries. There is deep historical evidence of coalitions and alliances being notoriously difficult balancing acts. Whether it was frictions within the Delian League during the Peloponnesian War generated by Athenian use of its navy or the "caveat management" of NATO leaders for the fifty countries engaged in Afghanistan operations in the twenty-first century, coalition management is a tricky business.[4] This is mirrored in Daenerys's experiences and the challenges of the changing affiliations of the Dothraki and the slave masters and will potentially manifest in the future in her relationship with the conniving and vicious Cersei Lannister.

Third, practical necessity and shared goals dictate the formation of most coalitions. Once they are formed, coalitions need coordination of effort to achieve their agreed common objectives.[5] For Daenerys, her all-consuming goal is gaining the Iron Throne. While achieving this often requires subsidiary efforts, she never veers away from this single goal. It provides the clear and unifying vision for how she views coalition formation and provides the rationale for her relationship building and maintenance for coalition formation.

Fourth, coalitions must be underpinned by cultural awareness. In seeking to build and sustain a consensus around strategic objectives, it is critical that coalition members demonstrate understanding of the cultural norms and sensitivities of their partners. During the Peloponnesian War, the Athenians were not always the masters of this, even though they managed to keep the Delian League together until their eventual defeat. The khaleesi displays an early appreciation for this aspect of coalition building and leadership.

She learns and mimics Dothraki habits and traditions and develops a deep empathy for partners such as the Unsullied, freed slaves, and Jon Snow's forces. As such, she increasingly establishes the capacity to balance her own objectives with the different cultural mindsets and approaches of the members of the collation she leads.

Finally, coalitions are built on personalities. Whether it is the modern example of General Dwight D. Eisenhower's masterful orchestration of partners for the liberation of Europe or the ancient example of Philip II of Macedonia and his League of Corinth, personal relationships matter in building and sustaining coalitions.[6] History's most outstanding coalition builders and leaders deeply appreciate how their personal leadership approach complements the national imperatives of each nation for joining the coalition. Tolerance, cultural awareness, empathy, good leadership, and courage (physical and moral) have defined the great coalition leaders of history. So too is this the case with Daenerys. While these qualities are not evident early in the series, she develops and hones these qualities over multiple years to eventually lead a powerful invasion force to Westeros. These personal qualities put her very close to achieving her goal of the Iron Throne at the end of season 7, before the intervention of the Army of the Dead.

Conclusion

The growing maturity of Daenerys's strategic decision-making manifests most clearly in the coalition that she has assembled by the end of season 7. From innocent young princess at the start of the series, she progresses through a broad range of experiences that hone her ability to build coalitions of different groups in order to ascend the Iron Throne. This demanded a significant level of personal resilience but also enhancing a variety of interpersonal skills that underpin her management of the key leaders in her coalition force that is now lodged in Westeros.

Daenerys demonstrates a growing sophistication in her approach to coalition building and leadership. Maintaining her ruthless focus on the goal of gaining the Iron Throne and applying different methods for different coalition partners, her actions offer a range of insights for contemporary strategic leaders and thinkers. And while the eventual outcome of her campaign to regain the Iron Throne is yet to be revealed, Daenerys Targaryen, khaleesi and Mother of Dragons, offers us an outstanding exemplar of a coalition builder and commander.

NOTES

1. Wayne A. Silkett, "Alliance and Coalition Warfare," *Parameters* 23, no. 2 (Summer 1993): 74–85.

2. Jim Mattis, *Summary of the 2018 National Defense Strategy* (Washington DC: U.S. Department of Defense, 2018), 8, https://www.defense.gov/Portals/1/Documents/pubs/2018-National-Defense-Strategy-Summary.pdf.

3. One useful history that cover this aspect of the Cold War is John Lewis Gaddis, *The Cold War: A New History* (New York: Penguin Press, 2005). See also Frank N. Schubert and Theresa L. Kraus, eds., *The Whirlwind War: The United States in Operations Desert Shield and Desert Storm* (Washington DC: Center for Military History, 1995).

4. For more, see Robert B. Strassler, ed., *The Landmark Thucydides: A Comprehensive Guide to the Peloponnesian War* (New York: Free Press, 1998). Details of the fifty coalition members can be found at "NATO and Afghanistan," North Atlantic Treaty Organization, last updated November 27, 2018, https://www.nato.int/cps/en/natohq/topics_8189.htm.

5. Silkett, "Alliance and Coalition Warfare."

6. Among the references of Eisenhower's coalition building, see Louis Galambos, *Eisenhower* (Baltimore MD: Johns Hopkins University Press, 2018); Carlo D'Este, *Eisenhower: A Soldier's Life* (New York: Henry Holt, 2002); Dwight D. Eisenhower, *Crusade in Europe* (New York: Permabooks, 1952). For a useful examination of Philip II and the League of Corinth, see Nicholas Hammond, *Philip of Macedon* (London: Bristol Classical Press, 1998).

28

Arya Stark's Targeted Killing and Strategic Decision-Making

CRAIG WHITESIDE

House Stark's fall from grace in *Game of Thrones* is a shocking and tragic event for a family whose lineage as the Kings (and more recently Warden) of the North dates back eight millennia. Following the execution of Eddard (Ned) Stark by the Lannisters and the massacre of Robb and Catelyn Stark at the Red Wedding, the bleak prospects of the splintered family, made worse by mistaken reports of the demise of several of the Stark siblings, serve as a foundation for a powerful subplot of redemption and triumph as they eventually reunite and regain their lost inheritance and authority over the North.

Arya Stark plays a significant role in this restoration, even though her journey back to Winterfell, the ancestral home of the Starks, is strange and dark. Her one-woman war, waged behind the lines against unsuspecting Stark enemies, peaks with her murder of Walder Frey, the architect of the Red Wedding, as well as the males of his line—serving as a poignant warning to potential challengers of Stark suzerainty in the future. The irony here is great; while the men of the Stark family serially fail to achieve success by arms and honor, Arya—an unlikely warrior to be sure—used deception and the heart of a cold-blooded killer to achieve some important results on behalf of her family. What should we make of this contrast in approach? Has Arya discovered a new way of war for her house, one that might prove more successful in a changing Westeros?

While it is necessary and fair to judge leaders like Arya on outcomes, this doesn't help us understand basic strategy. Instead, it is more instructive for us to deconstruct decisions in order to learn leader intention, preparation, and execution of strategy. Did her decisions lead to the restoration of her house, or did it happen in spite of her efforts? And what was the cost of her decisions, both long-term and short? I found Arya's personal journey to be a cautionary tale, with a distinct disconnect between her actions and a renewal of political power for her family. Arya Stark's choice to start a solitary campaign of revenge against her family's enemies, over other more conventional options, has disastrous consequences for her personally—and for her family's political future—that should not be overlooked despite the successful restoration of one of the great houses of Westeros.

Emotions and Strategy

The crafting of strategy, at its heart, is often perceived as a rational process. Leaders match ideas on how to achieve a realistic goal with the minimum resources to achieve it. This process, although intuitive, is sometimes criticized for its formulaic nature.[1] For political leaders like the Starks, these goals are linked to aggregating more power relative to internal rivals and external foes. While leaders are influenced by nonrational elements in their goal selection and willingness to expend resources, an appropriate balance between rationality and emotional influences is ideal. In contrast, Thucydides highlighted the dangers of a military strategy driven by popular passions when he described the disastrous Sicilian Expedition in his history of the Peloponnesian War.[2]

The remnants of the Stark family, while not specifically trained in any of this strategic calculus, nonetheless benefited from what could be described as a strategic family culture.[3] Ned Stark, the family patriarch, worked tirelessly before his demise to impart to his children a series of general strategy lessons rooted in family lore, stressing preparation for hardship ("Winter is coming" is the house motto) and the need to work together in times of crisis. This canon is overcome by events when the family crisis hits unexpectedly and overwhelmingly, atomizing the group and precluding much collaboration between key members. The loss of successive Stark family leaders in quick order forced the remainder of the siblings to act independently and prioritize survival over family goals. Each chose different paths to adapt to the new reality. Jon Snow chose political sequestration in the Night's Watch before returning to the family, and Sansa Stark chose to submit to adversary families in the hope of creating new opportunities. Arya's unexpected choice to seek revenge for what was done to her and her family makes for compelling drama, but using it as the basis for a strategy is a terrible idea.[4]

Arya as a Strategic Leader

In some ways, Arya's youthful insistence to her father to be treated as an important member of the Stark's political-military unit is vindicated when she is thrust in the critical role as a Stark survivor, with the legacy of the family to uphold. Of the three able-bodied siblings, she alone sought out training and dedicated mentorship from the likes of master swordsman Syrio Forel and Jaqen H'ghar, one of the Faceless Men of Braazos. This training is directly correlated to the path she chooses to follow and in this sense is a pretty reasonable series of acts.

Selection of an attainable goal while balancing other factors like resources, time, and acceptable risk is the most crucial aspect of strategy making. Considering Arya's decisions after the fall of House Stark, discerning any political or military goal that advances the interests of the Stark family is difficult, if one exists at all. What passes for an overarching vision guiding her actions is a virtual list of individuals who played a part in the misfortunes of the Starks and need to be tracked down and killed. Worse from a strategic perspective, the list grows with the addition of insignificant actors, like the random Lannister soldier whom Arya watches mocking the Stark slaughter at the Red Wedding. This event triggers Arya's decision to give up reuniting with her family and become a professional assassin, with the young soldier as her first victim. Her path back to her family suffers a willful and lengthy detour at this point that tests her mettle and teaches her valuable skills for a fighter who cannot rely on brawn. At this critical juncture, Arya recovers good sense and rejects the false objective of becoming an assassin, renewing her desire to return to her family.

Another key aspect to strategy formulation is the development of a shared faith in a series of actions that in concert should produce concrete results in the attainment of the objective. These steps answer *how* the goal will be accomplished. While Arya never wavers in her conviction of what must be done to her enemies, as demonstrated regularly in her bedtime death-list recitation, she has no idea how any of it will be done. Instead, she adds new people to the list as quickly as others are removed. Nor is there any priority for this list, which even her companion the Hound makes fun of. The events happen randomly, as she careens from city to city with little appreciation for her own agency or her own input into what she will do the next day. Her departure from Westeros to train with the Faceless Man is symbolic of her desertion from the field at a critical time for the Stark family. Lost in the pursuit of her private ambition, she has become what she originally hated in others, like the Hound—an unfeeling, unthinking killing machine.

Inexplicably, she is rescued from an unenviable fate as a life-term member of an assassins' guild by her belated recognition of her true identity as a Stark and the responsibility that comes with it. Finally reunited with her family, she is able to use some of her newfound skills to defend against Petyr Baelish's intrigues and help her sister Sansa's regency of House Stark while Jon Snow is away dealing with the White Walker threat. The family reunion of three tried and tested siblings, assisted by a fourth sibling with incredible powers of sight and knowledge of the past, makes the house a formidable player once again in the Westeros political landscape. It is hard to argue that this happened by design instead of by chance, and Arya is fortunate that her siblings are so happy to see her that they inexplicably fail to ask the hard questions about her choices.

Arya's Game of Many Faces

Arya's list of enemies and her decision to target them individually have some fairly obvious parallels to conflict today. Targeted killing is used by both the strong and the weak in what scholar Tom Greer calls "mirror images [of] terrorist campaigns." Both sides in this asymmetric battle use clandestine methods to strike the other, in the hope that the relentless fear of an unexpected death will terrorize the other side, causing them to quit the fight. These actions could take the form of suicide bombings, drone strikes, or small-scale raids targeting individuals. This would be in contrast to the large-scale bombing campaigns of World War II, whose goals were more linked to psychological warfare than an effective means of hitting military targets. Targeted-killing tactics can be part of a larger strategy of attrition of an enemy force or exhaustion of the enemy's will to fight, and a viable option for actors of any size.[5]

There are valid criticisms regarding how well these strategies work, or if they are even counterproductive in other ways.[6] Nonetheless, they are used extensively, even predominantly by some countries and groups, so Arya's choice to engage in a campaign of targeted killing has some merit. To use this tactic as part of a larger strategy, however, the decision maker must have some idea of whether the end state is achievable and the costs are bearable, as well as the additional risks that might develop from the use of these tactics. These risks can come in the forms of failing to achieve the end state, experiencing excessive casualties to the friendly force or to civilian populations, losing public support, and increasing moral injury among those executing these missions. Slow, deliberate campaigns of attrition or exhaustion are notoriously hard to measure, with seemingly little correlation between individual deaths and the termination of the campaign. How does this one death secure a better peace?[7] More importantly, when is killing in war justified, and when is it murder or assassination?[8]

Critiquing Arya's focus on securing vengeance for her family, often described in dismissive terms as irrational, seems reasonable until one considers the U.S. decisions to use force in the past two decades. The official wording in the congressional Authorization for Use of Military Force passed in the wake of the 9/11 terrorist attacks is brief, and today it is still used as the legal justification for military action on multiple continents. Devoid of many qualifications, it authorizes "the use of United States Armed Forces against those responsible for the recent attacks launched against the United States."[9] Of note, there is no strategic guidance in this document, and the only restriction presented by its authors refers to the existing requirements of the War Powers Resolution, which are too frequently ignored by presidents anyways.

This American policy to use force—constrained by congressional spending limits and the occasional threat to produce a new, more limited authorization—is often justified as an effort to protect the country from attack by external enemies that have demonstrated ill will and a real capability to reach the homeland. Yet it can also, more honestly, be described as revenge for the original attacks and a demonstration of will to deter future acts of terrorism. Security studies scholar Thomas Waldman calls one subsequent campaign—the 2003 invasion of Iraq—"an ideologically driven war of revenge that was only possible in the unique political conditions of the immediate, emotionally charged aftermath of 9/11."[10] In this light, our judgment of Arya's various diversions needs to be tempered by an acknowledgment that she made the necessary course correction in a reasonable amount of time. In contrast, the war against global jihadists continues, with no end in sight.

All strategies have opportunity costs. Arya lost time in her journey that could have been used for better purposes. The current U.S.-led campaigns against global jihadists, as terrorism experts Daniel Byman and Will McCants argue, are too expansive, unjustifiable, and unsustainable. A new strategy that prioritizes efforts to disrupt foreign operations cells, deny militant control of major population centers, and prevent genocidal campaigns would be a better use of time and resources, while keeping the United States and its partners safe.[11] The need to regulate this limited campaign against a dispersed foe is stronger than ever as more important threats to U.S. interests arise.

Much like Arya's misadventures in Braavos, the current fixation with global jihadi movements has possibly obscured the rise of credible threats to the liberal global order as understood by policy makers. Although the rise of China has inspired U.S. strategic shifts toward the Pacific in previous administrations, these efforts have been frustrated by continued diversions to stamp out fires in the Middle East. Efforts to engage China have largely failed, requiring additional thought, an alternative approach, and a laser-like focus.[12]

Our Own Game of Thrones

As a character, Arya never seems interested in the game of thrones, even after becoming an important role player in the struggle. Loyal, smart, and willing to kill for her family without remorse, she has become an ideal functionary for a traditional power family that is desperate to reassert itself. She has learned a great deal and has become a better decision maker through experimentation and experience—the gift of combat, if you will, for those who survive. On the other hand, like her siblings and many others in Westeros, she has survived horrific encounters and seen unforgettable events in her journey. There is a chance that she has suffered what is called moral injury, with consequences yet to be seen.[13] There is also the possibility that her past as an assassin will reflect poorly on the reputation of her house, which has a culture that has stressed honor and integrity. Finally, her connection with figures like the Faceless Man will most likely return at the worst possible moment, with requirements that will conflict with her duty to her family.

Judging Arya for her detour into the heart of darkness is easy for us when we examine her decisions from the basis of normative strategic models. It is well understood that basing strategy on emotions can lead to bad results. And yet a comparison of Arya's decisions with our own struggles to craft a limited and efficient strategy to fight al-Qaeda and ISIS found many more similarities than one would think. While we can take little solace in this revelation, it is possible to use this critique of a young woman and her evolution into a political and military strategist to honestly assess and adjust the conduct of our own efforts to keep the peace in our version of Westeros.

NOTES

1. Jeffrey W. Meiser, "Are Our Strategic Models Flawed? Ends + Ways + Means = (Bad) Strategy," *Parameters* 46, no. 4 (Winter 2016–17): 81–91.

2. Thucydides, *History of the Peloponnesian War*, trans. Rex Warner (London: Penguin Classics, 1974), 414–26, 536–37.

3. Colin S. Gray writes about strategic culture as context in *Modern Strategy* (New York: Oxford University Press, 1999), 129–51.

4. While it might seem unfair to critique Arya's choice here, Arya believes she is the sole remaining Stark not in enemy hands or in the Night's Watch, making her the de facto political leader of House Stark. The merits of her choice to wage a solitary, irregular warfare campaign against her enemies are worth examining here. Revenge as a motive for strategy could be justified, but often the logic of strategy is lost.

5. Tom Greer's book review of Antulio Echevarria's *Military Strategy: A Very Short Introduction* argues that targeted killings are not a strategy but that they fit better under larger categories like attrition and exhaustion; see Tom Greer, "Book Notes—Military Strategy: A Very Short Introduction," *Scholar's Stage*, May 1, 2018, http://scholars-stage.blogspot.com/2018/05/book-notes-military-strategy-very-short.html.

6. Recent scholarship differs on the efficacy and long-term impacts of removing leaders. See Jenna Jordan, "Attacking the Leader, Missing the Mark," *International Security* 38, no. 4 (Spring 2014): 7–38; Jenna Jordan, "When Heads Roll: Assessing the Effectiveness of Leadership Decapitation," *Security Studies* 18 (2009): 719–755; Byran Price, "Targeting Top Terrorists: How Leadership Decapitation Contributes to Counterterrorism," *International Security* 36, no. 4 (Spring 2012): 9–46; Michael Freeman, "A Theory of Terrorist Leadership and Its Consequences for Leadership Targeting," *Terrorism and Political Violence* 26, no. 4 (2014); and Patrick Johnston, "Does Decapitation Work? Assessing the Effectiveness of Leadership Targeting in Counterinsurgency Campaigns," *International Security* 36, no. 4 (Spring 2012): 47–79.

7. James Igoe Walsh, "The Rise of Targeted Killings," *Journal of Strategic Studies* 41, nos. 1–2 (2017).

8. Tom Junod, "The Six-Letter Word That Changes Everything," *Esquire*, June 11, 2008.

9. 107th Congress, Pub. L. No. 107-40, Joint Resolution, 115 Stat. 225 (September 18, 2001).

10. Thomas Waldman, "Vicarious Warfare: The Counterproductive Consequences of Modern American Military Practice," *Contemporary Security Policy* 39, no. 2 (2018): 181–205.

11. Dan Byman and Will McCants, "Fight or Flight: How to Avoid a Forever War against Jihadists," *Washington Quarterly* 40, no. 2 (Summer 2017): 67–77.

12. Aaron L. Friedberg, "Competing with China," *Survival: Global Politics and Strategy* 60, no. 3 (2018): 7–64.

13. Nancy Sherman, *Afterwar: Healing the Moral Wounds of Our Soldiers* (New York: Oxford University Press, May 2015).

29

Ned Stark, Hero of the Seven Kingdoms, and Why the Good Guys Win (in the End)

ML CAVANAUGH

"Heroes do things and they die," Daenerys explained to Tyrion, because they compete to see "who can do the stupidest, bravest thing."[1]

To many fans, Ned Stark, Lord of Winterfell, was just such a fool—more heroic in his convictions than strategic at his core. At least one critic has pointed out that Ned was apt to "confuse nobility with stupidity," while another has assembled a list of Ned Stark's "political missteps" during the first season of *Game of Thrones*.[2] The way this telling goes, in step with Cersei's assessment, Ned was "just a soldier, following orders," and marched to the beat of his own mindlessly moralistic drum—right up to the gallows and his own beheading.[3]

But while some see Ned as naive, others find in him the "show's moral compass," the "one character who's truly unforgettable" and an "undeniable hero."[4] The actor Sean Bean, who played Ned Stark, has said in an interview that Ned was an "anchor" to many fans due to his "principles and morals and values" in contrast to so many of the other "poisonous" characters that populated the show.[5]

So which is it? Was Ned a moralizing moron or a hardened hero? Or is it a little bit of both? Just what can the case of Ned Stark—Lord of Winterfell, the Hand of the King to Robert Baratheon, husband to Catelyn, and father to Robb, Sansa, Arya, Brandon, and Rikkon—teach us about heroes, good guys, and victory at war?

It turns out the answer is "a lot," because even in a digital age full of advanced drones and artificial droids, thinking about heroes still matters. As one political scientist has pointed out, we "can't understand any number of wars and conflicts without paying attention to duty and honor and other romantic notions."[6]

That's because when humans go to war, heroes rise. Heroes inspire others through myths and unify disparate allies. And these two characteristics—willpower and allies—often mean the difference between victory and defeat at war.

Heroes without Capes

The word the ancient Greeks used for "hero" translates, in English, to "protector."[7] The mythologist Joseph Campbell has described the hero as "someone who has given his or her life to something bigger than oneself" and sometimes even "performs a courageous act in battle or saves a life."[8]

So a hero is someone who serves and sacrifices for the protection and betterment of others. This is, biologically speaking, a little strange. Charles Darwin's theories about natural selection ran counter to such an instinct, and he wrote, "He who was ready to sacrifice his life, as many a savage has been, rather than betray his comrades would often leave no offspring to inherit his noble nature."[9] Or more bluntly, as the writer Chris McDougall put it, "Selfish Bastard's kids would thrive and multiply, while Hero Dad's kids would eventually follow their father's example and sacrifice themselves into extinction," and so "if natural selection eliminates natural heroism, why does it still exist?"[10]

Think of the Lannisters' self-interested behavior. Tywin Lannister fretted constantly about the good of the family. Darwin's theory might predict that his offspring would do very well in a harsh world. But it's not quite so simple—in many ways, Ned Stark's children had more wind in their sails.

That's because it appears that humanity's social instinct has won out over our individual, selfish needs. We are, after all, the "most helpful species that's ever existed," and at war "we unite in fantastic numbers."[11] And while natural selection remains generally predominant, humanity's social development does favor traits that "introduce highly cooperative behavior into the physiology and behavior of group members," according to Harvard biologist E. O. Wilson's theory of eusocial evolution.[12] That's why two species have essentially conquered our planet—the ants and us.

Society's designated warriors developed codes, or ethos, to push back against the instinctual desire for self-preservation.[13] And looking back over the long sweep of history, Amy Chua has pointed out that each and every world power that has "achieved global hegemony" and dominance was relatively tolerant and able to achieve some degree of loyalty and unity out of very diverse coalitions.[14]

There's a deep tension, then, between the self-inclined, selfish individual and the self-abnegating, self-sacrificial person willing to give all for their society. So there are two ways of looking at the hero. Viewed narrowly through a focused, individualistic lens, Ned's choices may appear foolish, naive, even stupid. But by looking more broadly, at the value of his behavior to a society and group (i.e., the Starks, Winterfell, the North, and the Seven Kingdoms), we might see Ned's choices in a different light.

And this is what heroes do. The Greeks saw that the empathetic drive and urgency to protect others gave heroes their greatest strength.[15] The same idea runs through G. K. Chesterton's well-worn aphorism that the "true soldier fights not because he hates what is in front of him, but because he loves what is behind him."[16]

Ned Stark, Hero of Winterfell and the Seven Kingdoms

Ned Stark was a hero because he served causes greater than himself—his family, his house, and the Seven Kingdoms—and he was willing to sacrifice for them.

Right from the beginning, Ned's actions were consistent with his values, as when he taught his children that the one "who passes the sentence should swing the sword" or the moment he told Arya, "The long winter is coming," and, "We must look after each other, protect each other."[17]

Perhaps Ned's service to others was most evident when his friend and king, Robert Baratheon, asked Ned to be the Hand of the King, the individual responsible for security and defense of the Seven Kingdoms. Ned did not want the job but could not turn it down, because he had sworn an oath to serve the sovereign. He told his wife, Catelyn, that he didn't "have a choice." Catelyn argued, resisted, and said that she could not run Winterfell without him, and yet Ned left anyways to take the job—even though it clearly came at a painful cost to both him and his family.[18]

Ned's service as Hand of the King was sorely tested when King Robert wanted to take an action that violated Ned's ethical code. King Robert learned that Daenerys Targaryen was pregnant with a child that might grow to threaten his throne, and so King Robert wanted Ned, as Hand of the King, to endorse and oversee the killing of the rival house's mother and child.

Ned pointed out that this assassination would have been dishonorable and made the case that it would also be unwise because the two young Targaryens were not a strategic threat, as the Dothraki horde they were allied with would never be able or willing to cross the Narrow Sea and attack into Westeros.

Still, though they acknowledged Ned's point, the Small Council unanimously decided to authorize the killing. Ned resigned as Hand of the King, removed his symbolic fist pin, and then gave King Robert some final, direct, unvarnished criticism: "I thought you were a better man."[19]

Ned was willing to serve, but within moral boundaries. Moral frameworks are important as guideposts that signal to others stable behavior that builds trust and confidence. The deed—to kill a young mother and unborn child—was wrong in itself but also a poor strategic choice. While it may have had some near-term upside (removal of threat), that would have been overwhelmed by a significant long-term downside in the likely blowback as well as in the fear of coalition partners, who would look to hedge their loyalty out of concern for who might be next.

Perhaps most importantly, Ned showed that he was willing to give up his powerful position, and prestige, for principle.

Later, after King Robert's death, when Ned was wrongly chain-bound because he knew the throne claimed by Joffrey (and Cersei) was Stannis Baratheon's by right, Lord Varys went to the dungeon to visit and convince Ned to falsely confess to treason, plea for his life, and "bend the knee" to Joffrey.[20]

Ned refused and responded, "You think my life is some precious thing to me? That I would trade my honor for a few more years of what—the Wall? You grew up with actors, you learned their craft, you learnt it well. But I grew up with soldiers. I learned how to die a long time ago."

At this point, Ned appeared resigned to his fate. Unbowed "in the face of death," Ned showed a type of courage that, Steven Pressfield has written, "must be considered the foremost warrior virtue."[21] Ned was willing to stand on principle all the way to his death. But Varys made one last argument as he left the dungeon: "What of your daughter's life? Is that a precious thing to you?"

This was the comment that convinced Ned to change his mind, to abandon his own hard-edged rejection of the lying, deceitful conduct of Cersei and Joffrey and the Lannisters. Ned was willing to confess to a crime he did not commit and to lie in order to protect his daughters.[22] Ned was an ethical pragmatist, willing to die for his beliefs but willing to be persuaded by the exigencies of life to abandon those beliefs, when necessary, not for personal gain but to protect others.

Why Heroes Never Really Die (and Usually Win)

Heroes inspire others to carry on and unify around certain ideals. Sean Bean once pointed out that Ned was the heart of the show long after his death and that Ned "posthumously guid[ed] the Stark children throughout their own journeys."[23]

The psychological damage caused by Ned's death was truly traumatic—Bran and Rikkon Stark saw, in their dreams, a supernatural Ned moving about the family crypt. Catelyn and Robb could not contain their grief, and both experienced extreme, spontaneous outbursts.[24]

But it was less in the initial moments of grief, which are to be expected, than in the longer shadow of his example that Ned impacted his children. Robb said that Ned was the "best man" he ever knew and that he taught Robb about leadership and fear and how to conduct himself as the King in the North.[25]

Arya and Sansa reminisced about their father's manner and how Ned would secretly watch Arya practice her skills with the bow.[26] Ned's memory, his ideals, impacted them deeply.

Through Jon Snow, of course, we find the greatest remembrance and connection to Ned Stark. From Ned, Jon learned a sense of duty, a sense of law, a sense of justice. Jon repeatedly references Ned in his journey to leadership, from offhand comments in which he cites Ned's aphorism that "true friends" are found "on the battlefield" to Jon's visit to Ned's crypt at Winterfell to Jon's stirring speech in defense of blunt honesty with allies: "I'm not going to swear an oath I can't uphold. Talk about my father if you want; tell me that's the attitude that got him killed. But when enough people make false promises, words stop meaning anything. Then there are no more answers, only better and better lies. And lies won't help us in this fight."[27]

To Jon especially, who called Ned "the most honorable man I ever met" and who acknowledged that he felt Ned was a part of him, Ned's impact drove Jon's life in many important ways.[28]

Jon's leadership is a direct continuation of Ned's tutelage and ideals. That's because Ned inspired Jon and he taught Jon the right way to live, focused on a purpose (and a "Why?") as opposed to narrow considerations centered on short-term gains and tactical considerations (i.e., "What's in it for me?"). Simon Sinek, a writer on modern leadership, refers to this distinction as the playing of finite versus infinite life-games.[29]

Ned Stark and his direct extension, Jon Snow, practice leadership that lives on because they put principles first. And people are loyal to them for that reason.

The Lannisters—Tywin, Jamie, and Cersei in particular—provide a useful contrast. They seek cheap victories through indirect methods, which, in some ways, Sun Tzu would likely appreciate. When Tywin struck a deal with Walder Frey to put down the Stark threat in the infamous Red Wedding; when Jamie used leverage and trickery to break the Blackfish's grip on the castle at Riverrun; when Cersei wielded wildfire to blow up a significant part of King's Landing to wipe out her rivals—these were short-term gains with long-term consequences. And that long-term consequence is clear—nearly nobody wants to ally with the devil.

As Cersei put it, "When you play the game of thrones, you win or you die. . . . There is no middle ground."[30] This is the Lannister fallacy—that leadership is zero sum, all or nothing, and focused on limited gains.

The reality, which Ned Stark shows us, is that heroes unify others through their good will and principled leadership. King Robert once tried to teach this principle to Cersei, who apparently did not learn it, when he asked her whether five or one was the "greater number." That's when he held up a hand, with the five fingers splayed, and then balled them together into a fist—a perfect representation of the military principle of unity of command.[31]

That's what heroes do. They unify.

And they inspire myths. We live by myths, much more than we know, and myths go on to inspire new heroes.

Yuval Noah Harari's influential book *Sapiens* noted that humanity's rise is "rooted in common myths."[32] According to Joseph Campbell, myths are "stories about the wisdom of life" that have a sociological function in that they often validate a "certain social order."[33] They also can serve a pedagogical purpose—to teach us to live better lives. Historian William McNeill once argued that such myths are at the "basis of human society."[34]

Ned Stark was a hero who served and sacrificed. He did not win, in the classic sense, in his lifetime.

But because he unified others through his conduct and principles and inspired others through his life and the mythmaking that extended his life's example, he gave rise to others who took up and carried on with the cause after he fell.

That's the lesson we can take from Ned Stark, hero of the Seven Kingdoms—especially if Jon Snow and the Starks' partners are successful in gaining the Iron Throne. The good guys usually do win in the end; it just takes a little longer.

NOTES

1. David Benioff and D. B. Weiss, "Beyond the Wall," season 7, episode 6, dir. Alan Taylor, *Game of Thrones*, aired August 20, 2017, on HBO.

2. Paul, "My New Favorite Thing, Stupid Ned Stark," *Unreality Magazine*, 2011, http://unrealitymag .com/television/my-new-favorite-thing-stupid-ned-stark/; Dan Selcke, "And the Dead Game of Thrones Characters Fans Miss the Most Is . . . ," *Winter Is Coming*, February 3, 2016, https:// winteriscoming.net/2016/02/03/and-the-dead-game-of-thrones-characters-fans-miss-the -most-is/.

3. Bryan Cogman, "Cripples, Bastards, and Broken Things," season 1, episode 4, dir. Brian Kirk, *Game of Thrones*, aired May 8, 2011, on HBO.

4. Cicero Estrella, "'Game of Thrones': Is Ned Stark Being Resurrected for the Final Season?" *San Jose (CA) Mercury News*, March 14, 2018, https://www.mercurynews.com/2018/03/14 /game-of-thrones-is-ned-stark-being-resurrected-for-the-final-season/; Leigh Blickley and Bill Bradley, "Sean Bean's Role in 'Game of Thrones' Was Much Bigger Than You Thought," *Huffington Post*, March 17, 2018, https://www.huffingtonpost.com/entry/sean-bean-game-of -thrones_us_5aa6b621e4b087e5aaeca1fc; Rod Lurie, "Rod Lurie (*Straw Dogs*) Talks David Benioff and D. B. Weiss' Game of Thrones," *Talkhouse*, May 23, 2014, https://www.talkhouse .com/rod-lurie-straw-dogs-talks-david-benioffs-game-of-thrones/.

5. Blickley and Bradley, "Sean Bean's Role."

6. Brian Rathbun, "Ned Is Dead, Baby. Ned Is Dead," *Duck of Minerva*, June 14, 2011, http:// duckofminerva.com/2011/06/ned-is-dead-baby-ned-is-dead.html.

7. Christopher McDougall, *Natural Born Heroes: How a Daring Band of Misfits Mastered the Lost Secrets of Strength and Endurance* (New York: Alfred A. Knopf, 2015), 26.

8. Joseph Campbell, *The Power of Myth*, with Bill Moyers (New York: Anchor Books, 1991), 151–52.

9. Charles Darwin, quoted in McDougall, *Natural Born Heroes*, 26.

10. McDougall, *Natural Born Heroes*, 26.

11. McDougall, *Natural Born Heroes*, 205.

12. See E. O. Wilson, *The Social Conquest of Earth* (New York: Liveright, 2012).

13. Steven Pressfield, *The Warrior Ethos* (New York: Black Irish Entertainment, 2011), 12–13.

14. Amy Chua, *Day of Empire: How Hyperpowers Rise to Global Dominance—And Why They Fall* (New York: Doubleday, 2007), xxi, xxiv, 330, 336.

15. McDougall, *Natural Born Heroes*, 204.

16. G. K. Chesterton, *Illustrated London News*, January 14, 1911, available at "Quotations of G. K. Chesterton," American Chesterton Society, https://www.chesterton.org/quotations-of-g-k -chesterton/#War%20and%20politics.

17. David Benioff and D. B. Weiss, "Winter Is Coming," season 1, episode 1, dir. Tim Van Patten, *Game of Thrones*, aired April 17, 2011, on HBO; David Benioff and D. B. Weiss, "Lord Snow," season 1, episode 3, dir. Brian Kirk, *Game of Thrones*, aired May 1, 2011, on HBO.

18. Benioff and Weiss, "Winter Is Coming"; David Benioff and D. B. Weiss, "The Kingsroad," season 1, episode 2, dir. Tim Van Patten, *Game of Thrones*, aired April 24, 2011, on HBO.

19. David Benioff and D. B. Weiss, "The Wolf and the Lion," season 1, episode 5, dir. Brian Kirk, *Game of Thrones*, aired May 15, 2011, on HBO.

20. David Benioff and D. B. Weiss, "Baelor," season 1, episode 9, dir. Alan Taylor, *Game of Thrones*, aired June 12, 2011, on HBO.

21. See Pressfield, *Warrior Ethos*, 13.

22. To forestall his execution, Ned Stark confessed to a crime he did not commit to save his family during season 1, episode 9. He said, "I am Eddard Stark, Lord of Winterfell and Hand of the King. I come before you to confess my treason, in the sight of gods and men. I betrayed the faith of my king and the trust of my friend Robert. I swore to defend and protect his children, but before his blood was cold, I plotted to murder his son and seize the throne for myself. Let the High Septon and Baelor the Blessed bear witness to what I say. Joffrey Baratheon is the one true heir to the Iron Throne, by the grace of all the gods, Lord of the Seven Kingdoms and Protector of the Realm."

23. Blickley and Bradley, "Sean Bean's Role."

24. Robb Stark repeatedly hits a tree with his sword and says: "I'll kill them all. Every one of them"; David Benioff and D. B. Weiss, "Fire and Blood," season 1, episode 10, dir. Alan Taylor, *Game of Thrones*, aired June 19, 2011, on HBO.

25. David Benioff and D. B. Weiss, "Prince of Winterfell," season 2, episode 8, dir. Alan Taylor, *Game of Thrones*, aired May 20, 2012, on HBO.

26. Benioff and Weiss, "Beyond the Wall."

27. David Benioff and D. B. Weiss, "The Winds of Winter," season 6, episode 10, dir. Miquel Sapochnik, *Game of Thrones*, aired June 26, 2016, on HBO; David Benioff and D. B. Weiss, "Dragonstone," season 7, episode 1, dir. Jeremy Podeswa, *Game of Thrones*, aired July 16, 2017, on HBO; David Benioff and D. B. Weiss, "The Dragon and the Wolf," season 7, episode 7, dir. Jeremy Podeswa, *Game of Thrones*, aired August 27, 2017, on HBO.

28. Benioff and Weiss, "Beyond the Wall"; Benioff and Weiss, "Dragon and the Wolf."

29. By focusing on "why," you acknowledge principles and ideals that essentially have no end. But by overemphasizing short-term, narrow objectives, like money or power, you focus on finite issues that are ultimately unsatisfactory. Simon Sinek, "Simon Sinek with Arthur Brooks: 92Y Talks Episode 131," *92Y Talks*, podcast, MP3 audio, 1:20:32, February 22, 2018, http://92yondemand .org/simon-sinek-arthur-brooks-92y-talks-episode-131.

30. David Benioff and D. B. Weiss, "You Win or You Die," season 1, episode 7, dir. Daniel Minahan, *Game of Thrones*, aired May 29, 2011, on HBO.

31. Benioff and Weiss, "Wolf and the Lion."

32. See Yuval Noah Harari, *Sapiens: A Brief History of Humankind* (New York: Harper Collins, 2015), 30.

33. Campbell, *Power of Myth*, 39.

34. William H. McNeill, "The Care and Repair of Public Myth," *Foreign Affairs* 61, no. 1 (Fall 1982), https://www.foreignaffairs.com/articles/1982-09-01/care-and-repair-public-myth.

30

White Walkers and the Nature of War

PAUL SCHARRE

When Jon Snow comes face-to-face with the Night King and his army at Hardhome, it's clear they are an enemy like nothing he has seen before. Defeating the White Walkers will require new weapons, such as dragonglass, and new tactics, like using fire against the wights, the White Walkers' army of undead foot soldiers. But even more than that, the enemy's inhumanity means that the fundamental nature of the conflict Jon Snow is engaged in is different from other wars against humans. The wights show no fatigue or fear, and at least at the start of season 8, the White Walkers' aims are unknown. They seem uninterested in negotiation and immune to the political intrigue, subterfuge, and shifting alliances that are so common among the human wars of Westeros. The war Jon Snow and his allies are fighting against the White Walkers is unlike any other war they have fought in the past, if it is a war at all.

The Character of Warfare and the Nature of War

In Western military circles, it is common to speak of the ever-changing character of warfare and the immutable and unchanging nature of war.[1] *Warfare* refers to the means and methods of fighting and is constantly in flux as militaries develop new tactics, technologies, and strategies. The essential nature of *war*, however, is timeless. War is a violent struggle among competing groups of people for political power.[2] Or as the Prussian strategist Carl von Clausewitz wrote, "War therefore is an act of violence to compel our opponent to fulfil our will."[3] Even while the means and methods of fighting (the character of warfare) change over time, all wars have common characteristics that stem from its unchanging, underlying nature. One of the U.S. Marine Corps' fundamental doctrine publications, *Warfighting*, states in its chapter on the nature of war, "The essence of war is a violent struggle between two hostile, independent, and irreconcilable wills, each trying to impose itself on the other. War is fundamentally an interactive social process."[4]

It may seem strange to describe war as an "interactive social process," but as practitioners and observers know, war is a human endeavor.[5] It is a struggle between people, even if the tools they use evolve over time. Because of the human nature of war, some elements of war are constant. Wars are motivated by, as Thucydides wrote some 2,400 years ago, some combination of "fear, honor, and interest."[6] Once underway, violence, uncertainty, and chance rule the battlefield. The life of the warfighter across all ages has been marked by danger, physical exertion, exhaustion, and suffering. And battlefields are home to what Clausewitz described as friction, which is best summed up in his statement, "Everything is very simple in War, but the simplest thing is difficult."[7] Friction is the message that didn't make it through to a unit, the supply train that got lost in the night, the vehicle that got stuck in the mud, and the battle that was lost as a result.

Could the Nature of War Change?

There is great value in differentiating between continuity and change in war. War is the most extreme of human endeavors, taxing individuals and even entire nations to their maximum limit with the gravest of consequences on the line. Yet militaries, in truth, rarely fight wars, or at least not big ones. Most of the time—thankfully—nations are at peace and militaries occupy their time with training and preparing for war. Knowing how best to prepare, however, is an immense intellectual challenge, akin to training a professional sports team for a game that is played only once a generation, where the rules are unknown and constantly changing and where losing a play could mean death. Military scholars have quite reasonably sought to distill from the millennia-long history of war some lessons to guide their planning.

There is danger, however, in leaping from the well-founded observation that wars in the past have always had certain commonalities to a future-looking statement that the nature of war can *never* change. If the nature of war is to mean anything, it should be possible to define conditions under which it might change, even if those conditions seem unlikely. To assert simply that it cannot change, no matter what, is not a scientific statement—it's a faith-based statement. Then military thinkers are no longer studying war, but war becomes a religion and Clausewitz a prophet. If scholars of war want to truly understand it, then they must open their minds to the possibility that the nature of war might change.

James Mattis, retired general of the U.S. Marines and secretary of defense under President Donald Trump, has raised precisely this intriguing possibility. During a conversation with reporters about artificial intelligence, he remarked, "I'm certainly questioning my original premise that the fundamental nature of war will not change. You've got to question that now. I just don't have the answers yet."[8] Mattis's statement is a bold proposition in Western military circles and one that challenges a tightly held dogma about the unchanging nature of war. Yet there are a number of disruptive technologies, including artificial intelligence and synthetic biology, that are certain to change the character of warfare and quite possibly raise intriguing questions about the nature of war. It's a bold assertion, but one worth considering. What would it mean for the nature of war to change?

The War against the White Walkers

Game of Thrones gives us a good vehicle to consider this question. We can examine a conflict—albeit a fictional and fantastical one—in which the nature of war might be different. So what is the nature of the conflict Jon Snow is fighting against the White Walkers?

There are many elements of the fight against the White Walkers that illustrate the changing character of warfare. The wights are already dead, and so they are unbothered by wounds that would kill a human, like an arrow to the head. Wights move with an unnatural speed. White Walkers' weapons will shatter a traditional sword. And the White Walkers can be harmed only with dragonglass or Valyrian steel (and possibly dragon fire). Jon Snow takes these lessons learned at Hardhome and other battles to refine his army's tactics and weapons. These are examples of the changing character of warfare in action.

But the White Walkers and their wight soldiers present a much deeper and more fundamental challenge to the nature of war—they are no longer human. Again, war—at least war as we conceive of it now—is a human endeavor. This is not merely a minor definitional issue, arguing that all wars have in the past been between humans. The fact that war is fought by humans against other humans is foundational to its nature. War is political—"a continuation of policy by other means," as Clausewitz described it.[9] But what are the White Walkers' aims? Are they also motivated by some combination of "fear, honor, and interest"? Do they seek power in a sense that the Westerosi lords would understand? At the outset of season 8, we simply do not know. It is possible that they have humanlike aims and motivations. It is also possible that they have no more desires than a virus has.

Even if their motivations could be understood in human terms, the inhuman nature of the White Walkers and the wights means that many commonalities in wars against people do not apply. Strategy often involves anticipating an enemy's move and using deception to trick an enemy. The ancient Chinese strategist Sun Tzu stated, "All warfare is based on deception."[10] Anticipation and deception require a working theory of mind in order to predict how an enemy thinks. While White Walkers are clearly sentient, it isn't clear how similar their thought processes are to humans. Some fan theories speculate that they can even see the future, which would fundamentally change essential elements of warfare, like deception.

In battle, the undead wights are immune to many of the challenges that human warfighters face. The U.S. Marine Corps' *Warfighting* manual observes that "individual conscience, emotion, fear, courage, morale, leadership, or esprit" are important, intangible "moral forces" in war that exert an even greater influence on the outcome of war than physical forces.[11] On fear in particular, the manual states, "Since war is a human phenomenon, fear, the human reaction to danger, has a significant impact on the conduct of war. Everybody feels fear. Fear contributes to the corrosion of will. Leaders must foster the courage to overcome fear, both individually and within the unit. Courage is not the absence of fear; rather, it is the strength to overcome fear."[12]

The wights do not feel fear, fatigue, conscience, or emotion. Their morale cannot be sapped; their esprit de corps cannot be broken. They are an unthinking and unfeeling wave of partially decayed flesh, more like a natural force than a human opponent. When Jon and his band of raiders are trapped beyond the Wall, there is never a sense that the wights might tire of their siege or succumb to fatigue or exhaustion. The Marine Corps manual points out that (for humans) "it is physically impossible to sustain a high tempo of activity indefinitely. . . . The tempo of war will fluctuate from periods of intense combat to periods in which activity is limited to information gathering, replenishment, or redeployment."[13] The wights do not need to rest, however. They are unburdened from supply lines or the need to tend to their wounded and bury their dead. They are already dead. These moral forces of war still weigh on Jon and his comrades and are an aspect of war for them, but not for their enemy. The nature of *this* war is different.

The war against the White Walkers is a kind of war, but it is different than any of the wars among the humans of Westeros. The inhuman nature of the enemy means that some elements of the nature of war have changed. Definitionally, this presents something of a challenge. If it does not meet all the criteria that define war, then what is it? The most sensible approach would be to define it as another kind of war, broadening the horizon for what war is into two categories—human wars and wars against nonhumans.

Prospects for Changes in the Nature of War

Short of a White Walker invasion, it is possible to envision scenarios in the real world where evolutions in technology do indeed truly lead to changes in the nature of war itself. Five possibilities are outlined below. None of these possibilities are necessarily likely, either in the short term or the long term. They are most certainly not predictions. Rather, they are merely thought experiments to help conceive of developments that might require a rethinking of the nature of war.

War against a Nonhuman Adversary

The most obvious candidate for a nonhuman adversary in war would be advances in artificial intelligence that could lead to the creation of an artificial entity that would pursue its own aims in a conflict. These aims need not be aligned with human desires or even appear sensible from a human standpoint. In science fiction, AI is often depicted as "waking up" and turning against humans, but that need not be the case. AI threats could come from nonsentient but intelligent AI systems, like an adaptive cyberweapon that is capable of resource acquisition, planning, and causing harm and is pursuing its own aims. While such an AI system would originally be designed by humans, it could slip out of control due to an accident. In fact, designing goal-driven intelligent systems that stay within the bounds of intended human design is an unsolved problem in machine learning and artificial intelligence.[14]

Changes in Human Nature

Synthetic biology offers the potential to alter humans directly, leading to the prospect of wars in the future that are still fought by humans, but humans who are unlike those who fought wars in the past. While still science fiction today, it is possible to imagine a world in which biological advances empower humans to fight without fatigue, exhaustion, conscience, fear, or mental weakness. Such a development would change the nature of war, humanity's relationship with it, and even humanity itself.

Changes in Human Organization

War is not merely violence. It is organized violence among competing groups for political aims. Social media is a new tool of organizing humans, and its introduction is as profound as that of the printing press. Already, social media has demonstrated a radically democratized information landscape where ideas and memes can spread virally without any hierarchical human organization to promote them. This has, among other things, led to a transformation in the nature of terrorist threats. The Islamic State is both an organization and a decentralized global movement that can inspire people around the globe through social media to carry out lone-wolf attacks on their own. The organization can be destroyed. Defeating the ideas is much harder. In the space of ideas (but not yet violence), competing ideologies and memes spread and evolve on social media in cycles of reaction and counterreaction. While organizations and groups may participate in these cycles of ideas, generating hashtags and arguments, they do not control the spread of ideas. No one does.

Changes in the nature of war are unlikely at the current state of social media, but we are only at the beginning of a new age of human communication. It would be unwise to anticipate that social media in its current incarnation will remain static. As digital technology evolves, the depth and breadth of human communication will continue to evolve as well. It is possible to conceive of future forms of democratized human communication that could lead to viral outbreaks of violence by individuals radicalized by social media. If this violence caused reactions and counterreactions, it is conceivable that it might occur on the scale of what we think of as war, particularly if other advances in future technology increase the destructive potential of individuals (for example, if advances in synthetic biology made it possible for individuals to create virulent pathogens in a garage that could target certain racial or ethnic groups). Such an activity would have many characteristics of war—violence, uncertainty, suffering, friction, political motivations, and human aims—but not the organization that has characterized wars in the past. This could make it uniquely difficult to control or end such wars, since it would not be a war among any groups or entities as they have traditionally been conceived—such as nation-states, tribes, religions, or paramilitary organizations. Rather, it would be a violent struggle for political supremacy among competing ideas. Individual humans would be both the authors and agents of those ideas, but there would be no organizations to sit at a negotiating table or declare an end to the war. The nature of such a war would be different than that of wars in the past, driven by an unprecedented change in human organization and communication.

Weapons Whose Destructiveness Renders Politics Irrelevant

The twentieth century saw the advent of nuclear weapons whose destructive power eclipsed human understanding, and the twenty-first century has the potential for even more transformative weapons in artificial intelligence and synthetic biology. It is possible to imagine weapons so destructive that they render politics irrelevant, since everyone would be dead. A hypothesized doomsday device that destroyed humanity would be such a weapon. There could be no rational policy aims for actually using such a weapon, since there would be no political outcome to achieve after its use. There might be reasons to threaten to use such a weapon and even to brandish one, as a threat of mutual suicide, but none for its use. Many wars have been fought in which both sides came out worse than before, but a war that was certain to obliterate both sides would be a war unlike any other. It would shift conflict to coercion and brinkmanship beforehand, a contest not in violence but in risk-taking. The nature of this contest would have some similarities to war but would be different in other ways. And if such a war were actually fought, it would be unprecedented—a war without any purpose.

Nuclear weapons flirt with this threshold of destructiveness, with some defense intellectuals arguing that the only purpose of nuclear weapons is to prevent the other side from using them.[15] Certainly, no rational policy aims could be achieved in a mass exchange of nuclear weapons among superpowers. Even more destructive weapons are conceivable. During the Cold War one conceptualized weapon was a salted nuke, which would leave radioactive fallout that could render an area uninhabitable for generations and an arsenal of which could extinguish humanity. Other potential dooms-day devices include bioengineered plagues or AI weapons.

War without Political Aims

Another conceivable development in weapons could be automation that led to automatic war without political aims—that is to say, a set of machine-enabled reactions and counterreactions that led to a war without human intent. Humans would have designed the system, but once in place, the system would spring into action of its own accord. If everything works according to plan, then the automation would be the embodiment of human intent. But if things were to go awry—if this automated network of reactions were to interact with the enemy or the real world in some unexpected way leading to a reaction that was *not* intended by humans—then the result would be something else entirely: a war without political aims.

While mishaps from malfunctioning machines are a part of everyday life in the form of software bugs and frozen computer screens and occasionally lead to fatal accidents, such as from self-driving cars, large-scale mishaps are rare. Few domains are so automated that humans cannot step in and correct errors. Stock trading is a rare exception, and machine-driven accidents like flash crashes have come hand in hand with the rise of algorithmic trading.[16] Should militaries automate their forces to a similar degree, perhaps driven by an arms race in speed as was the case in financial markets, then a comparable accident could result—a flash war.

Once underway, humans may be able to regain control of their systems and shut them down, but the damage could already be too great. An opponent may not be willing to ignore an incident simply because "the machines did it." With passions and tensions inflamed, machine-generated war could give way to a more traditional human war. Or a machine-initiated war could simply subside, a spasm of apolitical violence. Such a concept is not entirely new. In his escalation ladder of levels of war, nuclear strategist Herman Kahn put at the top a "spasm or insensate war," a nuclear strike delivered by virtue of automatic protocols put in place ahead of time by leadership but devoid of considered intent or political purpose. Kahn described such a war as "blind and irrational."[17] War without political purpose is not war as it is traditionally understood, and an insensate war would be of a fundamentally different nature than wars in the past.

Humility in Our Vision of the Future of War

None of these five visions presented above is necessarily likely, but defense thinkers should keep their minds open to the possibility that future technological developments *might* change the nature of war. To believe otherwise is to willfully blind oneself to possible risks. The future is, as always, uncertain. In his essay "War—Continuity in Change, and Change in Continuity," the strategist Colin Gray remarked, "We know everything there is to know about war, unsurprisingly, since we have variable access to at least 2,500 years of bloody history. But we know nothing, literally zero, for certain about the wars of the future, even in the near-term."[18]

Ironically, Gray goes on in his essay to reiterate the claim that the nature of war is immutable. But we cannot know that. Scholars would be well served to keep in mind Gray's observation of our profound uncertainty about the future. For thousands of years, the nature of war—a violent clash of wills between opposing groups of people for political power—has not changed. Might it change in the future? It is possible. Jon Snow's war against the White Walkers is a vivid illustration of the possibility of a war of a fundamentally different nature than wars in the past.

NOTES

1. For example, see Colin S. Gray, "War—Continuity in Change, and Change in Continuity," *Parameters* 40, no. 2 (Summer 2010): 5–13; U.S. Marine Corps, *Warfighting*, Marine Corps Doctrinal Publication 1 (Washington DC: U.S. Government Printing Office, 1997); and Christopher Mewitt, "Understanding War's Enduring Nature alongside Its Changing Character," *War on the Rocks*, January 21, 2014, https://warontherocks.com/2014/01/understanding -wars-enduring-nature-alongside-its-changing-character/.

2. While the political nature of war is taken as an unquestioned assumption in contemporary Western defense circles, it is worth noting that there are dissenting points of view. Historian John Keegan opens his sweeping tome *A History of Warfare* by stating, "War is not the continuation of policy by other means. The world would be a simpler place to understand if this dictum of Clausewitz's were true. . . . War embraces much more than politics: . . . it is

always an expression of culture, often a determinant of cultural forms, in some societies the culture itself." John Keegan, *A History of Warfare* (New York: Alfred A. Knopf, 1993), 3, 12.

3. Carl von Clausewitz, *On War*, trans. James John Graham (London: N. Trübner, 1873), bk. 1, chap. 1, available online at the Clausewitz Homepage, https://www.clausewitz.com/readings /OnWar1873/BK1ch01.html#a.

4. U.S. Marine Corps, *Warfighting*, 3.

5. For example, see H. R. McMaster, "The Pipe Dream of Easy War," *New York Times*, July 20, 2013, https://www.nytimes.com/2013/07/21/opinion/sunday/the-pipe-dream-of-easy-war.html.

6. Thucydides, *The Peloponnesian War*, trans. Richard Crawley (London: J. M. Dent; New York: E. P. Dutton, 1910), bk. 1, chap. 76, online at Perseus, http://www.perseus.tufts.edu/hopper/text?doc= Perseus%3Atext%3A1999.01.0200%3Abook%3D1%3Achapter%3D76%3Asection%3D2.

7. Clausewitz, *On War*, bk. 1, chap. 7.

8. Aaron Mehta, "AI Makes Mattis Question 'Fundamental' Beliefs about War," *C4ISRNET*, February 17, 2018, https://www.c4isrnet.com/intel-geoint/2018/02/17/ai-makes-mattis -question-fundamental-beliefs-about-war/.

9. Clausewitz, *On War*, bk. 1, chap. 1.

10. Sun Tzu, *The Art of War*, trans. Lionel Giles, chap. 1, online at http://classics.mit.edu/Tzu /artwar.html.

11. U.S. Marine Corps, *Warfighting*, 16.

12. U.S. Marine Corps, *Warfighting*, 15.

13. U.S. Marine Corps, *Warfighting*, 10.

14. Dario Amodei et al., "Concrete Problems in AI Safety," preprint, submitted July 25, 2016, 4, https://arxiv.org/pdf/1606.06565.pdf; Stephen M. Omohundro, "The Basic AI Drives," *Self-Aware Systems*, 9, https://selfawaresystems.files.wordpress.com/2008/01/ai_drives _final.pdf; Stuart Russell, "Of Myths and Moonshine," *Edge*, November 14, 2014, https:// www.edge.org/conversation/the-myth-of-ai#26015; and Nick Bostrom, *Superintelligence: Paths, Dangers, Strategies* (Oxford: Oxford University Press, 2014).

15. Associated Press, "McNamara Calls on NATO to Renounce Nuclear Arms," *New York Times*, September 15, 1983, https://www.nytimes.com/1983/09/15/world/mcnamara-calls-on -nato-to-renounce-nuclear-arms.html.

16. U.S. Commodity Futures Trading Commission and U.S. Securities and Exchange Commission, *Findings Regarding the Market Events of May 6, 2010* (Washington DC, September 30, 2010), 2, http://www.sec.gov/news/studies/2010/marketevents-report.pdf; Maureen Farrell, "Mini Flash Crashes: A Dozen a Day," CNNMoney, March 20, 2013, http://money.cnn.com/2013 /03/20/investing/mini-flash-crash/index.html; Matt Egan, "Trading Was Halted 1,200 Times Monday," CNNMoney, August 24, 2015, http://money.cnn.com/2015/08/24/investing /stocks-markets-selloff-circuit-breakers-1200-times/index.html; Todd C. Frankel, "Mini Flash Crash? Trading Anomalies on Manic Monday Hit Small Investors," *Washington Post*, August 26, 2015, https://www.washingtonpost.com/business/economy/mini-flash-crash -trading-anomalies-on-manic-monday-hit-small-investors/2015/08/26/6bdc57b0-4c22 -11e5-bfb9-9736d04fc8e4_story.html?utm_term=.c12bdb13b4e2.

17. Herman Kahn, *On Escalation: Metaphors and Scenarios* (London: Pall Mall, 1965), 194.

18. Gray, "War—Continuity in Change, and Change in Continuity," 5.

Epilogue

Down from the Citadel, Off the Wall

What happens when a society is cut off from its wisest and bravest members?

Game of Thrones addresses this very question. When the end-of-the-world threat arrived, those in critical professions were either too self-interested or so far removed that they couldn't connect when it counted.

As the White Walker army continued its ceaseless march south, the amiable Samwell Tarly tried to convince the archmaesters at the Citadel (the unequal-parts Westerosi blend of Harvard, Oxford, and Hogwarts) to wield their considerable intellectual powers to defeat the threat from the undead.[1] Yet instead of helping, a committee of maesters laughed off Tarly's call to academic arms, went back to their dusty books, and essentially decided to leave Westeros without its sharpest minds in the war to come.

Tarly learned of the White Walker threat while in service with the Night's Watch on the Wall. The Night's Watch are the sworn defenders of the realm, stationed on the remote, icy barrier that separates the Seven Kingdoms from the Free Folk (and whatever else threatens from the frigid far north). The Night's Watch was neglected for decades and generations by the rest of Westeros, and over time what began as a legitimate frontier force devolved into a small slice of unfortunates who were involuntarily split off from society and summarily shipped off to serve. And when frightful threats emerged, the Night's Watch sent ravens to warn the rest of Westeros. Nearly nobody listened.

We see some of the same in the real world. Too often, academic experts are unavailable when society needs them the most.[2] Instead of "the Citadel," however, the derisive term we typically use for the place highfalutin academics occupy is "the ivory tower." Or today, expertise itself is questioned.[3] And the military is becoming smaller and smaller and more separated from the rest of society.[4] Here, instead of a "Wall," though, when we describe the distance between civilians and soldiers, academics prefer a term like "the gap."[5]

If anything, *Game of Thrones* can teach us that we must find better ways to come together. In an age when deadly technologies become less expensive and more destructive—insanely cheap and ridiculously powerful—scholars and soldiers must collaborate with society to inform the body politic and help them decide on critical issues of national defense and even, in extreme cases, national survival. And if pop culture is where these groups intersect— where we can find common ground to talk about modern war—then perhaps series like this are indeed more useful than they might otherwise appear.

Of course, the look of a book can deceive. Retired general Stanley McChrystal, former commander of all forces in Afghanistan, wrote recently, "Wisdom is where you find it. Don't be afraid to look in unexpected places."[6] Sometimes, popular fiction, like *Game of Thrones,* can reveal hard truths.

That's because we can use art to teach a thing or three about modern conflict and strategy. When the distinguished Cold War historian John Lewis Gaddis wrote his end-of-career, long-view book on grand strategy, he made heavy use of film and fiction to describe the concept.[7]

Why? Because as authors and screenwriters well know, fiction can make us *feel* in a way that raw data simply cannot. Writer Tim O'Brien has said that he uses stories to tell others about the Vietnam War because fiction can help us experience war as close as possible, to the degree that the reader feels partly in it.[8] This bestows a sense of empathy, says author Dave Eggers, as it "allows us to look through someone else's eyes and know their strivings and struggles."[9]

More than that, art can convey complex ideas about war to democratic societies that must make difficult decisions on dangerous threats. For example, at the dawn of the nuclear age, the famed doomsday clock, which portrayed the impending likelihood of nuclear war as a clock approaching midnight, debuted in 1947 on the first cover of the *Bulletin of the Atomic Scientists*. The clock was designed by the oil painter spouse of one of the magazine's scientist members.[10] That potent, artful image has served the public interest ever since by providing a concise, easy-to-understand mental image of the estimated proximity of nuclear war.

Film and fiction can also predict what's to come and inspire us to meet that future. Novelist and science-fiction writer Ray Bradbury's books *Fahrenheit 451* and *The Martian Chronicles* were well ahead of their time and stimulated his readers to confront the consequences of where those roads might lead.[11]

When it comes to war and strategy, art, film, and fiction can teach us, make us feel, reach others, contemplate what may pass, and even propel us to prepare for the upsides and the downsides to come. That's because war fiction is "not an escape from reality"; as the philosopher Christopher Coker has said, "it animates reality."[12]

And *Game of Thrones* is the series that launched a thousand lessons. A quick query online suggests that the show and books can teach us about subjects as diverse as debt, the workplace, flexible learning, digital marketing, game theory, the Magna Carta, parenting, the "perfect" wedding, and, yes, even the meaning of life.[13]

Of course, whatever the series might offer in the way of helpful hints for matrimonial bliss or rat racing, the truth is that *Game of Thrones*, at its core, is about human conflict. We can see this in the show's incredible scripts, which contain a seemingly endless source of quotations that provoke thought and stimulate debate.

Take the slippery Petyr Baelish, who said, "If war were arithmetic, mathematicians would rule the world."[14]

Other, less important characters also provide quotable wisdom. Braavosi swordsman Syrio Forel, Arya Stark's combat instructor, dispensed this gem:

"Watching is not seeing. That is the heart of true swordplay," an observation as useful for strategy as it is for swordplay.[15]

Maester Aemon Targaryen, learned advisor to the Night's Watch, pointed out that "love is the death of duty," a comment that would likely sting the ear of every warrior who has left home for war.[16]

In a more lighthearted way, every soldier turned parent would nod at Ned Stark's comment that "war was easier than daughters."[17] And even the show's combat sounds and visuals can teach us a bit of always useful trivia, like how many arrows it takes to put down a giant. (The answer is thirty-six, plus a spear.)[18]

Who could forget Tyrion Lannister's mighty wisdom? When he said, "I drink, and I know things," it was funny, but we also took seriously his lifelong commitment to sharpening his truest weapon when he said that "a mind needs books like a sword needs a whetstone."[19]

Likewise, Tyrion's sister, Cersei Lannister, observed that "when you play the game of thrones, you win or you die. There is no middle ground."[20] (One must acknowledge that there are, in fact, exceptions to Cersei's theorem—in pursuit of titles and lands, poor Theon Greyjoy seems to have lived an excruciating nightmare in which he has claimed neither victory nor death . . . yet.) But Cersei's comment is undoubtedly right in at least one way—at war the stakes are high. Indeed, they are the highest, both in our world and in the *Game of Thrones* universe. This fact alone should keep us glued to the lessons of modern war embedded in the strategic storytelling in *Game of Thrones*.

First, we should remember that all war is relative. Strategy is always practiced against some competitive enemy or within a cruel environment. In short, there is always some opposing force, and so there is no such thing as "good" or "bad" strategy.[21] There is only "superior" or "inferior" strategy, because we're constantly made to measure our relative performance against our opposition. Translated into *Game of Thrones* speak, it is of no use to look at Daenerys Targaryen or Jon Snow in isolation—you've always got to measure their performance against their opponent(s).

Second, mind the map.[22] Geostrategy is the relationship between force and space—or as the scholar James Kurth has put it, where history, geography, and culture intersect, the "realities and mentalities of the localities."[23]

The importance of geostrategy has been hammered into viewers every time the show's opening credits fly across the map of all the contending factions and warring parties. If, as the adage goes, "where you stand depends on where you sit," then in *Game of Thrones* how you fight depends on where you're from. The Northerners do well in winter weather, while the Baratheon and Lannister (or southern) armies struggle in the frost. And the Dothraki horsemen, content to raid and ride across Essos, have never considered crossing the Narrow Sea into Westeros (that is, until they meet a certain khaleesi). Each distinct group of people thinks differently, fights differently, and thinks about fighting differently—which is why they could be said to have distinct strategic cultures.[24]

We also see the role of chance and contingency at war—the iron law of unintended consequences. These are the factors beyond one's own control. For example, it's clear that Cersei did not intend to kill Ned Stark, yet her son Joffrey's decision to execute the Stark patriarch set in motion a series of events that shook all of Westeros and ultimately resulted in Cersei's unlikely ascension to the Iron Throne.

Nobody is safe, and "once you realize that heroes die," as *Game of Thrones* showrunner David Benioff has said, "everything becomes that much more terrifying."[25] So it goes in modern war.

Distant events that matter greatly to us all are happening all the time, hidden by the limited range of our own view. Consider the average Westerosi citizen, minding her own business as a shopkeeper in King's Landing. Just think about all the far-flung occurrences that are coming together from all directions to impact her life.

From the north the White Walkers and Free Folk from beyond the Wall now head her way. From the south, in Dorne, vengeful plotters threaten to shake up the kingdom. From the east rises Daenerys and her dragons, and from the west the berserk Euron Greyjoy commands an immense fleet of Iron Islanders to accompany his sizable appetite for pillaging. All the while, at home, just up the hill at the Red Keep, Cersei considers the destruction of all those ill-intentioned comers.

For our unsuspecting shopkeeper, this multidirectional gathering storm is certain to have some sort of impact. In our world, we should take heed the shopkeeper's predicament—the farthest clouds may yet bring the most lightning, thunder, and rain to our own lives.

These principal lessons from this "reel" war, especially its visual aspects, have been molded by some true creative genius. Showrunners D. B. Weiss and David Benioff have shepherded the HBO series from a relative success to a global cultural phenomenon that demands discussion, and they ought to be commended for their efforts in so doing.

Even more credit is due to author George R. R. Martin, who originally envisioned and wrote this series. Martin said that he is "fascinated by war" and pointed out that armed struggle "brings out the best and worst in people."[26] In that same interview, Martin also said, "Literature of the past used to celebrate the glory of war; then the hippie generation in the 1970s wrote about the ugliness of it. I think there's truth in both." He's right. War can be both dark and beautiful, and he has shown both sides of the war coin.

There's an irony to Martin's success in propagating so many lessons about war. The series that has inspired millions to learn a little something about war was conceived by someone who sat out the biggest conflict of his own youth. Though he is not and never was a pacifist (he's always felt "that sometimes war is necessary"), Martin asked for and was awarded conscientious-objector status during the Vietnam War and chose alternate national public service in Chicago during that war.[27]

With *Game of Thrones*, George R. R. Martin and Weiss and Benioff have brought war and human conflict into the homes of many millions. They've used art to fuse entertainment and education in a way that has brought in multitudes of fans to watch the course of one long struggle and war. And while Martin may have chosen to sit Vietnam out, he merits some recognition for his service to the public in this creative endeavor.

He's given those of us locked away in the Citadel or stuck far atop the Wall the opportunity to come down from our high-up and far-off places, to connect with society again, to talk about the threats to come in our real world.

He's reminded us that winter always returns.

And to win in Westeros, as in our world, we'll need all the help we can get.

NOTES

1. Dave Hill, "Eastwatch," season 7, episode 5, dir. Matt Shakman, *Game of Thrones*, aired August 13, 2017, on HBO.

2. Nicholas Kristof, "Professors, We Need You!" *New York Times*, February 15, 2014, https://www .nytimes.com/2014/02/16/opinion/sunday/kristof-professors-we-need-you.html.

3. See Tom Nichols, *The Death of Expertise: The Campaign against Established Knowledge and Why It Matters* (Oxford: Oxford University Press, 2017).

4. See James Golby and Hugh Liebert, "Midlife Crisis? The All-Volunteer Force at 40," *Armed Forces and Society* 43, no. 1 (2016), 115–38; Conrad Cranes, "The Future Soldier: Alone in a Crowd," *War on the Rocks*, January 19, 2017, https://warontherocks.com/2017/01/the-future -soldier-alone-in-a-crowd/.

5. See Kori Schake and Jim Mattis, eds., *Warriors and Citizens: American Views of Our Military* (Stanford CA: Hoover Institution Press, 2016).

6. Stanley McChrystal, foreword to *Strategy Strikes Back: How Star Wars Explains Modern Military Conflict*, ed. Max Brooks, John Amble, ML Cavanaugh, and Jaym Gates (Lincoln: University of Nebraska Press, 2018), xii.

7. John Lewis Gaddis, *On Grand Strategy* (New York: Penguin Press, 2018), 17. Gaddis glowingly cites screenwriter Tony Kushner's take on strategy in Kushner's work on the script of the 2012 film *Lincoln*, when one character asks President Abraham Lincoln how Lincoln can reconcile a righteous aim with less-than-lofty methods. In Kushner's words, the character Lincoln recalls his younger days as a surveyor: "[A] compass . . . [will] point you true north from where you're standing, but it's got no advice about the swamps and deserts and chasms that you'll encounter along the way. If in pursuit of your destination, you plunge ahead, heedless of obstacles, and achieve nothing more than to sink in a swamp . . . [then] what's the use of knowing true north?"

8. Tim O'Brien, "War and Literary Fiction," Pritzker Military Library and Museum, November 3, 2017, https://www.pritzkermilitary.org/files/8915/1922/7865/2017_Symposium_Tim _OBrien_transcript.pdf.

9. Dave Eggers, "A Cultural Vacuum," *New York Times*, June 29, 2018, https://www.nytimes.com /2018/06/29/opinion/dave-eggers-culture-arts-trump.html.

10. Rachel Bronson, "Can We Turn Back the Hands of the 'Doomsday Clock'?" Commonwealth Club of California, YouTube video, 1:05:46, June 13, 2018, https://www.commonwealthclub .org/events/2018-06-13/bulletin-atomic-scientists-ceo-rachel-bronson-can-we-turn-back -hands-doomsday.

11. See Ray Bradbury, *Ray Bradbury: The Last Interview*, ed. Sam Weller (London: Melville House, 2014), 4–6. In *Fahrenheit 451*, published in 1953, Bradbury envisioned earbuds, flat-screen televisions, extreme school violence, and the fall of the American newspaper. In the same interview, Bradbury alluded to the fact that the earliest American astronauts read *The Martian Chronicles* and were inspired by his book to explore space.

12. Christopher Coker, "Men at War: What Fiction Tells Us about War," Oxford University, *Changing Character of War*, podcast, MP3 audio, 54:23, October 28, 2013, http://podcasts.ox .ac.uk/men-war-what-fiction-tells-us-about-war.

13. Using the Google search engine, the author performed web searches for "*Game of Thrones*" and each of these subjects on June 1, 2018, finding relevant content for each.

14. Vanessa Taylor, "Garden of Bones," season 2, episode 4, dir. David Petrarca, *Game of Thrones*, aired April 22, 2012, on HBO.

15. George R. R. Martin, "The Pointy End," season 1, episode 8, dir. Daniel Minahan, *Game of Thrones*, aired June 5, 2011, on HBO.

16. David Benioff and D. B. Weiss, "The Watchers on the Wall," season 4, episode 9, dir. Neil Marshall, *Game of Thrones*, aired June 8, 2014, on HBO.

17. David Benioff and D. B. Weiss, "Lord Snow," season 1, episode 3, dir. Brian Kirk, *Game of Thrones*, aired May 1, 2011, on HBO. See also ML Cavanaugh, "Sixteen Lessons on War from a Three-Year-Old," Modern War Institute, August 27, 2014, https://mwi.usma.edu/2014827sixteen -lessons-about-war-from-a-three-year-old/.

18. David Benioff and D. B. Weiss, "Battle of the Bastards," season 6, episode 9, dir. Miguel Sapoch-nik, *Game of Thrones*, aired June 19, 2016, on HBO. Using the highly sophisticated, advanced technological approach of freeze-framing this episode at 53:29, just after the giant has crashed through the front gate of Winterfell, one can see that the giant has twenty-five arrows embed-ded in his body at that moment. Ten more are then fired into the giant's massive frame, in addition to a spear that pierces his hand. That makes thirty-five arrows, and the thirty-sixth and final arrow is Ramsay Bolton's into the giant's eye.

19. George R. R. Martin, "Blackwater," season 2, episode 9, dir. Neil Marshall, *Game of Thrones*, aired May 27, 2012, on HBO; David Benioff and D. B. Weiss, "The Kingsroad," season 1, episode 2, dir. Tim Van Patten, *Game of Thrones*, aired April 24, 2011, on HBO.

20. David Benioff and D. B. Weiss, "You Win or You Die," season 1, episode 7, dir. Daniel Minahan, *Game of Thrones*, aired May 29, 2011, on HBO.

21. Steven Jermy, "Strategy for Action: Using Force Wisely in the 21st Century," Oxford University, *Ethics, Law and Armed Conflict*, podcast, MP3 audio, 41:30, October 26, 2011, http://podcasts .ox.ac.uk/strategy-action-using-force-wisely-21st-century.

22. See "The Geopolitics of Ice and Fire," *Geopolitical Futures*, April 1, 2017, https://geopoliticalfutures .com/geopolitics-ice-fire/.

23. James Kurth, quoted in Ronald J. Granieri, "What Is Geopolitics and Why Does It Matter?" Foreign Policy Research Institute, YouTube video, 1:00:51, February 25, 2015, https://www .fpri.org/multimedia/2015/02/what-is-geopolitics-and-why-does-it-matter/.

24. "Strategic culture" refers to the "beliefs and assumptions that frame" a particular country or culture's attitudes toward war. Stephen Peter Rosen, quoted in Jeffrey S. Lantis and Darryl Howlett, "Strategic Culture," in *Strategy in the Contemporary World: An Introduction to Strategic*

Studies, ed. John Baylis, James J. Wirtz, and Colin S. Gray, 4th ed. (Oxford: Oxford University Press, 2013), 80.

25. D. B. Weiss and David Benioff, "Game of Thrones Interview: DB Weiss and David Benioff," interview by Ed Cumming, *Telegraph*, April 10, 2012, https://www.telegraph.co.uk/culture /tvandradio/game-of-thrones/9195683/Game-of-Thrones-interview-db-Weiss-and-David -Benioff.html.

26. George R. R. Martin, "Game of Thrones: Interview with George RR Martin," interview by Jessica Salter, *Telegraph*, March 25, 2013, https://www.telegraph.co.uk/culture/tvandradio /game-of-thrones/9945808/Game-of-Thrones-Interview-with-George-rr-Martin.html.

27. Martin, "Interview with George RR Martin."

CONTRIBUTORS

JOHN AMBLE is the editorial director at the Modern War Institute at West Point and codirector of the Urban Warfare Project. A military intelligence officer in the U.S. Army Reserve, he is a veteran of the wars in Iraq and Afghanistan. He holds a BA from the University of Minnesota and an MA in intelligence and international security from King's College London.

J. DANIEL BATT is a writer, artist, and futurist. He serves as creative and editorial director for 100 Year Starship, creating visual engagement for 100YSS programs and activities. He also serves as a lead researcher with Deep Space Predictive, focusing on developing tools and systems to ensure success in human group dynamics on deep space missions. His books include the novel *Young Gods: A Door into Darkness* (Sacramento CA: Storyjitsu, 2015) and the children's book series *The Tales of Dreamside*. His short fiction has been published in *Bastion Science Fiction Magazine, Bewildering Stories,* and other periodicals. He edited the science fiction anthology *Visions of the Future,* published through Lifeboat Foundation, and is coeditor of the anthology *Strange California* (Charlotte NC: Falstaff Books, 2017).

LIONEL BEEHNER is an assistant professor at the Modern War Institute at West Point and teaches courses on military innovation and research methods. He holds a PhD in political science from Yale University and is formerly a fellow at the Truman

National Security Project; a member of the *USA Today* Board of Contributors; and a term member with the Council on Foreign Relations, where from 2005 to 2007 he worked as a senior staff writer for its award-winning website, cfr.org. He holds an MA in international affairs from Columbia University. His research examines the transnational nature of conflict and combat, civil-military relations, and limited military interventions. His writing has appeared in *Orbis*, the *Atlantic*, *Foreign Affairs*, the *New York Times*, the *Washington Post*, the *National Interest*, and the *New Republic*, among other publications.

BENEDETTA BERTI is a foreign policy and security researcher, analyst, lecturer, and author. She got her BA in Oriental studies at the University of Bologna and achieved her MA and PhD in international relations at the Fletcher School at Tufts University. She has written four books and was awarded the Order of the Star of Italy in 2015. Her work has been published in *Al-Jazeera*, *Foreign Policy*, *Foreign Affairs*, the *New York Times*, the *Daily Beast*, and the *Wall Street Journal*. While being both a TED senior fellow and an Eisenhower global fellow, Berti has also maintained positions at West Point, the Institute for National Security Studies, the Foreign Policy Research Institute, and Harvard University. She is currently a lecturer at Tel Aviv University and was appointed as a member of the Commission on the Study of Radicalization in 2016 by the Italian government.

CHUCK BIES is an armor officer in the U.S. Army. He serves as study manager for the Army Science Board and holds a BS in engineering from Duke University and an MA in diplomacy and military studies from Hawaii Pacific University. He previously served as an assistant professor in the Department of History at the U.S. Military Academy. He won the 2016 Gen. George S. Patton Award at the U.S. Army Command and General Staff School as the best tactician in his class of 1,300.

JONATHAN BOTT is special assistant to the commander in the Fourth Fighter Wing at Seymour Johnson Air Force Base in Goldsboro, North Carolina. He has five combat deployments in the F-15E Strike Eagle. Lieutenant Colonel Bott received his master's degree from the U.S. Army School of Advanced Military Studies.

MAX BROOKS is an author, public speaker, nonresident fellow at the Modern War Institute, and senior resident fellow at the Atlantic Council's Art of Future Warfare Project. He is the author of *World War Z* (New York: Three Rivers Press, 2006) and *The Harlem Hellfighters* (New York: Broadway Books, 2014).

JOE BYERLY is an armor officer and recently served as a special advisor within U.S. Special Operations Command. He received his bachelor's degree from the University of North Georgia and his master's degree from the U.S. Naval War College. He is a nonresident fellow at the Modern War Institute at West Point and the founder of From the Green Notebook, a website emphasizing military leadership and professional development. His writings have been published in *War on the Rocks*, ARMY magazine, *Strategy Bridge*, and *Small Wars Journal*.

ML CAVANAUGH is a U.S. Army strategist with global experience in assignments ranging from the Pentagon to Korea and Iraq to Army Space and Missile Defense Command. A nonresident fellow with the Modern War Institute at West Point, he has written for the *New York Times*, *Washington Post*, and *Wall Street Journal*, among other publications. For more, visit MLCavanaugh.com.

KELSEY CIPOLLA is a writer and editor who has covered topics ranging from food and fashion to nonprofits and social issues. She is currently the communications coordinator at the University of Kansas School of Business and a writer for *In Kansas City* magazine.

LIAM COLLINS is a career Special Forces officer who has served in a variety of special operations assignments and conducted numerous combat operations in Afghanistan and Iraq as well as operational deployments to Bosnia, Africa, and South America. He is a graduate of numerous military courses, including Ranger School, and his military awards and decorations include two valorous awards for actions in combat. He is the director of the Modern War Institute at West Point and previously served as the director of the Combating Terrorism Center at West Point. He has a BS in mechanical engineering from the U.S. Military Academy and an MPA and PhD from the Woodrow Wilson School at Princeton University.

MICK COOK is an Australian writer, digital content producer, and veteran of the war in Afghanistan. He hosts *The Dead Prussian* podcast and is passionate about encouraging critical thought on war among military professionals, policy makers, and the wider community.

JONATHAN E. CZARNECKI is currently a professor of joint maritime operations at the Naval War College in Monterey, California. He is a retired U.S. Army and Army National Guard colonel with more than twenty-seven years of experience in the field and on staff. He received his MA and PhD in political science and applied social statistics from the State University of New York at Buffalo and his BS in social sciences–industrial management from Clarkson University. He has published numerous articles on the topics of joint operations, organizational behavior, and operational art.

GREGORY S. DROBNY was an Airborne Infantryman at 6th Ranger Training Battalion, a private security contractor in Central America, and a psychological operations team chief during Operating Iraq Freedom; he currently works as an assistant operations manager and range marshal at Makhaira Group. He holds a BA in history and an MS in organizational psychology, has written extensively for *The Rhino Den* and *Unapologetically American*, and contributed to *War Stories: New Military Science Fiction* (Lexington KY: Apex, 2014) and *Redeployed: How Combat Veteran Can Fight the Battle Within and Win the War at Home* (Dallas TX: Frisco House, 2013). He currently blogs at *Havok Journal*.

JAYM GATES has spent a decade as a science fiction editor, game developer, and author, with over a dozen anthologies and more than fifty published short pieces of fiction and nonfiction to her credit. She is a coeditor of *War Stories: New Military Science Fiction* (Lexington KY: Apex, 2014) with Andrew Liptak, has judged writing contests for the Atlantic Council, managed media relations for Uplift Aeronautics/ Syria Airlift Project, helped develop a crisis simulation role-playing game for Harrisburg University, and is a juror for the Canopus Award for Interstellar Fiction.

ANDREA N. GOLDSTEIN is an officer in the U.S. Navy Reserve and a nonresident fellow at the Modern War Institute at West Point. A nonprofit leader, military strategist, and veterans' advocate, she has published widely, with bylines in the *New York Times*, *Task & Purpose*, *Proceedings*, the *Fletcher Forum of World Affairs*, *War Horse*, and *Business Insider*, and with reports for the Center for a New American Security, Joint Special Operations University, and the *International Feminist Journal of Politics*. Andrea is a Pat Tillman Scholar and holds a master of arts degree in law and diplomacy from the Fletcher School at Tufts University and a bachelor's degree in history and classics from the University of Chicago. She lives in upstate New York.

ANDREW A. HILL is the chair of strategic leadership at the U.S. Army War College and founder and editor-in-chief of *War Room*, the Army War College's online journal. His research focuses on strategy and innovation in organizations. He received his doctorate in management from Harvard Business School.

THERESA HITCHENS is a senior research associate for the Center for International and Security Studies at the University of Maryland, where she focuses on space security, cyber security, and governance issues surrounding disruptive technologies. From 2009 through 2014 Hitchens was the director of the United Nations Institute for Disarmament Research Geneva. A former journalist, she spent eleven years at *Defense News* covering issues ranging from U.S. Air Force programs to arms-control treaties; she served as editor from 1998 to 2000.

ERICA IVERSON is a U.S. Army strategist with a range of strategic career assignments spanning the globe in Asia, Europe, and the Middle East. An experienced speechwriter for several U.S. Army four-star commands with combat deployments to both Afghanistan and Iraq, she recently completed a year serving in the U.S. consulate in Jerusalem. She is presently assigned to the Pentagon.

MIKE JACKSON is a lieutenant colonel in the U.S. Army. He holds a master of arts degree in liberal studies, with a concentration in international affairs, from Georgetown University and a master of military arts and science degree from the U.S. Army Command and General Staff College. Lieutenant Colonel Jackson has combat experience spanning the levels of platoon, company, brigade, division, and corps, during five deployments to Afghanistan and Iraq as an infantry officer and U.S. Army strategist (FA-59). He has also served with the chief of staff of the U.S. Army's Strategic Studies Group, in an interagency fellowship as the special advisor for manufacturing policy to the U.S. secretary of commerce, and as deputy director of the Modern War Institute at West Point. His areas of academic interest are international affairs and security studies.

MICHAEL JUNGE is a surface warfare officer and served afloat in USS *Moosbrugger* (DD 980), USS *Underwood* (FFG 36), USS *Wasp* (LHD 1), and USS *The Sullivans* (DDG 68) and was the fourteenth commanding officer of USS *Whidbey Island* (LSD 41). He also served with U.S. Navy Recruiting, Assault Craft Unit Four, the Office of the Secretary of Defense, Headquarters Marine Corps, and as the deputy chief of naval operations for communication networks (N6). He is the author of numerous articles that have been published in the U.S. Naval Institute's *Proceedings* magazine, as well as a monograph on command responsibility, *Crimes of Command.*

JONATHAN P. KLUG is a U.S. Army strategist. He has extensive overseas experience, and he taught military and naval history at the U.S. Air Force Academy and at the U.S. Naval Academy. Currently, he is in the U.S. Army War College Professor Program and a PhD candidate at the University of New Brunswick.

NINA A. KOLLARS is an associate professor in the U.S. Naval War College's Strategic and Operational Research Department and a published researcher and writer with a specific concentration on cyber security and military innovation. She is currently an editorial board member for the *Special Operations Journal.* Her work has been included in various publications, such as the *Palgrave Handbook of Security* and the *Special Operations Journal.* She is also a member of the Committee for the Analysis of Military Operations and Strategy.

STEVE LEONARD is an author, a speaker, and currently the director of the graduate program in business and organizational leadership at the University of Kansas. After serving for twenty-eight years in the in the U.S. Army, he made a career in writing and speaking and is the cofounder of Divergent Options and a founding member of the Military Writers Guild. An alumnus at the School of Advanced Military Studies, he led the interagency team that authored the U.S. Army's first stability operations doctrine and penned the doctrinal principles for the army design methodology. His writings on foreign policy, strategy, and leadership have been published numerous times, and he is currently the author of four books.

BRYAN MCGRATH is the founding managing director of the FerryBridge Group, specialists who concentrate primarily on naval and national security issues, including national and military strategy, strategic planning, and executive communications. After twenty-one years of service, he is now a retired U.S. Navy officer. McGrath is the deputy director of the Hudson Institute's Center for American Seapower. He is also a published commentator in the fields of national and maritime strategy.

RICK MONTCALM is a lieutenant colonel in the U.S. Army; he most recently served as the deputy director of the Modern War Institute at West Point and is currently a PhD student at Vanderbilt University. He received a master's degree in policy management from Georgetown University and a bachelor of fine arts degree from Austin Peay State University. Before his West Point assignment, Lieutenant Colonel Montcalm served as an executive officer in the U.S. Army TRADOC Command Group, following his key developmental assignments as a squadron executive officer and an executive officer in the First Brigade of the 101st Airborne Division. He has also been on armor, Stryker, and infantry brigade combat teams with positions held in Iraq and Afghanistan.

MAGNUS F. NORDENMAN is a writer, speaker, and noted NATO and maritime affairs expert. He has served, among other positions, as the deputy director of the Brent Scowcroft Center on International Security at the Atlantic Council in Washington DC. He graduated from the Virginia Military Institute and the University of Kentucky. He is the author of *The New Battle for the Atlantic: Emerging Naval Competition with Russia in the Far North* (Annapolis MD: Naval Institute Press, 2019).

JOSHUA D. POWERS is an infantry officer in the U.S. Army and founder of *The Field Grade Leader*, a blog focused on organizational leadership in the military. Captain Powers has been in the U.S. Army for nearly fifteen years. He received a bachelor's degree in history from the Virginia Military Institute and a master's degree in military art and science through the School of Advanced Military Studies. Josh is currently assigned to the headquarters of U.S. Army Pacific in Hawaii, where he serves as an operational planner.

MICK RYAN is an Australian Army officer and currently commands the Australian Defence College in Canberra. A distinguished graduate of Johns Hopkins University, the U.S. Marine Corps Staff College, and the U.S. Marine Corps School of Advanced Warfare, he is a passionate advocate of professional education and lifelong learning.

PAUL SCHARRE is a senior fellow and the director of the Technology and National Security Program at the Center for a New American Security. He is the author of *Army of None: Autonomous Weapons and the Future of War* (New York: W. W. Norton and Company, 2018), and his articles have been published by the *New York Times*, CNN, *Time*, Fox News, *Foreign Affairs*, and various other media outlets. He is a term member of the Council on Foreign Relations. He received his MA in political economy and public policy and a BS in physics from Washington University in St. Louis.

P. W. SINGER is a strategist at the New America Foundation and professor at Arizona State University. He was recognized by the Smithsonian as one of the nation's one hundred leading innovators and by Defense News as one of the one hundred most influential people in defense issues. He has written award-winning books, including *Corporate Warriors: The Rise of the Privatized Military Industry* (Ithaca NY: Cornell University Press, 2003); *Children at War* (Berkeley: University of California Press, 2006); *Wired for War: The Robotics Revolution and Conflict in the 21st Century* (New York: Penguin, 2009); *Cybersecurity and Cyberwar: What Everyone Needs to Know* (Oxford: Oxford University Press, 2014), with Allan Friedman; *Ghost Fleet: A Novel of the Next World War* (Boston: Mariner Books, 2016), with August Cole; and *LikeWar: The Weaponization of Social Media* (Boston: Houghton Mifflin Harcourt, 2018). He has held positions at the Office of the Secretary of Defense, *Popular Science*, and Harvard University and was the founding director of the Center for 21st Century Security and Intelligence at Brookings.

JOHN SPENCER is a retired U.S. Army infantry major currently serving as the chair of urban warfare studies at the Modern War Institute at West Point. He served over twenty-five years in the U.S. Army, including two combat deployments to Iraq. An expert on urban warfare, his writing has appeared in the *New York Times*, the *Wall Street Journal*, *Politico*, *Foreign Policy*, and other publications.

ADM. (RET.) JAMES STAVRIDIS is the twelfth and current dean of the Fletcher School of Law and Diplomacy at Tufts University. He served in the U.S. Navy for more than thirty years and retired in 2013 after completing a four-year tour as supreme allied commander of NATO. He has published six books, including most recently *The Leader's Bookshelf* (Annapolis MD: Naval Institute Press, 2017) with R. Manning Ancell and *Sea Power: The History and Geopolitics of the World's Oceans* (New York: Penguin, 2017). He received his PhD from the Fletcher School. He tweets at @stavridisj.

JESS WARD is an Australian Army officer in the Royal Australian Electrical and Mechanical Engineers. She is currently serving as an instructor at the Royal Military College at Duntroon and has over ten years of military experience, both in Australia and on operations in the Middle East. Jess is the founder and chief editor of the Junior Officers' Book Shelf.

CRAIG WHITESIDE is an associate professor at the Naval War College, where he teaches national security affairs to military officers as part of their professional military education. He is a fellow at the International Centre for Counter-terrorism–The Hague. Whiteside's current research focuses on the Islamic State's grand strategy and military doctrine. A graduate of the U.S. Military Academy at West Point, he has a PhD in political science from Washington State University and is a former U.S. Army officer with combat experience in Iraq.